EDUCATING FOR HUMANITY

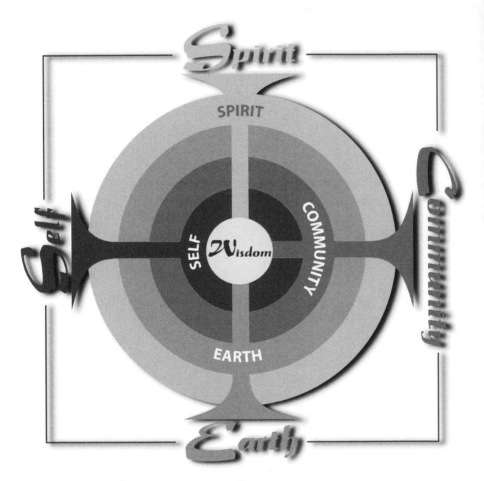

Educating for Humanity

EDUCATING FOR HUMANITY

Rethinking the Purposes of Education

edited by
Mike Seymour

Paradigm Publishers
Boulder • London
The Heritage Institute
Clinton, Washington

KH

Published in the United States by Paradigm Publishers, 3360 Mitchell Lane Suite C, Boulder, Colorado 80301 USA and The Heritage Institute, 4777 Commercial Road, Clinton, Washington 98236 USA.

Paradigm Publishers is the trade name of Birkenkamp & Company, LLC, Dean Birkenkamp, President and Publisher.

Library of Congress Cataloging-in-Publication Data

Educating for humanity / edited by Mike Seymour.
    p. cm.
    Includes bibliographical references and index.
    ISBN 1-59451-064-4 (cloth cover : alk. paper) — ISBN 1-59451-065-2 (paper cover : alk. paper)   1. Education, Humanistic.   2. Education—Aims and objectives.   I. Seymour, Mike, 1943–
LC1011 .E38 2004
370.11'2—dc22

                                    2004007875

    Printed and bound in the United States of America on acid-free paper that meets the standards of the American National Standard for Permanence of Paper for Printed Library Materials.

Designed and Typeset by Straight Creek Bookmakers.

08 07 06 05 04
5 4 3 2 1
ISBN 1-59451-064-4 (cloth)
ISBN 1-59451-065-2 (paper)

10/24/05

Contents

Foreword

Henry M. Levin

Several weeks ago I visited an elementary school that had met all of the requirements of "No Child Left Behind" (NCLB). Although the school was in an inner-city with more than half of the students on a reduced-cost or free lunch and 70 percent drawn from minority populations, it had met all of its academic growth targets under the law. The school was heralded in the local press as an exemplar that demonstrated what a dedicated school could accomplish.

On my visit I spoke with teachers and the principal and observed several classrooms. I also spoke with students. What was clear was the extent of strict devotion to success as defined by NCLB. According to teachers and students, each day began with a pre-test of material that was to be covered over the next days or a post-test of what had been covered in one or another subject. Both pre-tests and post-tests followed the state test formats. The curriculum was modeled after the test domains and items, and emphasis was placed on test performance. Teachers were required to follow scripted approaches to both language and mathematics in terms of the units and their presentation and activities. Worksheets that reinforced the content of each unit and test format were employed extensively. I observed little discussion. Questions emanating from the natural curiosity of the children were not forthcoming.

I asked teachers how they covered poetry and what kinds of projects the students were undertaking. Teachers reported that they had dropped coverage of poetry because it was not reflected on the tests, and that a vocabulary project for each national holiday was all that time permitted. Although they did not feel comfortable with "narrowing" the curriculum, as a school-wide effort, they were pleased with the test results.

The principal was very proud of her school-wide approach, telling me that more than 90 percent of instruction was well-aligned with the test. Her view was that she was doing what was expected to achieve success as defined by state standards and

NCLB. Although students told me they wanted more art and "fun" activities, they agreed that the school was good because they had heard this repeated by parents and teachers. Overall, about 60 percent of students met state "proficiency" standards in reading and mathematics. The principal sympathized with student views on broadening the curriculum, but she said that "they had a job to do" and that after-school programs, recess, and summers could be used to do other things. Besides, their present success was evidenced by unending requests by potential visitors to observe the school as well as a backlog of applicants for transfer from other schools in the district.

On leaving the school I was reminded of a scene from the movie, *Hans Christian Anderson* (1952). This fanciful film on the Danish writer of children's stories starred Danny Kaye as Anderson. Presumably, Anderson was a cobbler in a small village who had hired a young boy, Peter, as a part-time, cobbler's apprentice. Peter was a dreamer. He found school to be boring and looked forward to his afternoon apprenticeship with a regular dose of Hans's far-fetched stories. One morning the young Peter arrived at the gate of the village school, late by an instant. The stern schoolmaster reprimanded him and barred his entry. Disconsolately, Peter sauntered to an open window to listen to the lesson. Passing by, Hans discovered Peter there, and the two of them knelt by the open window to listen to the instruction, surrounded by the marigold garden bordering the school.

As they crouched among the marigolds, they observed an inchworm, maneuvering its body in measured fashion across the giant orange blossoms. Just at this moment, the school children broke out in recitation: "Two and two are four. Four and four are eight. Eight and eight are sixteen. Sixteen and sixteen are thirty-two." Repeated again and again.

With this recitation as chorus, Hans directed a song at the insect: "Inchworm, inchworm, Measuring the marigolds, You and your arithmetic will probably go far. Inchworm, inchworm, Measuring the marigolds, Seems to me you'd stop and see how beautiful they are."

The contrast between the mechanical recitation inside the schoolhouse and the boundless world of beauty and curiosity facing Peter is poignant. Outside of the window, Peter is immersed in nature, aesthetics, and humanity. He can realize the proportions of the flower from the inchworm's movement in ways that cannot be seen by the children in their recitation and memorization. He is ready to learn from Hans's stories and experience in a way that is precluded by drill and memorization. And, shortly thereafter, Peter gives up his formal schooling as the two of them set off for Copenhagen to see the larger world. In this clever scene one can see the poverty of limiting learning to the traditions of the schoolhouse, the present tradition being imposed on schools by NCLB, and the possibilities that can only be found when learning is elevated to a larger stage in which student experience and participation are the enabling ingredients and activities that are intrinsically valuable are the aims.

Mike Seymour and his talented colleagues believe that all children are left behind by NCLB. *Education for Humanity* has the purpose of providing educational aims for all of our children through democratic classrooms that commit themselves to all children and a present and future society that is robust, healthy, and sustainable. By creating schools that are devoted to all dimensions of the human condition, all students will be engaged collaboratively to succeed by a caring educational community. To do this, our children must be made aware of both the threats to such a society and the opportunities and possibilities that education provides to create a world that is prosperous, equitable, peaceful, and sustainable from an ecological perspective. This is an education that engages all of us in recognizing both the challenges and opportunities before us and provides us with the tools of analysis and action.

In Chapter Eight, "Aims in Education" of his classic book, *Democracy and Education,* John Dewey discusses aims in education. Dewey refers to good aims as follows:

> The aim set up must be an outgrowth of existing conditions. It must be based upon a consideration of what is already going on; upon the resources and difficulties of the situation. Theories about the proper end of our activities—educational and moral theories—often violate this principle. They assume ends lying outside our activities; ends foreign to the concrete makeup of the situation; ends which issue from some outside source. Then the problem is to bring our activities to bear upon the realization of these externally supplied ends. They are something for which we ought to act. In any case such "aims" limit intelligence; they are not the expression of mind in foresight, observation, and choice of the better among alternative possibilities. They limit intelligence because, given ready-made, they must be imposed by some authority external to intelligence, leaving to the latter nothing but a mechanical choice of means.

Much of what is done under NCLB is done to increase scores on stultified tests, not to engage students in a world in which they will succeed. In Dewey's terms these are "externally supplied ends." Although done ostensibly to prepare students for labor markets, the evidence linking the test scores to economic success is meager. High productivity workplaces want workers who can undertake responsibility, plan a project, evaluate the quality of their work, cooperate with others, and anticipate problems and solve them. Where do students get experience doing these things with a scripted curriculum broken down into units contained between bookends of pretests and post-tests where everything has a fixed answer that can be captured in a multiple choice answer? This is not to say that many of the skills are unimportant. It is to say that they should be learned in a context that allows thinking, planning, risk-taking, and meaningful applications, and above all they must allow for participation and democracy and moral determination.

The thrust of this volume is the quest to open the school experience to a different reality for students; a world that poses many contradictions that need resolution. Students need to consider the presence of material abundance alongside poverty, massive conflict and insecurity alongside desire for peace and stability, and natural beauty and order amidst environmental degradation and destruction. Only through confronting the challenges can these contradictions be overcome by human community. Education for humanity is awareness of both the problems and possibilities that we face and the proactive tools and courage to act together. It is the provision of educational tools and processes that make the world a better place for humanity through serving human needs and those of community. It is an education dedicated to awakening and empowering our spiritual sensitivities, our relation to human community, our connection to nature, and our values as human beings dedicated to a healthy society, present and future.

Sadly, such aims are noticeably absent from the official accountability standards of contemporary educational systems, the tests that measure their attainment, and the curriculum and instruction that slavishly pursue these narrow ends. In a Deweyan world, the test results that are worshipped presently by the political process should be viewed as mere by-products of the educational process, regardless of their value as by-products. Surely our children and the future of our society are worthier of much more than the delivery of by-products that can be validated by the scratch of a number-two pencil on a multiple-choice test form. Mike Seymour and his colleagues make a powerful case for a highly attractive alternative vision in what follows.

Introduction

Educating for Humanity: Rethinking the Purposes of Education

Mike Seymour

By all accounts, humankind finds itself at a life and death turning point in the twenty first century. We are on a course of unprecedented environmental destruction in terms of species extinction, global warming, and natural resource depletion. Population and consumption trends predict that humans will overshoot the earth's carrying capacity in many areas within the next century.

Humanity is at war with itself in escalating numbers of regional, ethnic, and religious conflicts. Moreover, the global economy and institutions of modernism—like education—have fallen prey to shortsightedness and a mostly economic agenda. The result is a growing gap between both rich and poor, loss of cultural diversity, and self-sustaining livelihoods. An unstoppable appetite for economic growth undermines attempts to safeguard the environment and, ultimately, our own lives.

These problems seen in the world at large can be found right here in America. What a great tragedy in this, the richest, most diverse country in the world! Einstein said, basically, the mind that got us into this mess is not the mind that will get us out of it. Humanity needs a change of mind fostered by a change of heart.

This book is about a new frame of mind, or consciousness, and how education can help us get there. I suspect that Einstein, who also said, "Education is what remains after one has forgotten everything he learned in school," might raise his eyebrows at my optimism about the possibilities for education.

It seems school hasn't changed much since Einstein's time. Daily, we read about low test-scores, parent backlash against new reforms, our continued failure to reach a

1

diverse student body, and persistent school violence. Too many kids sit in boring classes or skip school, adding to the epidemic dropout population. In the public mind, stories of outstanding teachers, engaged classrooms, and memorable student experience seem rather pale stars that are overshadowed by the dim skies under which public education is often pictured. And too often, I believe, education is shown worse than it actually is.

Regrettably, human suffering will likely increase in the coming centuries as we struggle toward a more equitable, sustainable way of life for all living beings. I am firmly convinced that we cannot make this global transformation to a new way of thinking without also making a radical change both in our conception and practice of education. The shift in our thinking that is needed to meet the complex, new realities of both our present and future simply cannot be accomplished within the prevailing mindset and practices of our current schools. But are we up to the task? Is education up to the task? More to the point, is society up to the task?

The contributors to these pages, and the growing number of progressive schools around the country and the world, give us reason to hope that a transformation in how we educate is possible and, in some small measure, already underway. A main focus of this book is to renew our faith in ourselves and our ability to realize the kinds of schools we want and need.

We live in a time that cultural scholars refer to as the biggest evolutionary change in human history. Growing global interdependence, combined with increasingly intolerable economic and social injustices, world health crises, and the threat of ecological self-destruction are forcing humanity toward the brink of a new age of enlightenment or an age of potentially irreversible darkness. While others speculate on how this will unfold, I believe, unequivocally, that an evolution to a more sustainable and meaningful way of being and thinking will only occur with a parallel change in our concept and the practice of education.

We must not just educate "better," as we have been trying to do, but educate *differently*. It's not a matter simply of finding fault with the current educational system (which has made positive contributions to individual and social well-being both here and around the world over the last one-hundred years). We must revisit our essential assumptions, values, and visions about what education is, and ask "what is an educated person" given what we know is most important to people anywhere and given what we know about the state of the world today. Tinkering with school structures and pedagogical practices will have limited success until enough people come to an all-encompassing agreement that addresses what is most important for our children and for humanity's future. We desperately need a vision that—regardless of social, religious, ethnic, and economic circumstances—serves to bring us into a sustainable, meaningful, and just future. To arrive at such a vision, we must reckon with our current social, economic, ecological, and spiritual realities—locally and globally.

This is a tall order. Achieving this consensus in our pluralistic and deeply divided society is no easy task. It is, nonetheless, one that bears a great moral imperative, given the state of the world and the fact that the United States, as the most powerful nation on Earth, serves as a model (both good and bad) for many nations. To redeem our view of the possibilities in education, we need to explore common ground and allow our differences to recede enough to achieve unity of purpose. It is my firm conviction that noteworthy change will occur if youth, parents, teachers, school boards, and community leaders reach within themselves to find their own deeper understanding of what is really important and then exercise the courage needed to put those convictions into action.

Imagine such a group assembled for a "town hall" meeting to explore a new vision and plan for its school district. Facilitated by a different sort of conversation than the usual one about "success" or "achievement," participants are asked to sit quietly and reflect on several questions, write down their thoughts, and then share them within a small group. The process culminates with a whole-group discussion.

The questions: What are your highest wish and hope for the lives of your young people, grandchildren, nieces and nephews, and any of the young people in your community, including those present? What do you want our young people to become as they mature and take over responsibilities from our generation? What do you want them to care about—what values do you want to guide their lives?

Now suppose we gather these answers and analyze the results, looking for common themes. It is likely that we would see a surprising degree of similarity—regardless of political stripe or religious affiliation—in what most people think and feel is important for young people. I imagine that the slips of paper would read:

- I want our children to be happy.
- I want our children to accept themselves.
- I want our children to feel like they are going somewhere in life.
- I want our children to be honest, respectful, and responsible.
- I want our children to experience happy, loving relationships and family lives.
- I want our children to have good jobs and enough money.
- I want our children to be kind and caring to others.
- I want our children to care about the world, not just themselves, and work to make the world and their communities a better place in which to live.
- I want our children to be kind to animals and nature.
- I want our children to succeed in life and achieve their dreams.
- I want our children to know their lives count for something.

Were this scenario to take place in a typical school district, one wonders how this group would translate this list into workable values and practices in schools. It would be a troublesome process. The vision of our hypothetical group would be hard to reconcile with the aims and practices common in most schools. Meeting these aims would require giving young people and their teachers far more say in what goes on at school than what they currently enjoy. So much of what goes on in schools today is mandated from "on high"—limiting teachers' and students' freedom of choice. Our imaginary group has said that human qualities such as happiness, self-fulfillment, and sense of purpose are of primary importance. But such a person-centered idea of education stands little chance against the policies and practices that strongly emphasize academic achievement and tend to either thwart human development or leave it to chance.

Educating for personal development—not for just what students can know and do—would be impossible if we taught as if children were empty vessels to be filled with socially useful knowledge. We aspire for our young to be in healthy relationships, parts of happy families, to be communally active, and to care about others and social equality. However, while social values are acknowledged as important in education, social and emotional learning are rarely pursued as educational ends in themselves. More often, they are only hoped-for byproducts of defined "academic" purposes of education.

We may value nature, but few schools have a truly comprehensive understanding of ecological literacy and how to impart it to young people. As for helping youth find meaning in experience, that is left mostly to chance or to the occasional social studies or English teacher who is gifted in helping students find themselves by probing big life questions raised in well-selected curriculum materials.

What currently survives the list of hopes for our children are those items that are the easiest to negotiate. In our materialistic, consumerist society, the educational path (of least resistance) settles for enabling kids to support themselves with decent work. This economic agenda is the "bottom line" that directs many private and most public schools.

Rather than educating for humanity, we school for the skills and knowledge needed to work and function at an "economically sound" level in society (and we don't do that very well either). By educating primarily for economic being, as opposed to human being and belonging, our system of education has relegated the development of a child's sense of self, his or her ability to make meaning of life and to love and respect others to family and/or civil society. Thus, education has played its role in the appalling losses we witness when we survey the landscape of shallowness, moral ambiguity, commercialism, and meaninglessness that pervade society today.

How can we expect children to become the type of adults we want them to be when one-third of their waking lives (in their most formative years) is spent in forced schooling that does not honor their humanity? From classical times to the early 1900s, education has been as much about ethics and character as it has been about content. In fact, reading, writing, history, and the humanities were not viewed as ends in themselves, but as means to cultivate a person of knowledge, decency, moral character, and higher purpose. We must realize anew that we only affirm a division between ourselves and society when we give school the job of the three Rs without requiring that it partner with family and civil society in nurturing the heart, character, and deeper thinking of our young. It *does* take a whole village to raise a child, including its schools. Fractious as our villages may be, our knowledge that a people divided cannot stand must impel us to conjoin education, family, and civil purpose for the sake of our children and also to enable a human future.

Family, civil society, and school represent three sources influencing the mind of America. Renewing harmony of purpose among these disparate spheres first requires healing the disharmony within ourselves. Embedded in the very paradigm of Western thought is a division between mind and body, spirit and matter, who we are and what we do, our ideals and reality, and "*talk*" versus "*walk*." All fissures in society stem from these fractures within ourselves. This is the illness of our times—of all times.

Out of this divided self, our "town hall" community agrees that even as the humanity of our children is most important, we do not attend to that humanity in the one-third of their life which is lived at school.

As we look closely at the alternative vision of education presented throughout this book, we'll see that this divided self is the root for most, if not all, of our personal, interpersonal, national, global, ecological, and spiritual crises.

The divided self shows up in our society's epidemic spiritual malaise, experienced as life lived without deeper (or any) meaning. Rather than working to integrate the needs and desires of our superficial selves with those of our deeper selves, we try to ameliorate any inner void with work, financial success, social recognition, love or lust relationships, or intoxicants—all of which become more frenzied and less satisfying with each attempt and through each successive generation.

This divided self is apparent in nearly all of our life experiences. We see it in the conflict between our concern for the environment and our attachment to ecologically destructive lifestyles. Though we think that increasing specialization and more data makes us smart, we recognize that we are being "dumbed-down" and are blinded to the larger picture. We espouse racial equality, yet resist seeing our own biases. When we meet people who are different from ourselves, we focus on the differences rather than celebrating inclusiveness of spirit and the common ground we share. We act as divided when we try to solve problems but fail to include all stakeholders, which leads to yet more complex problems. At the level of state politics, nationalism, which works for the good of a people, has increasingly negative consequences for that same people, the more the well-being and destinies of all nations become intertwined, as they have become in our time.

How do we bridge these troubled waters of a deeply divided self? It will certainly take the whole village, including its schoolhouse, to raise generations of hearts that understand the unity in all things and minds that think systemically. When I write, in this book about educating for humanity, I am envisioning how we can think, live, parent, and teach in ways conducive to the emergence of an integral, deeper, more inclusive, and systemic mind. In this sense, we empower our children to have a whole experience of life. To realize this dream, our generation must strive to close the split within ourselves, between ourselves and others, between ourselves and nature, and between ourselves and some form of higher meaning and common spirit which serves to bind us together.

Signs of an emerging integral mind can be seen everywhere in society, including in education. In education, for instance, integrated curriculum, community in school, inquiry-based and student-centered learning, social and emotional learning, teacher renewal and presence, holistic education practices, whole language, systems learning, and ecological school design are examples of a larger social movement throughout the world to make connections and find deeper meaning. But this movement in education has a tenuous foothold in the larger culture that is dualistic and at odds with the emerging, unified view of life and its accompanying values.

Arnold Toynbee's *A Study of History* describes our times well:

> [W]hen civilizations have reached a peak of vitality, they tend to lose their steam and decline . . . social structures and behavior patterns become so rigid that the society can no longer adapt to changing situations. . . . Whereas growing civilizations display endless variety and versatility, those in the process of disintegration show uniformity and lack of inventiveness. . . . The dominant social institutions will refuse to hand over their leading roles to the new cultural forces, but they will inevitably go on to decline and disintegrate, and the creative minorities may be able to transform some of the old elements into a new configuration. (1974, 9)

These kind of tectonic shifts in society today are marked by conflict and greater imposition of control as the dominant forces sense a threat to their ways of life. This reactive control is reflected in education in the current top-down, standards-based reform that has been building steadily since the Reagan years (the Bush administration's No Child Left Behind being the latest "act" in this drama) and before that, since the early 1900s. In this scenario, the integral view emerges amidst conflict and confusion, in piecemeal fashion, like small islands in schools, only to be washed away by staff turnover or budget cuts. Thus, many integral-type reform efforts, as far back as John Dewey's time, have proved hard to sustain within the larger dualistic, predominantly three Rs system that is fighting for its life.

We're witnessing the struggle between two civilizations and their attending values, with people gravitating to one or another paradigm, or way of thinking, as part of making sense of life. The dominant civilization we all grew up in is dualistic, scientific, and looking at the world in terms of separate objects. We would call this the "technoscientific" mind that divides, categorizes, and analyzes, believing this will lead to greater truth—which, in a way, it does, but at the cost of seeing the whole. The emerging civilization, which I'll call integral, is searching for meaning in a larger whole, perceiving the interconnection between all things.

Thomas Berry describes the shift to an integral world in his chapter, *Ethics and Ecology* (this volume): "Indeed, we must say that the universe is a communion of subjects rather than a collection of objects."

There's no past-bashing here. All the dynamics of the technoscientific civilization that we need to leave behind have served humanity well but have now outlived much of their usefulness. Who could deny the gains from democracy, respect for individual freedom, a better material life, and technology made possible by the movements that had their origin in the Renaissance, the Reformation and the Age of Reason? But neither can we deny the tremendous costs to all of life and life's very meaning, having now reached the decaying end of the technoscientific way of seeing and being.

I cannot stress enough the importance in this new paradigm of respecting the whole of reality. Merely railing against the dominant technoscientific civilization creates counterproductive resistance, unless we are able to recognize the good along with the bad. True power comes from compassionately embracing all views. The great challenge of our day is to find in our humanity the common, sacred ground on which we are all revealed to stand with noble purpose: finding a common vision for our children that will bring us together.

My quest for a common ground relative to education started several years ago, as the inner ruminations of many years in continuing education for teachers came to the surface. On a flight home to Seattle, I was working on a new philosophy statement for the Heritage Institute,[1] which I direct and which has a legacy of place-based environmental and community learning for teachers from holistic and progressive perspectives. Out of my search for the meaning of education came "Educating for Humanity," which I hastily scribbled on the rear jacket cover of the book I was reading.

I understood humanity in its fullest dimensions, in my own case, shaped by having been a family therapist, student of Jung and process-oriented psychology, and my lifelong quest for spiritual meaning. I mused that educating for the humanity of one child benefits all of humanity. All children, opened to the fullness of their own beings, bring blessing to whomever and whatever they touch. To be fully human, in my understanding, means feeling and acting as part of a larger whole. Much like the indigenous perspective, an integral and human way of thinking and being would connect first with self and, through that, connect to others, the natural world, and to something larger that gives life its meaning.

From these reflections emerged the concept of an ecology of learning with four interdependent domains: self, community, Earth, and spirit (see the illustration opposite the title page). Our lives unfold in circles beginning with ourselves and our inner aliveness, moving next to the life we have in those we are connected to, rooted in the earth which is our home and, finally, encompassed altogether in spirit—or that which gives meaning, coherence, and energy to everything. This ecology of learning renders us fully human. It does so by helping us to connect with our callings in life, to others in the local and global community, to Earth and ecological responsibility, and to a common sacred ground of being in which our unique religious and spiritual expressions are felt to have one heart with many-limbed expressions.

It is important to understand that this family of purposes does not fully come to life unless they operate together. Without connecting to self, our connection to others is impaired. Can we commune with others, nature, or spirit without having deepened communion with our own soul? The reverse is also true. Without connecting to other people, the earth, and a spiritual meaning, we cannot realize the most expansive aspects of self, but get stuck in self-centeredness and its destructive projections onto others.

This ecology of learning says that self and world are one whole. "We are the world," as the song goes—the microcosm in which the universe meets itself. Being human means being in harmony with all. The deeper we reach within our own soul and its many potentialities, the more we realize our essential harmony with others, nature, our home, and the cosmos. The more we contemplate truth in the world about us, the more we find a deeper, truer self reflected in what we see. Essentially, we and everything else are stardust and the ground from which the universe arose. A deep and open heart allows us to walk in the shoes of all that is. In those shoes, we feel into the being of all we encounter.

Are we ready for this kind of thinking in our communities and schools? We know from our "town hall" meeting that the network of values represented in self, community, Earth, and spirit are important. The question is whether we dare to make these the core purposes of education—and whether we can grasp how education must be related to the most significant dimensions of life in order for school to really work.

This leads to a related question—whether we can wake up from our cultural trance and understand that who we are is vastly bigger and more important than "what we can know and do," which is the current standards-based refrain in most states. Can we realize that skills and knowledge, while important, mean little in a soul-deprived person?

We must see that we are so much more than we ever imagined, that we feel compelled to respond to our own magnificence in the way we educate. The question becomes one of trust that there is something so good and unique in each child that we feel morally obligated to dedicate the adventure of learning to its discovery—as opposed to paving over that gift with some technocrat's dream-become-nightmare that exacts conformity and expects what it never can get, namely, a zest for life and learning.

Putting the moral urgings of such "town hall" conversations into practice will not be an easy process. It will call upon us to step over our fears into the bigger person we suspect ourselves to be, but may have lacked the courage to realize. We will land right in the middle of those chilling existential issues we may have avoided— questions like: Who am I? Where am I going? Am I doing what I want in life? Does my life have meaning? and What in me am I resisting that would make me a bigger person? This kind of thorny inquiry can wound our self-confidence and send chills down our solar plexus, causing us to shrink and live divided lives, as Parker Palmer is known to say. Or, this bold look in the mirror could bring a wonderful new life. Our individual and collective futures will be made at this threshold where we turn toward life or turn away in fear.

It remains to be seen how our public schools will unfold, but I am happy to say that there are people of courage all over America who have asked those deep existential questions in their own way, and who have voted for life. We see some of those words fill the pages of this book with hope, stories, and exhortations.

We don't have to reinvent the wheel. There are growing numbers of public and private schools with a whole variety of educational models to learn from that engage the whole child and embody a meaningful, communal, just, and ecological approach to education.

THE ORGANIZATION AND USE OF THIS BOOK

I have assembled a broad selection of articles and interviews from respected leaders in education, from those whose work concerns youth and from others who speak about the great cultural transformation that is called for in our time. To my knowledge, the people who speak and write in these pages have never before appeared in one volume. Their depth and diversity add a richness this subject deserves.

I have organized these articles and interviews according to the ecology of learning—self, community, Earth, and spirit—which I would propose as a starting point in thinking again about what education should be for.

The Great Work of Reconnecting to Self, Community, Earth, and Spirit, part I, launches us into the big picture behind the global crisis and the possibility for transformation before humanity today. Noted physicist and author, Fritjof Capra, talks about the revolution in scientific thought that underlies the kind of integral culture and thought we need to realize in ourselves and in our institutions. Writer and cultural analyst, Duane Elgin, gives us a way to look at this evolutionary threshold we've arrived at with new eyes, and the hope that our double wisdom as homo "sapiens sapiens" will prevail.

Part II, Educating for Self: Being Called into Life, begins by drawing from the ecology of learning that I originally envisioned as circles-within-circles, as depicted opposite the title page, to illustrate the interconnected nature of all four purposes—self being the innermost circle.

We hear about the necessity of drawing forth the callings in our young people by nurturing their interests, the hearts of teachers, and the kinds of person-centered environments where soul feels at home.

Part III, Educating for Authentic Community: Holding Space for the Heart, recognizes that people and schools are profoundly social, and that learning rests upon the depth and strength of connections we make with others. This is true of relationships within the school, between the school and its community, and between ourselves and peoples in other countries—as we go beyond nationalism and affirm kinship with all the people of the world. In this light, a spirit of multiculturalism must become a priority in our thinking and made a reality in our schools by honoring social justice, addressing issues of racial and gender bias in our systems, and affirming the need for culturally sensitive curricula and instruction.

Part IV, Educating for Earth: Future Generations and All of Life, is, in my mind, both the most challenging and thought-provoking section. We have only barely begun what Thomas Berry says we must—to rethink who we are from the species level on up. Contributors to this section acknowledge the role of human ingenuity and technology in moving toward a sustainable society, but all agree that only a spiritual transformation will make a sustainable future for humanity. A purely technological fix still keeps humans in control of nature, as opposed to humanity seeing itself as one part of a wondrous Earth community whose combined elements make up the great web of self-sustaining life.

Educating for Spirit: The Question for Heart, Character, and Meaning, is both the title and subject of part V. Spirit is recognized in all prior sections as an essential, integrative presence within and among people, and between people and the natural world. Here, we understand how a school can and must make room for a language of the heart, a spiritual literacy, and ways in which meaning and character development must flourish for education to be life affirming.

In the appendix, I offer a list and brief description of progressive schools I have visited in the United States that reflect one or more of the four principles in educating for humanity. I have included a partial list of resource organizations that offer professional development, technical assistance, and/or research to schools in line with the thinking of this book. Lastly, the appendix contains a reading list of titles I have found particularly helpful in the evolution of my own thinking.

I apologize for not laying out at this time a more concrete path for schools to follow. It is not my intent to prescribe fixed methods and programs in this book. I prefer, instead, to offer schools a framework of both values and thought as a mirror to reflect upon the community's own values. This requires work and commitment, but can result in more authentic, homegrown improvement efforts.

May each of you who read this work find insight and affirmation in your personal and collective journeys—helping to make your work with young people, your communities, and our world something that fulfills the deepest part of who you are.

NOTE

1. For more information on the Heritage Institute, visit its website at www.hol.edu.

REFERENCE

Tonybee, Arnold. 1974 [1946]. *A Study of History.* Abridgement of Volumes I–VI. London: Oxford University Press.

PART I

The Great Work of Reconnecting to Self, Community, Earth, and Spirit

Mike Seymour

DISCONNECTIONS

The insight of this book is that the separation of people from their deeper selves underlies all other forms of disconnection. Being disconnected from oneself hampers true connection to others, to the natural world, and to a higher meaning that gives a sense of hope and fulfillment. These fissures in self show up as institutional dysfunctions and are the central problems in our schools. Reconnecting is the way to a more human, meaningful, and intellectually rigorous learning environment.

Disconnection permeates our conception and practice of education. There are many examples. Teaching subjects separately, without showing their relationship, reinforces a disconnected view of the world. Students are not connected to their subjects because we fail to help them connect with themselves and make learning relevant to their lives. Similarly, too many teachers have lost their connection to their calling and passion, performing functions prescribed largely by custom and the mandates of school boards—working under conditions they cannot control, with no voice in setting their objectives, time schedules, or criteria of evaluation. Students complain about not being connected to their teachers or to other students because school cultures reinforce superficiality, inauthenticity, competition, formality, and other forms of separation. School cultures, curriculums, and policies do not connect with young people of nondominant cultural backgrounds, but perpetuate the cultural racism embedded in our Eurocentric society. The traditional school is not connected in a viable way to its community, especially in terms of seeing the community as a context for learning outside the walls of the school. Most schools don't connect, in any significant way, with the culture, history, and nature of its place—which we simply take for granted as a backdrop for the so-called important learning. I know of hardly any schools that have revisioned their purposes with Earth in mind. Our education does not ask what it would mean to teach, learn, and live simply and with sustainability so that others on the planet may simply live.

All of these disconnections drain the learning community of spirit, meaning, and purpose. And, in the larger sense, they are part of enabling the titanic course humanity has mistakenly charted in our time.

I have, therefore, dedicated this book (and this section in particular) to the explanation of why the "great work of reconnecting" must become the central purpose of society and our schools.

THE LESSON FOR TODAY

Every epoch of human history has its own lesson for humanity to learn. In our time, humanity is trying to learn that all life, human and other-than-human, is one interconnected whole. This perception invites us into an experience of the sacredness of everything. Understanding one's connection to the whole brings an inner realization that each person, animate and inanimate thing has an essence of its own and a vital role to play in the web of life. With this comes a deep sense of respect, relationship, and personal responsibility to the whole. Today, we are embarked on a "great work," to use Thomas Berry's words, of reconnecting—not just to the natural world—to the whole community of life, beginning with ourselves.

To begin the work of reconnecting, we must first make an inward movement into the unexplored depths of our own souls. Being sight-dependent, people have always looked outward more than inward—a habit reinforced by our culture and our education. People who are comfortable with their inner life must first buck the societal norm and suffer through the dark aspects of their nature. It is hard to be honest about our insecurities—jealousy of others, feelings of shame, unworthiness, of having failed—and our feelings of hate, aggression, pride, and lust. We do our best to avoid and deny these parts of ourselves that are painful and don't fit into our ideal picture of who we are. So it takes great courage, loving friendships, and faith beyond ourselves to traverse the soul's dark night into the light of our deeper connection.

The hope in connecting to our deeper selves is to encounter something far bigger than the small, shallow "I" of our everyday banality and sufferings. Christians, Buddhists, Muslims, Jews—all the religions and indigenous traditions—express a notion of dynamic connectedness, "interbeing," or "ground of being" as an essential nature of reality. Going inward connects us with a spirit by which we are able to experience our connections to all other people and things. Similarly, when we truly commune with others and nature, we intuit a presence, a beauty, and the very same spirit we experience in deep moments of connecting to ourselves.

All life swims in the same great river of spirit, and with this realization comes a most profound transformation in human awareness. In this process, our identity, motivation, and purpose are no longer just of our own making or limited simply to notions of "I." Who we are becomes radically shaped by the people and the things to which we feel connected. Our sense of isolation disappears, and we begin to think and act responsively (and responsibly) in harmony with the whole. This is the ultimate purpose in educating for humanity, and in realizing our connections and responsibilities to self, community, Earth, and spirit.

CONVERGENCE OF SCIENCE AND PERENNIAL WISDOM

The reemergence of an integral culture in our time is a response to a world situation so precarious that humanity cannot go forward with its present way of thinking and living. The moral and intellectual dialogue around integral thinking has been shaped by a renaissance of thought in our time. Modern science has affirmed the picture of the unified reality we see in our perennial wisdom traditions (as well as through our common sense).

Interviewed for this part of the book, Fritjof Capra has shown how physics, Earth, and biological sciences reveal the unitary nature of reality. The wisdom of twentieth-century physical science and quantum physics (in particular, as represented by Einstein) have linked the seemingly fragmented parts of the world in a universal web of interrelated energy fields. The worldview of Newtonian mechanics, which portrays a world of separate objects, has fundamentally changed.

Similarly, the work of James Lovelock and Lynn Margulis (2000) in evolving the "gaia hypothesis" helped to revolutionize our view of Earth as a whole, living system. Looking for the evidence of extraterrestrial life on Mars, Lovelock observed Earth as an extraterrestrial might. He began to formulate a method to explain why Earth appeared not so much as a planet adorned with diverse life forms, but as a planet that had been transfigured and transformed by a self-evolving and self-regulating, living system. Earth, in this view, seemed to qualify as a living being in its own right.

Today, we have an impressive array of theory (general systems theory) and scientific evidence in molecular biology, cybernetics, brain research, earth systems, and physics that all point to what the ancients have long said: We are all connected.

IN SEARCH OF A NEW STORY—WHERE WE ARE TODAY

In spite of these revolutionary advances in thought, conventional thinking, institutions, ethics, and policy are still dominated by the dualistic, Cartesian paradigm underlying our materialistic, industrial society. Capra explains that we all bear a great burden from our education and (technoscientific) culture—which has been steeped in an atomistic view of the world. In his chapter, "Ethics and Ecology," Thomas Berry points us to a further reason. He decries the absence of ethical leadership from education and religion in regards to the environment as reflecting a lack of "an integral or a functional cosmology" (this volume). In other words, as advances in science and technology wore away at the Christian cosmology of the "great chain of being," we've lost the story we tell ourselves to explain the world and our role in it—a story that once provided a common spiritual and ethical framework. And we have not yet created a new, collective story.

Joseph Campbell, noted scholar and writer in comparative mythology, emphasizes that we need myths to survive like we need oxygen to breathe. Myths are a life force with which to understand our existence—past, present, and future. Without a widely accepted cultural myth, each person and group have to discover their own guiding story in ways that are authentic and meaningful.

A STORY FOR EACH COMMUNITY AND SCHOOL

So too, each school community must work out its own story that makes sense of the world. Deborah Meier echoes what I hear many educators saying today: We can't "cookie cut" success from one school to the next. Being inspired by models are great, but each school and each community must dig deep enough within its own heart to find that river of spirit, the common sacred ground out of which a functional cosmology will grow.

Our stories grow first out of our individual souls, then the ground of our collective being and, ultimately, out of the place on Earth we call home. Whenever I have facilitated community groups and schools, I have always started with the first point in the ecology of learning—self: Who are you deep down? What are the deeper, multigenerational streams that make you who you are and bring you to this place in your life? Amazing openings, stories, and wisdom emerge when a group of people allow themselves to become vulnerable with the trust and support of a heart-filled, respectful gathering.

We see how the individual stories, rooted in generations, become a communal story in the present moment. Invariably, we find a convergence of themes among people, much like in my "town hall" example in the introduction of this book. The deeper we go into our individual humanity, the more we connect with the humanity of others.

Finally, widening the lens, I would ask: What is it about this particular town, this particular place in nature that calls you? How does this place shape and explain who you are? What are the claims on your life being made by this place? Perhaps I would have people go into the nearby natural areas or bring to mind a cherished place in nature where they feel wonderfully connected to themselves or to all of life. I would ask them what nature, and the web of social relationships that has peopled this place, says to them about who they are.

These themes are echoed in the work of Duane Elgin, whose interview appears in this part. Elgin speaks about the "opportunity trends" or powers by which humanity can transform itself. He mentions first the power of perception—to see the relationships and commonality among us. This perception of our connectedness is more strengthened the deeper we go into our personal story and see its many connections within our life and the lives of those who've influenced us. So too, our power as a community grows in proportion to the common, sacred ground we make together.

Next, Elgin says we have the power of choice. Each school, like each person, can and must choose its own story—a story that evolves continuously through experience. Too many schools are not "about" anything—other than being a building in a neighborhood which kids go to because school is what we "have to" do at certain ages. There is little personal or collective significance to many schools apart from being a place where we go mostly because we want to get someplace else. A school cannot begin to serve its youth, teachers, and community unless its story reflects the heart, passion, and commitment of its members—unless it is rooted in the souls, soils, and spirit of its place. For school to be worth our own and our children's time, it must have intrinsic worth. It must stand for something of significance to all the people involved and to the larger community of life, which is influenced by human thought and activity.

Elgin then talks about the power of communication. Much of the discussion about school does not address what is most important in peoples' lives. Conversations of significance are too infrequent and often fail to include all the right people— current and former students, for example. We need to deepen the conversation and reach people in the most significant spaces in their lives. Educators, parents, and community leaders must create a space for dialogue that revitalizes and connects us in a common ground. It is then that we will begin to draw in larger numbers of people—people who are hungry for the truth and for real talk. It is then that our conversation space will be worthy of the youth we must also invite.

Finally, Elgin talks about the power of love—that consummate force that makes our inner and outer worlds cohere. I have always felt at home in every school I have visited which lives its own story from the inside out. Our schools should be about caring, as educator and author, Nel Noddings, has so eloquently told us. When they are, I can literally feel the love in my bones. The greetings of students, walls covered with soul-inspired art, the warmth in the receptionist's manner, the attentive, patient presence of teachers—all serve to remind me that the everyday tapestry of love is being woven well in this place—and woven from a larger pattern of meaning.

REFERENCES

Lovelock, James. 2000. *Gaia: A New Look at Life on Earth.* Oxford: Oxford University Press.

1

Networks and the Web of Life: The Science Behind an Integral, Sustainable Culture

An Interview with Fritjof Capra by Mike Seymour

I met Fritjof Capra in Berkeley at the Center for Ecoliteracy which he cofounded and which aims to "foster a profound understanding of the natural world, grounded in direct experience, that leads to sustainable patterns of living." They offer many grants and programs to K–12 schools. At the time, we were meeting with students from Common Ground, a school-within-a-school at Berkeley high that had been funded by the center. Fritjof has an intensity that is in accord with his reputation as a physicist and one of the leading figures in explaining systems theory and science to lay people. Author of the Tao of Physics, The Turning Point, The Web of Life *and, recently,* The Hidden Connections, *Fritjof has decisively explained the interconnectedness of life.*

MIKE SEYMOUR: I came to know you through your work in *The Tao of Physics, The Turning Point,* and *The Web of Life,* which I read with great enthusiasm. What are some of the notions of the worldview expressed in your early writing that figure prominently in your present thinking?

FRITJOF CAPRA: The central discovery in modern physics was formulated at the beginning of the last century in quantum theory, relativity theory, and quantum field theory. The discovery, which was very difficult for physicists to understand, is that you cannot see or understand the world in terms of isolated objects. Isolated objects with well-defined intrinsic properties do not exist. They are a feature of the world of

Newtonian physics that was based on macroscopic phenomena like billiard balls colliding or pendulums swinging. As physicists penetrated into smaller and smaller dimensions, to the subatomic level, they saw a need to describe reality as a network of relationships. Any node in this network has certain properties derived from the links to the other nodes. A subatomic particle is not a thing in itself. It is a set of relationships that reach outward to other things and those other things are relationships in turn, so you never end up with any well-defined fundamental objects; you always have to talk about relationships. I think that shift from objects to relationships is a central characteristic of systems thinking, which I have explored now for over twenty years.

SEYMOUR: I wonder why so much of the lay and scientific world doesn't accept the relational, interconnected nature of reality and its larger implications. What do you think lies behind the failure in so many to grasp this concept of the unified nature of reality?

CAPRA: I'm not sure if I have a clear answer, but one thing I would say is that Western intellectual history weighs very heavily on us. We have all been educated within the Cartesian–Newtonian paradigm. When we learn things in school, we start with the mechanistic worldview and rarely go beyond that. The whole conceptual framework of education, at all levels, is based on this mechanistic framework. When you talk about business for instance, managers are trained to be efficient and to run a corporation like a machine. Of course that doesn't work, because a company is not a machine. It is a system of living organisms interacting, forming communities and relationships. So, educated in a mechanistic view and given intellectual tools appropriate to study mechanical systems, we don't even have a very good language to analyze and study networks. We don't even have the tools to inquire into questions like: How many types of networks are there? Can you classify networks? What are their structures? What are their key characteristics? How does a living network differ from a nonliving network? In fact, we are just beginning to study these issues. The unusual nature of this perspective and the difficulty in finding the right language creates a great hesitancy among scientists and professionals to appreciate network thinking.

I also believe people are afraid of the uncertainty implied in a network or systems-view of the world. They want a world that is predictable and controllable. In complex systems, on the other hand, there is no straight line from a cause to an effect. Take the current insecurity and sense of vulnerability in the United States after the terrorist attacks of September 11. The White House portrays international terrorism as an evil force operating in a vacuum. Once we have identified the terrorists, they say, we can prosecute them and bring them to justice and we will eradicate evil. This is a simplistic linear analysis to ease people's fears and uncertainty.

SEYMOUR: On another note, in *The Web of Life*, you introduce ideas from Varela and Maturana that living systems are cognitive systems and that the organizing activity of living systems is a kind of mental activity. Could you explain that for us?

CAPRA: This major advance in our understanding of life has to do with the question of the nature of mind and how mind is related to matter, to the entire organism. This involves a whole set of questions that have puzzled philosophers and scientists for centuries, ever since Descartes made a strict division between mind and matter by postulating that they belong to two kinds of realities. One is the reality of matter, which he called the "extended thing" because matter has physical extensions. The other, the reality of mind, he called the "thinking thing." This division has kept Western thinking, for centuries, from seeing the unitary nature of life. The major advance has been the recognition that mind is not a thing but a process. In fact, it is the very process of life, as argued by Varela and Maturana. This is a radically new concept: Every living organism, from the simplest bacteria, is engaged in a cognitive process. The interactions of the living organism with its environment are cognitive interactions, or knowledge interactions. So, Varela and Maturana have identified the process of knowledge with the process of life. As they put it "to live is to know." This process of knowledge, or cognition, does not operate only through brains but through all organisms, like plants, for example, which don't have nervous systems but are still engaged in cognitive activity.

SEYMOUR: This view of the sentient and unitary nature of all life is echoed throughout our wisdom traditions and world mythologies.

CAPRA: Yes. In fact, ordinary people often have a direct experience of life and understand its integral nature of life. There are many examples of this in our folk wisdom.

SEYMOUR: One aspect that would trouble many people about Varela and Maturana's thinking is that there is no objective reality because the only world we know is one known through our perception. This flies in the face of most people's steadfast adherence to the fact that there is such a thing as an objective reality. So how would you explain that to people?

CAPRA: I would ask them to picture a tree and to consider how differently a dog, insect, or bird would see the same tree. They would perceive it differently since they have different sensory organs, perceiving different colors or shapes. We know from science that the shape, texture, and color seen by a bird, or any other animal, are very different from what humans see. Also, have a few glasses of wine and your perceptions will change. We know from these experiences that what we see depends on our state of mind. Taking into account evolution and development, we can say that what we see depends on who we are, how we have evolved, how we have developed.

SEYMOUR: The subjectivity in our ways of knowing has great implications for education. I move away from the idea of the objectified universe and understand that everything, including me, is part of a system of networks. For instance, by observing a particle, I am influencing the particle by virtue of the fact that I am seeing it. What does this say about learning and the process of education?

CAPRA: A living system is a learning system which responds in unique ways to its environments depending on its structure, and we know that the structure changes in this process. If you apply this to education, you realize that all children learn naturally, so it certainly doesn't make sense to force them to learn. They will learn because they are alive, and living systems learn. The question is: What do they learn? What will they learn from the teacher's body language about human respect, about authority, about prejudice, about honesty? This is what we call the "hidden curriculum." Children pick up all these unspoken cues which are the subtext of teaching.

Young people learn what they're interested in and what has relevance for them. Today, many teens know the lyrics to perhaps as many as fifty top songs. To inspire young people, we need to help them become full human beings and respect their natural curiosity as an aspect of the curriculum.

SEYMOUR: We need to respect young people's native interest and learn how to channel that to benefit both themselves and society.

CAPRA: The way I approach education and relate it to systems thinking is through sustainability and ecological literacy. The great challenge of our time is to build sustainable communities, designed in such a way that our lifestyles, technologies, social institutions, and physical structures do not interfere with nature's ability to sustain life. Sustainable living means living in such a way that we do not interfere with nature's ability to sustain life, which means that we first have to know how nature sustains life. This brings us to the study of ecosystems. By studying the principles and processes of organization in ecosystems, we can derive a set of key concepts which we call the principles of ecology.

SEYMOUR: I know that young people learn and are affected by their understanding of ecological concepts. But if this is just an intellectual exercise and not something that impacts them in a deep, emotional way, they would miss, if you will, the sacred experience of the web of life. What are your thoughts about the need for the more spiritual or intuitive dimension in learning ecoliteracy?

CAPRA: I think this is absolutely critical because kids could be brilliantly educated in principles of ecology; they could analyze ecosystems and tell you everything about primary producers, secondary producers, cycles, decomposing organisms, and so forth. And then they could go and become stockbrokers, buy their SUV, and care little about the environment. Knowing nature is not enough. One must also learn to care for and love nature, and that cannot be done intellectually. This is why we take kids out into nature. We take them out into the school garden, out into creeks, and give them a firsthand experience of the beauty of nature; give them a sense of responsibility that only comes when you feel connected to nature. So, there is a visceral experience that we are trying to elicit in young people that is absolutely critical.

SEYMOUR: I would like to turn now to your latest book, *The Hidden Connections: Integrating the Biological, Cognitive and Social Dimensions of Life into a Science of Sustainability.* It sounds like this is a magnum opus of sorts that builds on much of your past thinking and then goes further.

CAPRA: It didn't start out that way. When I started four or five years ago, it was just going to be a book about the latest from the forefront of science, but it turned into a theoretical framework that integrates three dimensions of life: the biological, the cognitive, and the social dimension. In the book, I apply this integrated framework to some of the critical problems of our times—economic globalization, genetic engineering, biotechnology, sustainability, ecodesign, and the management of human organizations.

SEYMOUR: Your central idea there is the concept that we are all involved in networks, and you compare biological networks and social networks. What are some of the similarities between social and biological networks?

CAPRA: The similarities are in the network pattern. Once you understand the network pattern—feedback, self-generation, emergence, and so on—you can apply these both to biological networks, which are networks of chemical processes, and to social networks, which are networks of communications. There are many differences too, and the key difference is that human networks of communication always involve meaning. We communicate meaning, we generate meaning, we generate contexts. So you need to understand the world of consciousness and culture to understand social networks. This is why I went into cognitive science and studied the nature of consciousness—to be able to deal with social networks.

SEYMOUR: Speaking of meaning and contexts, you elaborate on the great conflict in our time between the forces for a sustainable society and those for global capitalism, which are both networks in a contest for shaping the future of humanity and the world.

CAPRA: These two competing scenarios are the major developments of our time, and both are based on networks. We have the networks of global capitalism which are electronic networks of financial and informational flows; then we have the ecological networks of nature; and then there are the human networks of grassroots organizations that reject the current model of globalization and want to have different values integrated into it. We don't say that globalization is bad in and of itself, but global trade needs to take into account the values of human dignity and ecological sustainability. If we can build that into global trade, we can survive and live sustainably.

SEYMOUR: That leads us to the $64,000 question. How do we move to that new set of values? Some people say capitalism is simply hostile to essential human values, the same way they speak of our public schools as essentially broken and needing to be abandoned. How do you see us moving to a more sustainable future?

CAPRA: I believe this is already happening in the emergence all over the world of sustainable cultures and practices. The argument that things cannot be fixed is no longer valid. There are enough progressive organizations in all fields—in education, science, business, agriculture—that the question is no longer "What can I do?" but "Where can I join?" There are many organizations working on sustainable futures that are now globally linked. I describe this in my book as the new civil society—the global network of NGOs, grassroots organizations, research and educational institutions, and activists working on significant alternatives in many fields for a more ecological future. One example is the renaissance in organic farming, which is directly related to what we are doing at the Center for Ecoliteracy.

The future of all of this is certainly difficult to predict. It is going to be chaotic. But one of the lessons we have learned from complexity theory is that chaos is not all bad. Chaos has an inherent creativity.

2

An Evolutionary Threshold: Calling on Humanity's "Double Wisdom"

An Interview with Duane Elgin by Carter Phipps

Duane Elgin and I first met when he came to Whidbey Island and gave a talk about the ideas from his latest book Promise Ahead: A Vision of Hope and Action for Humanity's Future. *I recall him being introduced as "one smart dude," which only begins to give a clue to the awesome visionary intellect of this man who is also down-to-earth, caring, and self-effacing. Duane lives true to his calling as a friend of Earth and the ideas in his initial book,* Voluntary Simplicity: Toward a Way of Life That is Outwardly Simple, Inwardly Rich. *He described a life of courage and adherence to his vision in spite of financial uncertainties. This interview was first published in* What Is Enlightenment? *magazine (Spring/Summer 2001), Moksha Press, and was then titled "The Breaking Point." Thanks go to Carter Phipps, the interviewer. Used with permission of the publisher. Duane's website is well worth visiting: www.awakeningearth.org/. For more information see www.wie.org.*

CARTER PHIPPS: Many of today's leading thinkers, futurists, scientists, and visionaries are warning us that the next twenty to thirty years will be a testing time for the human species, a time of evolutionary crisis that will entail great, and potentially even catastrophic, change. Could you please describe what you feel are the key factors precipitating this crisis? What will we be facing in the coming years?

DUANE ELGIN: What we're really facing is the convergence of a number of powerful trends—climate change, species extinction, the spread of poverty, and the growth in population. All of these factors could develop individually, but what's unique about our time is that the world has become a closed system. There's no place to escape, and all of these powerful forces are beginning to impinge upon one another and reinforce one another. Our situation is something like a set of rubber bands that you stretch out and out and out until they reach the limit of their elasticity, which is the breaking point of the system. My sense is that we still have a fair amount of elasticity in the world system. It's going to be another couple of decades until we reach the breaking point.

PHIPPS: How would you respond to someone who said, "What crisis are you talking about? There may be a lot going on, but things aren't that bad. I'm sure we'll deal with it. No problem, we'll be okay." What would you say to that person to convince them that the situation is urgent and that we have to face it directly?

ELGIN: Let's take a look at these trends one at a time. First, climate change. I think it's clear that, by itself, this could change the entire situation in the world. If you look, for example, at carbon dioxide levels, they are very closely correlated with temperature levels over thousands of years. The carbon dioxide levels have fluctuated between 170 and 300 parts per million for the last twenty million years. And we are now outside of that range. We are at nearly 380 parts per million of CO_2, which means that we have created a situation that's beyond what has existed for the last twenty million years; a period in which there have been enormous fluctuations in glaciation on one hand and global warming on the other. And we're still shooting out the roof in terms of the amount of CO_2 we're putting into the atmosphere.

Now let's look, for example, at the Greenland ice cores and the way they indicate how quickly climate changes can occur. They show that the last great ice age, about 120,000 years ago, descended, scientists believe, in a period of two decades. It wasn't centuries; it was roughly twenty years. So we are creating a very critical situation. But my concern is not simply with warming and the oceans rising, but rather with changing weather patterns, precipitation patterns—how much rain and when. If it shifts radically, we will not be able to adapt global agriculture to respond to the new climate circumstances.

At the same time that climate change is under way, in the same twenty-year period, we're going to add roughly two to three billion people to the earth—that means the equivalent of another Los Angeles every month. We're going to be adding enormous numbers of people to the earth at the very time the climate is beginning to shift and make food-growing more precarious. It is also estimated that, in terms of resources, 40 percent of the people in the world will not have access to enough water by the 2020s to grow their own food. Forty percent of the world will not have enough water to grow their own food. And most of those people are going to be in the poorest parts of the world, in developing countries where they have moved to megacities and are living in the slums.

We can then factor in other impacts, like species extinction. It's estimated that as many as 20 percent of all plant and animal species could be extinct in the next thirty years, and half could be extinct within the next hundred years. Now let's put that into even more specific terms. It's estimated that roughly 25 percent of all mammals are threatened with extinction, 12 percent of all bird species, 25 percent of all reptiles, and 30 percent of all fish; this is the World Conservation Union's recent report. We are beginning to tear at the fabric of the biosphere at the very time that we're stressing it with climate change, at the very time that we're stressing it further with population, at the very time that we're diminishing the availability of critical resources like water. And then we factor in a final force, and that is poverty, which is extraordinarily massive in the world. I really had no idea until recently [when] traveling in India and seeing the magnitude of it. In the United States, the poverty line is about $11 a day per person. If we cut that poverty line by three-quarters, set it at $3 a day per person, and ask what percentage of the world lives on less than $3 a day, it's 60 percent of the world! And that means that whether it's a pair of shoes or a book to read, or glasses, aspirin, vitamins, et cetera—the basics of life that must be purchased at world market prices are not accessible to 60 percent of the world's population. But if you walk into the villages in India and Brazil, you see that even the poorest people have a television set. They are seeing, in living color, lifestyles that will never be accessible to them. And historically, those are the ingredients for revolution.

So there we have what I call the adversity trends, and we could talk about many others: Ozone depletion, ocean overfishing, deforestation, and on and on. And it's utterly clear that not only are these critical individual trends, but that, as you look at the dynamics of their convergence, we are facing an unprecedented whole-system crisis within the next few decades. Something powerful is going to begin happening at that point, and while right now we can turn away from this, in another twenty years, a systems crisis will be an unyielding reality that we will have to deal with. And we will either deal with it by pulling together as a human family to produce what I would call an "evolutionary bounce"—or by pulling apart to produce an evolutionary crash. If we pull apart, it will be an evolutionary dark age.

PHIPPS: In your book, you also mention several trends that potentially herald new opportunities for our collective evolution. What are those trends, and what do you think will be their impact on us in the near future?

ELGIN: I feel that there are a number of equally powerful opportunity trends that are cooking away in the world that have the power to transform what could be an extraordinary evolutionary crash into an evolutionary bounce. The first is the power of perception, the capacity to see the universe as a living system. The second is the power of choice, the power to choose different ways of life. The third is the power of communication, the power to use these incredible tools of communication for purposes way beyond commerce. And the fourth is the power of love, the ability to bring a spirit of reconciliation into relationships of all kinds. We could speak about each of these, but collectively, they are an extraordinary force for transformation in the world.

PHIPPS: Could you give a brief overview of each one?

ELGIN: First, there is the idea of a living universe. Science has traditionally regarded the universe as nonliving at its foundations, but it's extraordinary that now, at the frontiers of science, we're beginning to find out that the universe itself is functioning as if it were a living system. For example, the physics theory of nonlocality tells us that the universe is connected with itself, despite its enormous size. And physicists say that there are enormous amounts of energy at the foundations of the universe, the so-called zero-point energy. Also, consciousness appears to be present at every level of the universe, from the atomic scale (and the behavior of electrons that seem to have a mind of their own) on up through the human scale. So the universe has the properties of a living system; life exists within life. This is an amazing miracle, and as we discover this, I think that it is going to begin to shift who we think we are and what we think our life journey is about. It's transformative. The idea and the experience of a living universe is a powerful recontextualization of who we think we are and where we think we're going.

The next opportunity trend is the emergence of simpler ways of living that put less stress on the earth. These lifestyles of simplicity are not so much driven by sacrifice as they are by a new sense of where satisfaction is to be found. What I see emerging in the world now is what I call the "garden of simplicity." There are some people who are practicing a more frugal simplicity by cutting back on their spending and decreasing the impact of their consumption on the earth. They're choosing to live simply, in Gandhi's words, so that others may simply live. Someone else may be practicing a "political simplicity," feeling that we have to organize our collective lives in a way that enables us to live lightly and sustainably on the earth—and that means changes in our transportation, education, media, and so on. There's also an approach that I call "soulful simplicity," which means approaching life as a meditation and cultivating our experience of intimate connection with all that exists.

The point is that there is a whole shift in mindset now occurring. In the United States, for example, a conservative estimate is that about 10 percent of the American adult population, or twenty million people, are making a shift on the inside toward a more experiential spirituality and on the outside toward a more ecological approach to life. Taken together, these could transform the adversity trends into a great opportunity.

Opportunity trend number three is the communications revolution, and it is also a very powerful trend. We can already see it transforming the world. Whether we're going to use this for positive transformational purposes or whether it's going to use us and just transform the entire world into consumers, I don't know. It depends upon us as citizens to see that the power of these communications technologies is used for higher purposes.

PHIPPS: In your book, you connect the history of human evolution with our ability to communicate.

ELGIN: Yes, I think it was our ability to communicate that enabled us to get from hunter-gatherers to the verge of a planetary civilization. And it will also be our ability to communicate that will get us to a sustainable species civilization.

The fourth opportunity trend I see is reconciliation. If you look at the nature of violence and conflict in the world, I think it's actually shifting out of the adolescent reactive mode into the adult interactive mode of negotiation. We're recognizing the enormous cost of hostility. In South Africa, for example, there has been a shift away from apartheid to their new government. What an extraordinary transformation. In Northern Ireland, they are attempting to achieve some degree of peace, and it's coming along. Look at what's happened in the Middle East. They came close, and now they're seeing how painful it is to have missed that opportunity. And so there's a more mature consciousness that seems to be growing in the world—seeing that the power of love, of reconciliation, is fundamental to our future if we're going to live on this small earth together. And it's not only about ethnicity, gender, and race, but it's also about issues of income distribution, generational reconciliation, even other species that we're divided from—there are many dimensions of reconciliation.

PHIPPS: You have also stated in your book and elsewhere that you believe our current crisis is a crisis of spirituality or awakening. Could you explain why you feel the spiritual journey is inextricably linked to our collective success or failure as an evolving species?

ELGIN: We are not simply hitting an environmental wall, or the limits to physical growth, but we are hitting an evolutionary wall, which is the limit of our traditional image of who we think we are as a species, and the limit of that form of growth. And we are also hitting the limits of our life stories as nations, as races, as ethnic groups. We need to find our larger story as a human family. So when we look at our sense of identity as a species and our need for a larger story, then that invites us to look into the so-called spiritual realm.

PHIPPS: What do you mean by "our larger story as a human family"?

ELGIN: I mean, who are we? What are we doing here and where are we going? My sense of our larger story is beautifully summarized in the name that we've given ourselves as a species: *Homo sapiens sapiens*. "Sapient" means to be wise; "sapient sapient" means to be doubly wise. We're the species, by our own definition, which knows that it knows. So to fulfill our self-given name as a species, as *Homo sapiens sapiens*, to fulfill our capacity to be doubly wise, is to discover our place in this living universe. It utterly transforms the nature of the human journey. Then we can ask ourselves: Are we serving our capacity for double wisdom, for knowing that we know— in other words, for awakening? And can culture co-evolve with that awakening of consciousness? And if so, how can we best evolve the culture and consciousness in a way that really serves our collective awakening? Then that becomes the agenda, and at that point, all of these issues that we're struggling with now are put into a completely different context.

PHIPPS: What do you think has to happen practically to make these changes? How do we pass this evolutionary test?

ELGIN: I think there are different things that need to happen, obviously, but what it finally comes down to, I feel, is conversation. The tissues of our lives are our conversations and our stories. As individuals, whether it's in living rooms, boardrooms, or classrooms, we need to be having conversations about these adversity trends and opportunity trends, about the initiation that we're going through. We have to wake up to what's happening. We need to have face-to-face conversations that really anchor this in our personal lives. At the same time, we need to be having conversations in our public lives, through our mass media, that support people in seeing that in addition to a consumer world, there's another world happening out there that we have to pay attention to as well. With these, what I would call "reflective conversations," happening both on the local scale and the societal scale, I think we could rapidly reach a working consensus for moving along a very different track toward sustainability and a much more satisfying future for ourselves. But consciousness is the key. Waking up is the key.

PHIPPS: How do we create the sense of urgency that is so critical in terms of our collective consciousness?

ELGIN: We can either wait for the circumstances to impinge upon us so harshly that we wake up, or we can magnify the input regarding, for example, species extinction or climate change, or poverty, or resource depletion. We can magnify the input by putting those things into our consciousness via the mass media. And right now, all those factors are excluded from the mass media. We're regarded not as citizens who want to be informed but as consumers who want to be entertained. So a very powerful way to transform this would be to open up more time on the airwaves—which is really opening up our species mind, our collective consciousness—for these kinds of concerns, as well as for the wonderful opportunities that are out there for us.

PHIPPS: One way to look at the spiritual path is to see it as a journey from an egocentric, self-centered perspective on life to an ever-increasing care and concern for greater and greater dimensions of life as a whole. However, traversing the deeper dimensions of the spiritual journey in a way that truly frees one from an egocentric view of the world has long been considered to be a very arduous undertaking, involving a profound commitment on the part of any individual who would take up the path of transformation. While there is no doubt that the world is in dire need of spiritually mature individuals, the genuine article seems to be a rare commodity. So, given the urgent demand of our collective crisis, and yet at the same time, the profound challenge of real spiritual transformation, what gives you confidence and hope that the transformation you envision will take place in a significant enough number of individuals and/or institutions? How can enlightenment save the world?

ELGIN: Let me say that as I've gone around the world in the last five or six years, I've had the opportunity to ask people in very different places and circumstances the following question: If you look at the whole human family as a single individual, how old are we? Are we behaving like toddlers, teenagers, adults, or elders? And immediately, much to my surprise, people have had no problem understanding the question and overwhelmingly have said that we're in our teenage years as a species.

That prompted me to look at adolescent psychology. And, indeed, if you look at adolescents, they tend to be rebellious, just like we're rebelling against nature. They tend to feel that they're immortal, that they're going to live forever in their current form, and we are also living with disregard for the long-term consequences of our behavior. Adolescents tend to be into outward appearances—and here we are;

this materialistic, consumer-oriented culture. So there are a lot of parallels between teenagers and the behavior of the human family today. Now I have three sons in their late twenties and have seen them mature out of those adolescent qualities into [having] a real concern for their families, their future, their work, and their relationships with others. And if we, as a human family, make that simple shift from our teenage consciousness into our early adult consciousness, I think the results will be organic, very natural, and quite amazing.

So I take confidence from having asked people about the age of the human family and having heard people respond so enthusiastically and so quickly that we're in our adolescent years. That suggests to me that a very normal, organic process of development and growth is taking place. We are approaching our natural opportunity to wake up and come to our early maturity as a species, and I have confidence in the deep integrity of the universe and in our integrity, as a human family; in our journey.

PHIPPS: Social activists have often been harshly critical of the spiritual search as being overly narcissistic—concerned solely with the individual and indifferent to the larger concerns of society. At the same time, spiritual masters have long claimed that it is only through individual transformation that anything can ever truly change in society as a whole. For example, the highly respected master J. Krishnamurti is quoted as saying, "What you are, the world is. And without your transformation, there can be no transformation of the world." It is a question perhaps as old as the spiritual life itself: Do I change the world or do I change myself? Given our current evolutionary crisis, how do you understand the role of individual evolution versus that of collective change? For those individuals who have a powerful spiritual calling and who also care deeply about the state of the world, where should they put their energy and attention?

ELGIN: My sense is that it's a co-evolutionary process. We've thought that we could disengage from the world and have a spiritual enterprise that was our own process of awakening. It's wonderful to be awake in an ancient tradition, but it's also very important to integrate those lineages into the modern world. So we have a lot of bridging to do between the spiritual and the worldly, between the species mind and the species body, so to speak.

For example, if you look at the world's spiritual traditions and ask how many of them are looking at the mass media as an expression of the collective mind and therefore bringing insights from their traditions to help transform the mass media into a more enlightened, healthy expression of that collective mind—it's not happening. You don't read about this. But the mass media is a powerful tool for bringing the principles of insight developed in personal meditative practice into our collective practice of paying attention as a whole civilization. For example, in Buddhism, there is a list of factors of enlightenment or of a healthy mind, which include concentration, mindfulness, equanimity, etcetera. Now, let's apply those to our whole civilization and use television as the most obvious manifestation of our species mind. Are we using television to be mindful? No, we're not. We're being contracted into a very narrow, small, consumerist view of the world. We're practically disconnected from the world. We do not understand these larger adversity trends that are impacting upon us. Are we using television to cultivate the capacity for collective concentration on critical choices? No, we're fostering distraction and fragmentation. Are we using television—our social brain—to cultivate equanimity? No, we're fostering collective agitation in much of the media produced now. My point is that irrespective of the spiritual tradition, there are general qualities of an awakened species mind that we need to begin cultivating as a human family if we're going to really deal with these serious challenges.

So I think we're discovering that we're deeply immersed in the species mind and that the species mind is not terribly awake at this point. But those who are awake are experiencing the suffering, the tension, and the stress of that species mind, which is struggling to awaken. And it's important for those who are working on their own wakefulness to be attentive to the species mind and to recognize that they are pioneers in a larger struggle, in a larger process of awakening. In many ways, this is the call to species maturity that is being evoked by this time of initiation, this rite of passage as we move from a journey as individuals to a journey in communion with the rest of life, with other people, and with the species mind.

PHIPPS: Earlier you mentioned that to fulfill our purpose as *Homo sapiens sapiens,* or "doubly wise humans," is to "discover our place in this living universe." Could you explain how realizing our potential for double wisdom allows us to discover our place in the universe?

ELGIN: First, I think it's very important to look at nature's designs as we try to understand our evolutionary journey. And if we come into alignment with nature, my sense is that our evolutionary journey is going to be much easier and smoother. If you look at what nature's doing, whether at the atomic level, the human level, or the galactic [level], you see this common signature; a common shape that emerges, that, in a static form, looks like a doughnut and in its dynamic form could look like a tornado, a hurricane, or a whirlpool. Called a "torus," this is the simplest structure of a self-organizing system. Atoms have that structure; galaxies have that structure. And so what I infer is that at every level the universe has a central project, and what the universe is doing is creating self-organizing systems. Now, [being a] *Homo sapiens sapiens* involves the capacity to be consciously self-organizing. If you know that you know, you have the capacity to center yourself, to organize yourself, and to take charge of your life. Becoming a fulfilled *Homo sapiens sapiens* is the fulfillment of what the universe is all about. So as it turns out, we have given ourselves a name that is completely in alignment with the fulfillment of the universe's common purpose.

PHIPPS: You have also written about our common purpose in more explicitly spiritual language, suggesting that part of the human journey is the pursuit and discovery of who we are at the level of the soul, far beyond the confines of our physical bodies. In the evolutionary process, we can ultimately recognize ourselves to be, as you put it, "a body of light and knowing." Could you explain what you mean by this "body of light and knowing," and do you believe that this is the final endpoint of human evolution?

ELGIN: Physicists talk about the basic building block of this reality as being the photon, which is light. That means we already live in an ecology of light, and that means we already are beings of light—right now. It's just that it's fairly dense here. So you could say that the endpoint of evolution is already in front of us, in that sense. As we fulfill our potential for knowing that we know, often this awakening is described as being bathed by a light with immense wisdom and compassion. I feel that we are immersed in that light right now in the midst of a living universe. Evolution seeks to allow that light to flow into our being and then out into expression in the world. Now, is that the final endpoint of evolution? I don't think so. What I think is happening is something perhaps even more extraordinary. As we come to our center of knowing that we know, that's really just the beginning of evolution. When we are stabilized in our own deeper sense of self, we can then move in the deep ecologies of eternity as conscious, active, co-creative participants. So rather than the endpoint, it's really the starting point. I think the cosmos is a place for life forms to come to self-referencing knowing freely. Realizing our potential for double wisdom marks the beginning point of a whole new phase of evolution.

PART II

Educating for Self: Being Called into Life

Mike Seymour

WE ARE CALLED

Educating for self begins the journey to realize inner aliveness and purpose by finding ourselves through what we cherish and love. In this context, education is about who we are as well as what we can know and do. Educating is about drawing forth the callings within our own deeper nature.

Early on, parents notice seeds of calling in something special about their child. I am not talking about calling as job or career, but as the sense of urgency in us that seeks its own unique expression in life. The observant parent notices signs of calling in the idiosyncratic ways of each child, sometimes within hours of a baby's birth. As a family therapist, I would ask parents what gifts and leanings they noticed in their child. I have yet to meet a parent who had not recognized some quality and disposition peculiar to each of their children.

We all understand, at some level, that each child is born unique. We may also realize the otherworldly nature of this uniqueness—what makes a child distinct doesn't come from either nature or nurture. It cannot be explained simply by genetic inheritance or home and social influence. When we see beyond the surface and into the heart of each child, we sense something mysterious and sacred.

My sons, Malcolm and David, each revealed the distinctiveness of their personalities, their callings, within weeks of birth. Malcolm, the oldest, was colicky and a difficult baby—up every two hours for feeding. He showed precocious tendencies at eighteen months by learning the alphabet and using a board with wooden letters—and was argumentative, particularly with his mother. He did well in school and gravitated toward debate, at which he excelled. He loved the chance to do research, make cases, and hone his verbal arguing ability.

When Malcolm was in the ninth grade, I asked him to close his eyes and imagine what he would like to be when he grew up. I was less surprised by the answer he gave than the certainty with which he reported it. After pondering for a few moments, he said, "I want to be a Justice of the Supreme Court." Where did this come from? Certainly not from me, who has been skeptical of the legal profession. I acknowledged his call to advocate for fairness and justice while wondering what hand of fate had touched this young man's spirit. Today, true to his calling, he is completing law school with a focus on international human rights law.

At its simplest level, calling is about sensing something and responding to it. This is the relationship between self and the wondrous world about us, which starts with the mother and child regarding one another and then moves to outer objects that elicit interest, grasping, and movement toward. Being encouraged to sense and explore one's environment is essential in nurturing the capacities for openness, perception, self-trust, and curiosity that help a child become an adult of confidence and purpose.

As one matures, one grows interests and passions, shaped by values, talents, and what intrigues or compels us—all of which lay bare the image of something unique within our personal natures. Most of us consider ourselves fortunate if, somewhere along the way, we grow some life-defining purpose and meaning—something beyond ourselves that gives our lives its deepest expression. A calling.

Calling becomes shaped at the intersection of the individual's own soul and the needs of the world about us. The passion that brings a more expansive sense of life goes beyond self-interest and seeks goodness in the world—a love and desire to give to something other than oneself. Out of such altruism, each person assumes his or her place in the community and is recognized for the special gift they bring.

In the case of my sons, their callings are leading them into their professional careers. But this does not mean that calling is only about our work. The longings of the soul are much larger than any work, relationship, or place. Ultimately, the longing in us calls for realization of the beauty and sacredness in each moment; we are called to life itself, of which work, marriage, and home are particular expressions. When we understand calling primarily as any one thing, we divide our lives in ways that rob us of the fullness in all of life.

In his chapter Downside Up: Getting Education Right, Ron Veronda addresses this subject, suggesting we must protect ourselves and our kids from the dangers of literalism and the mistake of thinking that a job is what we're all about. We have to open up to the wider symbolic meanings of our young people's dreams. He tells of expanding Mike's dream of becoming a welder on union ships to a larger context in which many career choices would be possible. In a parallel way, my son Malcolm learned that the image he first held of a Supreme Court Justice was but one expression of a larger heart-calling to social justice and advocacy for those in need.

Therefore, we must break the chains of literalism to liberate the greatness in our youth and turn their attention to the wider meaning in their passion. We must allow them to learn in the context of the larger world to whose needs they are called. Finding one's piece of that "great work" of our day, as Thomas Berry suggests, bestows a dignity of spirit and largeness in life for which our souls have thirsted. Each child is born for big things. A secret part of every heart knows and yearns for this sense of spaciousness.

DEAFNESS TO CALLING AND THE SOULLESS SOCIETY

Not to realize one's gift—and be welcomed by others for the gift one has—brings great pain. Moreover, we all suffer the loss of any one person's gift, since each of us is connected in this vast web of life to every other person, being, and thing. The smiles or frowns of strangers, the beauty or devastation of nature together comprise the ocean from which we drink and draw our being.

To be born but not to have fully lived—not to realize, as Parker Palmer says, "the life that wants to live in us" is a terrible loss. Deaf to the callings of our heart, we grow insensitive to life itself and unresponsive to the joy, beauty, pain, challenge, and bigness that is ours to have.

Lacking true vitality, we substitute false pleasures, shallow interests, or addictions for that which would otherwise bring authentic fulfillment. By not living out their inner callings, generation after generation has made and remade the ideas, values, and institutions of the soul-depriving society we live in today. The current obsession with consumption—which powers our suicidal, global economy—arises from the ghosts of lost callings, and feeds on this pervasive spiritual deprivation.

There is an existential epidemic of people who feel lost or out of harmony with life. Many who felt a call at one time may have simply run out of water in the spiritual desert of our modern world. They may, in fact, be the lucky ones. At least they realize something is missing. More lost are those who do not know they are lost, but simply have accepted the cultural incantation that a job, a roof overhead, and the "American dream" of making money and having nice things is what it's all about. Whatever bigger truth may be felt inside is walled off, creating a divided self mentioned by Parker Palmer in my interview with him (this volume).

Walled-off, divided people make fertile soil for the seeds of dogmas and ideologies that divide one person against another, promoting distrust, hatred, and violence. When the deeper self is not listened and responded to, the soul's call becomes shadowy, showing up as boredom, shallowness, mischief, greed, infidelity, illness, conflict, anger, inhumanity, and violence. All negativity breeds more of the same until we return to our true roots. Either we pursue self and the inner life, or it haunts us in its dark ways. The measure of our flight from calling can be seen in the current social and ecological disasters that constitute the defining test of humanity in our time.

Nurturing the deepest part of who we are and finding our calling is essential for a peaceful, meaningful, and sustainable society.

TOWARD A BIGGER SELF

Our era of global interdependence calls us to realize that all of life, human and other than human, sinks or swims together. We need to go beyond every division (tribalism, regionalism, nationalism, humanism, and religious sectarianism) into a consciousness of what all people and life on Earth have in common. Just as the crisis in our time is a spiritual one, so the self we need today is an expansive and spiritual one. Our consciousness needs and wants to feel connected to things beyond us that also, paradoxically, make us feel more like who we really are. Therefore, we must resist the narrowing culture of hyperindividualism that has desecrated the social and natural landscape of our world and our schools. We must search for a more expanded or integral self.

Both Robert Bellah and others (*Habits of the Heart: Individualism and Commitment in American Life*) and Robert Putnam (*Bowling Alone*) agree that elevating the individual to a status above society causes related notions (self-reliance, individual wants, the corporate bottom line, the quest for achievement, rationality, and a sink-or-swim approach to moral development and economic well-being) to become enshrined as absolutes at the expense of communal values.

Seeing each individual as solely responsible for personal well-being hides the truth of our interdependence. It also disguises the culture's bias as an advantage, if you're part of the dominant culture, and as a disadvantage, if you're not. Hyperindividualism is a cornerstone in cultural and institutional racism, elitism, and all forms of separation that contribute to the loss of social capital, civic consciousness, trust in public life, and the sense that, together with our neighbors, we can make the world a better place for all.

Regaining our humanity means resisting the culture of "me-ism," comparison, competition, and achievement solely for individual benefit—which characterizes so much of our society and schools. It means educating for a bigger, more inclusive sense of self by highlighting the distinctions and gifts of all. It means seeing that our gains and losses are interdependent with others and a larger community of life.

TOWARD A DEMOCRATIC EDUCATION

Denying teachers and students a role in deciding what goes on in school is not only a bad lesson in democracy, but is also a sure way to dampen the natural curiosity by which children (and adults) come to know themselves and the world.

Letting students and teachers have a voice in education need not devolve into chaos and "everybody doing their own thing," as critics of democratic forms of education would like us to believe. It does take time and care, and what may seem like endless meetings to those who just want to get a decision made, get on with it, and go home. But the time and, yes, frustration, are worth it.

It is worth it if you believe that each person has something of value to contribute, that each person is worthy of being heard. The more people are not listened to, the more they grow mute and don't listen to themselves or start yelling in anger. These are two sides of the same coin.

AS WE THINK, SO WE ARE: MENTAL MODELS

Whether or not a child's authentic, deeper self finds a home in school depends upon the values and assumptions about human nature that guide our ideas of learning and teaching. If there is a strong belief that each child brings something special to school in the form of interests, cultural distinctions, and talents, then the job of teaching is about bringing these forth. On the other hand, if kids are seen more as empty vessels, albeit with unique talents and qualities, then the job of teaching is seen as filling them with socially useful information.

In the first case, education will be more student-centered, collaborative, and honoring of the student's voice and right to choose. I call this the "whole child" model. In the latter case, which I call the three Rs model, teaching tends to be characterized by lots of teacher "talk-time," memorization of disconnected facts, reliance on texts, and sorting of students through tests.

Given that most parents acknowledge something special about their child, I was pondering why the three Rs model has such a hold in America, when I interviewed Deborah Meier, known for her outstanding work in the Central Park East elementary and secondary schools in Harlem. I asked if parents were really interested in having a school that honors the special qualities unique to their child. She confirmed what I already suspected. Parents are aware of and value something special in their child, but see school as a place for "getting ahead—to become socialized—to become more like everyone else" and are "uncertain about their child's uniqueness and anxious about not failing them as parents, so they sometimes push more for achievement along accepted lines" (this volume).

It seems too many of us have settled for a job instead of calling, and therefore look at school for our children mostly as an economic ticket to get ahead. If we want a culture in which calling is drawn forth in our schools, we need the courage to respond to the truth that we and our children are far bigger than our current notions of education assume. We need the courage to live this bigger truth against the ground swell of materialist concerns that have swamped our culture.

DEEP CALLS TO DEEP

Only when our teachers' inner genius comes to life can they water the seeds of calling within their students. The unhappy inverse is also true: Teachers shut off from their passion in life too often shut down the kids they teach.

Young people learn to relate to themselves and the world through the example of others. We realize our callings in relation to the adults and friends whose own passions and teachings let us drink from many cups and sample new worlds. Students do best with teachers who care about kids and are passionate about what they teach.

Parker Palmer speaks about the Courage to Teach teacher formation program he initiated to help teachers rejoin "soul and role." Palmer's and similar work, like Sam Intrator's, *Stories of the Courage to Teach*, remind us that good education and soulful young people are more likely when teachers are supported in remaining alive to their own calling.

INWARDNESS

Inwardness and self-reflection in school need to grow in value and practice for schools to be hospitable to the calling of young people. The gentle voice of our deeper nature simply can neither be felt, listened to, nor appreciated in the din of a hectic, fast-paced life. If the life in school, like in society, is about "getting somewhere" more than it is about simply being in the present moment, we lose those delicate spaces in which our deeper self arises. We need not wonder why stress is pandemic, and why many kids, like their parents, feel emptier the more they both do and have. We are blindly groping outward for that which can only be found in our inner stillness.

The role of inwardness in education has been recognized for years within the holistic education tradition and, more recently, in the wealth of educational literature on bringing spirit and soul to education. Social and emotional learning, popularized by the work of Daniel Goleman, is now taking root in many classrooms throughout America and the world. Based on the thesis that emotional literacy and social skills make for success in school, home, and work, programs to help kids identify feelings, become aware of and control destructive impulses are widespread and have many proponents.

Inward people move more deliberately and mindfully through the day, noticing the pin Susie wears, the scratch on someone's knee, or the new shoots pushing through the soil in spring. The joy in small things that warms our insides never arises when our pace is inhospitable to the guest of little graces. Chip Wood, in *Time to Teach, Time to Learn: Changing the Pace of School*, confronts the epidemic of busy-ness in our schools and speaks to this need for slowing down. Curriculum coverage, more "time on task," and doing more, result in an illusion of accomplishment and an impoverishment of soul—and of real learning. In contrast, Wood describes a host of ways to make time for deeper reflection, more meaningful social interactions, restructuring how time is used in and between classes, and policy structures that value slowing down.

A culture of inwardness is the only basis for an intellectual rigor that has been lacking in our schools and in society at large. We can have all the curricula in the world for "higher order thinking skills," but we will not produce more thoughtful people without a culture of inwardness.

Americans, by nature, have not been much of an intellectual people. Deep thinkers are as out of favor today as when Adlai Stevenson ran and lost for president. We value action and bravery more than deliberation, discussion, or diplomacy. We tend to tire of extended dialogue and sustained intellectual activity. "My head hurts too much when I think" is a statement I once heard that reflects the anti-intellectual bias in this country.

Small-mindedness, bigotry, the inability to expand thinking and encompass other views are hallmarks of restrictive cultures that repress authentic self. On the other hand, breadth and flexibility of mind enable breadth of self and the respect for the individuality of others.

REFERENCES

Bellah, Robert, Richard Madsen, William M. Sullivan, Ann Swidler, and Steven M. Upton. 1996. *Habits of the Heart: Individualism and Commitment in American Life.* Berkeley: University of California Press.

Palmer, Parker. 2000. *Let Your Life Speak: Listening for the Voice of Vocation.* San Francisco: Jossey-Bass.

Putnam, Robert D. 2000. *Bowling Alone: The Collapse and Revival of American Community.* New York: Touchstone.

Wood, Chip. 1999. *Time to Teach, Time to Learn: Changing the Pace of School.* Greenfield, Mass.: Northeast Foundation for Children.

3

Authentic Living and Teaching: Rejoining Soul and Role

An Interview with Parker J. Palmer by Mike Seymour

Prior to visiting Parker Palmer at his home in Madison, Wisconsin, where this interview was done, I had the pleasure of hearing him speak at a Boulder, Colorado, conference on Spirituality in Education in 1997 and at a day-long presentation in Seattle. Parker fulfilled all the expectations I had of him from reading his many books, as a person truly big in heart, courage, and wisdom. He has evolved a language that makes self and spirituality accessible and relevant to both teaching and learning. Palmer is author of To Know as We Are Known: Education as a Spiritual Journey; The Active Life: A Spirituality of Work, Creativity, and Caring; *and* Let Your Life Speak: Listening for the Voice of Vocation. *He is best known among K–12 educators for his book* The Courage to Teach: Exploring the Inner Landscape of a Teacher's Life *and for the Courage to Teach teacher formation programs that he initiated with support from the Fetzer Institute. Reading over this interview, I have been amazed at how fluidly and coherently he speaks about the importance of joining soul and role as teachers and learners.*

MIKE SEYMOUR: In your book *Let Your Life Speak,* you talk about "calling" and our deep sense of self and ask us to consider this probing question: Am I living the life that wants to live in me? Could you open this up for us?

PARKER J. PALMER: We have a life independent of the "I" that thinks and plans. In Western culture, we're hung up on this notion that the self I'm mostly conscious of is the only self I've got. This ego self, however, is the shallowest part of us, not the "true

41

self," as Thomas Merton used to say. This is the same claim made in all the wisdom traditions, and it challenges the reductionism in our culture where the self is seen as raw material to be shaped by social forces. We are on dangerous ground when our concept of human beings is reduced to raw material that we are then free to shape in any way necessary to support a certain cultural, social, and political system. Wisdom traditions concur in the view that human beings are not raw material, but rather, have a unique nature, [unique] potentialities and limits, which are ours to discover over a lifetime's journey. It takes a lifetime to discover the underlying truth about ourselves that lies deeper than our ego wants and the expectations of others. The journey takes us toward understanding the mystery of our own selfhood and trying to live more deeply into it.

SEYMOUR: You speak about inauthenticity and the divided life as being a central, pervasive issue in society as a whole and in the lives of individuals.

PALMER: The divided or inauthentic life comes in a variety of forms. One of those [forms] is living the life that someone else hopes you will live, which is the simplest version, like the child who feels forced to live some unfulfilled part of the parent's life. In general, though, the divided life is more subtle and hard to detect because it is not always a life that I live simply to respond to someone else's expectations. The wall of separation between inner truth and outer act is often something we create ourselves because we don't want to live the truth that we know inwardly due to the risks involved. I think of Rosa Parks sitting at the front of the bus, deciding in that moment: I am no longer going to live a divided life. I am no longer going to act on the outside as if I were less than the full human being I know myself to be on the inside. That was a risky act. Many of us have sensed a truth in ourselves that, if acted on, could cost us friends, a job, income, or status. The dynamic of the divided life is rooted in protecting ourselves against risk by building a wall between the inner and [the] outer. Living an undivided life also requires that we open the shadow side of ourselves to communal scrutiny and questioning. It takes courage to face the shadow elements inside of us and our capacity for doing harm. But we can reduce the danger that comes from our own shadows by not hiding our faults from ourselves and others until one day all our pent-up darkness bursts out.

SEYMOUR: I wonder how many people believe they are being themselves without realizing the degree to which their self is shaped by the social convention of the culture? The opinion that they have a good life, by societal standards, is part of the wall denying access to a deeper part of themselves that wants to speak to their lives.

PALMER: It's much easier to live on the outside, settling for the minimums—a roof over our head, food in the stomach, and a decent job. But the kinds of crises many people experience—like depression, illness, the death of a loved one, loss of a job— make them more aware of some of the subtle symptoms of dividedness in themselves. The subtlest symptom is going through the day on automatic pilot. Here, you do what needs to be done, possibly even doing it as well as you know how, but you're not reaching for that growing edge of your existence. In this case, people become aware that things seem okay on the surface but inwardly, they are numb, anesthetized.

SEYMOUR: And that comes out in things like boredom, our addiction to entertainment, or feelings of restlessness. We have momentary feelings that things aren't quite okay, but then we go to the TV or do something to dampen the discomfort.

PALMER: Exactly—and sometimes we cover up with busy-ness and overwork. We know all about drug and alcohol abuse as ways of anesthetizing ourselves to our own dividedness. But I think the drug of choice for a whole lot of us is simply staying frenetically busy until we get so tired we have to crash—only to awake to another round of busy-ness.

SEYMOUR: Vocation today is often made synonymous with work, but I believe your understanding of vocation is far broader and derives its meaning from the more spiritual and existential sense of vocation.

PALMER: Vocation is one of those words we have diminished, so that now we talk about a vocational school as a lesser form of education where you learn to perform some practical task. The word *vocation* has its root in the Latin *vocare,* the same word that gives us voice, and it means to be called to some purpose, some truth, some depth of selfhood in your own life. This requires listening for that call, because the call does not come to us in thunder or Technicolor, but in a still, small voice, or through those symptoms of malaise we were talking about earlier. I think it is very important to restore vocation to its original meaning to help people understand that the journey, at any age, is not just looking for a job, however important that may be. Vocation is about seeking purpose and making a meaningful investment of one's life in ways of being and doing that are true to one's identity and [are] of service to others.

SEYMOUR: Vocation doesn't come from our willing it, but from receptivity and openness to hearing the voice of our own inner teacher or guide. In your view, what keeps us from this kind of attention to our own lives beyond what we've already talked about?

PALMER: We want to be in the driver's seat—and receptivity, especially among intellectuals in Western culture, takes away our control. We resist the idea that there is something larger at work in this universe than our own minds, thoughts, and plans—and "listening" assumes something that is more knowing than we are. We don't like to listen and we don't like to receive, because we might hear something that we don't want to deal with, something that would challenge and call us to a larger self. Wanting to stay in control is typically considered a sign of mastery, but it's actually a position of great fear and weakness. Out of fear, we try to control the unpredictable.

I see examples of this all of the time in the classroom. A professor stands behind the podium with his or her lecture notes and asks the students to be quiet and memorize what they need to know, and then spit it back out on the test at the end of the term. That's staying in control in a self-protective way so that that professor never has to confront something in dialogue that he or she wouldn't know how to handle. On the other hand, there are teachers who open the process up and say: "Here's the question. Here is the body of data or problem we're going to work on. Let's do this together. You bring your experience and knowledge to the table and I'll bring my experience and knowledge to the table, and we'll create a community of inquiry around this thing." Professors like that are taking the risk that someone in the room may know more than they do, or that some tense and messy conflict is going to emerge. But teaching like that educates students and demonstrates what it means to be a learned person in a much more vivid and compelling way than standing behind the podium, maintaining control. Translate that into parenting, supervising employees, or jobs of any sort and I think you would see the downside of overcontrol.

SEYMOUR: Talking about teaching, I want to quote from your book, *The Courage to Teach,* where you write: "When I do not know myself, I cannot know who my students are. I will see them through a glass darkly in the shadow of my unexamined life. When I cannot see them clearly, I cannot teach them well." Can you expand on this?

PALMER: Let's look first at authenticity in teaching from the student's side of things and then turn to the teacher. Whatever situation we are in, we ask a very simple question: Is what I see on the outside of this person the same as what is true on the inside? Children ask that about parents, students ask it about teachers, employees ask it about bosses, citizens in a democracy ask it about their political leaders. "Are they the same on the inside as they are speaking and behaving on the outside?" When the answer to that question is "no"—when we are getting an act on the outside that is different from what's on the inside—the situation, by definition, becomes dangerous. You don't know what you're dealing with in this other person, and that uncertainty makes people crawl into their foxholes. The child, student, employee, or citizen withdraws. They withdraw investment, energy, attention—and, in a democracy, they stop voting. Why bother to cast a ballot if you are voting for people who are putting on a false performance rather than telling you who they really are, what they think and feel, and what they are actually going to do?

In teaching and learning, the consequences of inauthenticity seem very clear. Students don't learn at any level of depth if they aren't invested—and they won't be invested with an inauthentic teacher. Suppose you're studying race relations in a society or racism in institutional life, and you've got students sitting in your class who are racists, or have been burned by racism, or are somewhere else on that continuum. They perceive the situation as so unsafe that they are unwilling to tell their truth, to bring their experience to the table. All they are getting is a head full of ideas from some book or some lecture that will never touch the truth of what is really going on in their lives. So, from the student's side, learning doesn't happen when the teacher is behind a wall.

I have vivid memories of times in my life as a teacher when my own inner dynamic and fears were so unexamined that I projected all kinds of false assumptions onto my students. I became afraid of my students, so concerned that they would wound me in some way, that I distanced myself from them. When that kind of disconnect occurs, I can't see who my students are; I can only see what I am projecting on them and [I] cannot connect with them in the way good teachers have to connect.

This is all tied in with my belief that we teach not through an abstract process of data transmission but by embodying a field of knowledge to which *we* become the bridge for our students. We connect to our passion and students are drawn to the subject by being drawn to our enthusiasm for it. For years I have collected stories from people about great teachers who touched their lives. It's amazing how often those stories say hardly anything about the field that was being taught, but they say an enormous amount about the personhood of the teacher. Often, people say they wanted to become a physicist or English literature scholar because they wanted to become like professor Jones. This is the bridge of selfhood that a good teacher creates to provide safe passage for fearful students into a fearsome field of knowledge.

Fear is one of the great unexamined topics in education. Being ignorant about something makes us fearful. A good teacher becomes a bridge across that chasm of fear by investing selfhood and teaching "from the heart." By heart, I don't simply mean the emotions. I mean heart in the more ancient sense—that place in us where intellect, emotions, will, and all our other faculties converge, where we are one with ourselves and what we are doing. When you see *that* in teaching, you see great teaching. This is not about personality. Students are able to sense authenticity not only in user-friendly teachers but in rigorous and demanding teachers as well. If they perceive authentic selfhood to be present, students don't get hung up on personality.

SEYMOUR: It is not just about being nice, which is a trap some teachers, especially new ones, fall into. The memorable teachers you refer to are courageous in terms of personal honesty. They model stepping over their fear into the truth and convey to students that they can do likewise.

PALMER: That is exactly right—and another word for this would be passion. These people are passionately present in the world. This is not only the Italian kind of passion where you wave your arms and raise your voice! It might be a Quakerly kind of passion where the inner light is glowing quietly but brightly from within, without a big show on the outside. Students recognize all these forms of passion and the authenticity or integrity that underlie them. The teachers that students don't trust are those who cloak themselves in distanced professionalism, a form of the divided self. Teachers like this are "phoning it in" or are on "automatic pilot." With such teachers, education becomes tedious and students don't rise to the occasion. And why should they?

SEYMOUR: Talking about being a bridge for students, you say teachers teach who they are, which means that beyond the subject matter, the message of teaching is our personhood. Students are reading us all of the time wondering if we're real and [if we] honestly care about them and, therefore, are safe to open up to.

PALMER: Young people have a built-in bunk detector. They are always asking: Is this person real? This happens especially starting in middle school, because that is when kids start wrestling with their own authenticity and start feeling the pain of the divided life. Up until middle school, kids are pretty much in the world as they are. You get a chance to see true self at work if you look at a two- or five-year-old. But as children enter the middle-school years, they start to question who they are, and have to deal with not only their own self-consciousness but with cliques and peer pressure. Even if they can't put the question into words, they are asking if it is possible to be who they really are, and they look to teachers as models. A teacher who can model authenticity is not only going to be liked by students, but will also make a big difference in the lives of some children at a very important time.

SEYMOUR: Many teachers see themselves as real people, but at the same time are also prone to professionalism, not relating to kids, and generally getting worn down by the dividedness in the bureaucracy. Is authentic teaching more of an ideal than a reality in our public schools today?

PALMER: I'll refer to The Courage to Teach program, where we help teachers "rejoin soul and role" through a two-year series of eight weekend retreats involving groups of twenty-five or so teachers. In this program, we hear teachers say that they were taught to distance themselves from kids. This was not part of the formal curriculum—which taught "best practices" in relating to students—but was in the hidden curriculum of what was modeled in their training. In other words, the academic culture itself was divided and was not walking its own talk. This is a common story with professional training in nearly every field.

After university, teachers often enter a school culture with little collegial support—not necessarily because their colleagues are uncaring persons, but because they are all being harassed by papers to fill out and hoops to jump through. All of this—on top of teaching thirty or forty students (and more in secondary education)—takes so much time and energy that teachers are left with very few reserves with which to support each other.

Also, the professional context in schools allows very little reflective time for the important questions of selfhood and meaning, which are exactly what the students want to explore. So when teachers go into the classroom, they are under considerable pressure to put on a professional mask rather than teach from the authentic self.

Take, for example, what has happened in our culture around teachers touching a child. When I was going to school it was common for teachers to use appropriate touch as a mechanism of reassurance, or guidance, or perhaps even a caution of some sort. Teachers today still have the human impulse to touch, but they are reluctant to do so for fear they will be accused of inappropriate touch, sexual harassment, physical abuse, and the like. We have created such a chill around authentic human relationships that many teachers feel on guard against the very impulses that are the core of our humanity.

SEYMOUR: You mentioned The Courage to Teach teacher formation program. Would you talk more about the kinds of transformation in teachers seen in this program?

PALMER: The Courage to Teach—which is now going on in about thirty cities—is a program that takes a group of twenty-five K–12 teachers through eight retreats over two years. Each retreat is three days in length, led by a trained facilitator, and is focused on the inner life of the teacher and reconnecting soul and role. It is a foundation-supported program, so we have been evaluated from the very beginning eight years ago. Our evaluations show a number of powerful and interesting things. First, many teachers come to our groups with more than five years of experience and are among the best teachers we have. But too many are about to leave because of the discouragement of working in the public school system. The evaluations show that this program renews their commitment to their vocation, which I think is very important.

Second, they become better colleagues—and we get this not only from their own testimony, but from the testimony of colleagues as well. They become more creatively involved in gathering colleagues together to make good decisions, to talk through problems, to share the journey.

Third, they become more deeply connected with their students. While most of this evaluation is credible self-testimony, we also heard the same thing when we talked with students.

Fourth, a lot of our teachers had bailed out on the politics of public education because it is so abusive to them. But through this program, they find ways to come back in a more creative mode—as peacemakers and as agents of change who know what they are talking about.

A final evaluation finding is that, when the two-year program comes to an end, the teachers who have taken that journey together want to keep on going. I led the pilot group in Michigan [in] 1994–1996, and some of its members are still meeting today because they learned to value community. It is a community of people who understand what it means to support each other's inner journey—not a community gathered to solve some external problem, or to achieve some external goal, but a community that helps each person learn to listen to his or her soul.

When people experience the power of doing that together, they don't want to let it go. They want to keep journeying with each other because they have found an invaluable support for more fully realizing themselves and fulfilling their own deep calling.

4

Mentoring the Genius of Our Youth: Watering the Seeds of the Future

An Interview with Michael Meade by Lauren de Boer

Michael Meade is a renowned storyteller, author, scholar of mythology, and student of ritual in traditional cultures. He has the unusual ability to illuminate how we live today through myth and traditional ways of knowing. Michael is the founder of the Mosaic Multicultural Foundation with a mission that includes a commitment to youth-at-risk, "genius-based" mentoring, and developing the "arts of community" in diverse organiza-tions and groups. He is author of Men and the Water of Life; Crossroads: Quest for Contemporary Rites of Passage; Holding the Thread of Life: A Human Response to the Unraveling of the World; *and coeditor of* The Rag and Bone Shop of the Heart. *The following chapter is adapted from an interview with Lauren de Boer,* Earthlight *magazine editor, that appeared in the Winter 2002 issue of* Earthlight *under the title "Youth Rising." Used with permission.*

"THE BANANA TREE AND THE MOON"—AN ORIGIN OF DEATH STORY FROM MADAGASCAR

Adapted by Michael Meade

> Once, before there was any time at all, when there was only one man and one woman who were in direct communication with the deities, it so happened that the deities said to those two people: "What do you prefer in terms of death?"

The first man and the first woman said: "Our preference is omission. We'd like to pass regarding any opportunities to die."

The deities answered: "This is understandable, and somewhat commendable in terms of its cleverness, but it's impossible. Life is fatal. Your choice is that you can die and then continue in the way that a banana tree does. Or, you can die and then come back in the way the moon does."

The first woman and the first man talked it over, and they decided that if they entered death and came back the way the moon disappears and leaves the sky dark and then is reborn, itself into itself, then they would always be just themselves, just by themselves, repeating themselves over and over. On the other hand, if they died the way a banana tree does, sending out shoots that then become other banana trees so that the first tree dies away but is followed by a multiplication of small banana trees, then the world would always be different. Besides, they wouldn't be doing everything alone; they would have children.

So, they went back to the gods and goddesses of that time and said: "We wish to die the way that trees die. We wish to die and leave sprouts that grow up and become other trees. And ourselves, we will go and take a rest."

The deities said: "That choice is good enough for us. Now that you have chosen it, you are already beginning to die."

As the first man and the first woman were growing, falling, walking their way toward death, they kept close to themselves the idea that they would be leaving children behind.

And that is the way both death and children came into the world.

LAUREN DE BOER: You tell the story of the banana tree and the moon where the gods give a choice to the first couple about death.

MICHAEL MEADE: It's one of our cosmological stories, from Madagascar. [The story says] that we've chosen this business of living and dying like the trees. We are like trees that produce fruit and seed; our living and dying fructify the world around us whether we know it or not. We have made, and keep making choices, that are related to the trees around us.

DE BOER: An interesting thing for me about that story is that it ties together the coming into the world of children and death. It seems to me it's a story about learning generosity toward future generations by making the choice of dying to our own lives, but spreading seeds that go on.

MEADE: When the idea comes up that we can make a new myth, I have to quibble over the words and some of the implications. I think, like the trees, we keep regrowing the same shape and similar forms. Yes, it's a new tree, but it's also the same apple tree that started all that trouble back in that other garden. We keep encountering the tree of knowledge of good and evil, keep missing the Tree of Life.

It's the second week of January now and right in front of where I sit and write, there's one apple left hanging on the tree. All around it, the bare branches, within it the seeds of time. That apple has in it the story of the original garden, but also the story of all other apple possibilities. There it hangs, both fruit and seed, impervious to winter and the flooding rains we've had. There's something persistent about cosmology and about myth, just the way there's something persistent about nature. A new myth is really the old myth telling itself in a way that engages us once again, taking us back to origins. Originality, so highly prized in the Western world, means "a return to origins."

It's like the trees and the seeds from the trees. We're handling old seeds and assisting new growth. Is it a new myth in the sense that it's another telling of the story? Yes. Is it an old myth in the sense that the story's telling itself again? Yes. Going back to the story from Madagascar, we participate in the ongoing creation by being and by saying that in order to be conscious of what we're doing, we must accept that we will die. We're going to continue this choice made by the original parents—to die and leave progeny, leave living seeds in the world. When that choice is made, we change the conversation from being about "me and my need" and "my culture and its hunger" to being about continuing the story in a way beyond oneself. [This] is part of the sense of cosmology as something that goes beyond oneself, of myth as telling the bigger story and of nature as life continuing its many forms.

DE BOER: To future generations.

MEADE: Including future generations of thought and of imagination. The seed opens up to mean everything from people to the seeds of thought.

DE BOER: If a new myth is about retelling the old stories in a way that's needed, then it seems to me that youth are one of our primary sources of what's needed.

MEADE: Youth are the edge of the story that the culture's telling itself. Youth are where the past and the future meet—the story is both being told and being found. It's like the making of a poem. It's a creation, but also a found experience. Youth live at that edge. They are strangers at the threshold of culture and at the threshold of nature, stumbling and striving into the story of their own nature, the nature around them, and the culture around them as well. Strangers at the threshold, they're an explosive act of nature, in flux and flood and growth. They're also the explosion of the culture. They're the past of the culture speaking its story in a new way, and the potential and future of the culture as well.

DE BOER: Are they a symptom of what needs to be healed, or what needs attention?

MEADE: A culture gets the youth it deserves, the youth it has made. They are always symptomatic, and a place where healing can begin. I've said to ecological groups that if you can get meaningful numbers of youth working at the story of ecology, change will occur more rapidly, more surprisingly, more beautifully.

DE BOER: You've said, in your tape "Throw Yourself Like Seed," that stories are about change and that ritual is the art of change. How can story and mythology help?

MEADE: Someone once described mythology as "the lie that reveals the truth." Mythology's modern connotation means "something false," but the word itself has to do with emerging truth. Something people usually see as fiction is actually carrying meaning and truth in the depths. Young people are just like that. People say, "They just want attention," and I say, "What's your point?" Attention is required for them to find themselves. "Themselves" is something that's a deeper story in them that modern culture would deny, reject, overlook.

People often send kids to camps in nature. It's a smart idea. They fit in with nature because they're exploring their own nature. I work with all kinds of young people. At fourteen, young people are having the seed ideas of their life. What we call middle school, early high school, is the time when the seed, the core imagination and seed ideas of their life are bursting within them and are seeking what I call the "waters of attention," the blessing, blessed waters from the culture around them that will allow those seed imaginations to grow.

DE BOER: What happens if they're not shown the recognition of that seed?

MEADE: Now, we're back to death. Blake said that the garden of the soul is already planted and is waiting for the water of life. Call it the water of attention. There are innate ideas, dreams, stories, buried in people. When we don't water those seeds, culture loses ideas. It loses imagination. It loses the capacity to dream itself forward. I mean that literally. What happens to someone whose innate core cannot grow?

The "second nature" of a person (the innate capacities) needs two kinds of attention. The person has to attend to it themselves. It also needs the other kind of attention which used to be called a blessing—the attention, especially from someone who's respected, someone who says, "I saw that. I heard that. I see the seed of life you're coming from." If these two kinds of attention don't happen, a kind of death is occurring, a withering.

DE BOER: The gift atrophies.

MEADE: Atrophy occurs and we it call depression and suicidal tendencies. For some, there's too much fire in the seed to simply atrophy and those burst into violence. Each young person is like an extreme story compelled into this world. Because of the intensity of life each person carries, there are two big tendencies, one toward suicide, one toward homicide. Either there is atrophy, withdrawal, and implosion or there is the explosion in which the seeds are cracked, blown, and strewn about to become the kind of seeds that don't find an earth in which to grow.

DE BOER: There's violence that comes from the lack of attention to one's seed. How does that relate to the violence from outside? What happens if we don't deal with the reverberations of violence from September 11 [2001] with young people?

MEADE: September 11 was a horrible thing, incomprehensible in many ways. At the time, I was doing work in South Central Los Angeles. When I'm there, I see terrorism every day. We have an internal terrorism in this culture. You can look in both directions—the outer terrorist and the homegrown, inner terrorist—both come from seeds of life so consistently rejected over generations or an extended period of time that they can't grow in a meaningful way. They can become dead seeds and seeds of death.

To my eye, a terrorist is someone who's already dead. That's why they're so hard to deal with. None of the things that normally apply to human psychology, apply to them. They found a suicide note in the car that a terrorist left in the Boston airport. It had been written two years before the attack. He was carrying his death note for two years . . . he was already dead. Terrorists are in the world of the dead, trying to drag other people there.

I've been with fifteen- [and] sixteen-year-old kids holding a gun, planning to go shoot someone based on some neighborhood revenge drama, and they intend to be shot while doing it. If you say to them, "What about your future?" they'll say, "I don't have one." If you say "Isn't there anything you want out of life?" they say, "I won't get anything out of this life." It's a tragic, grievous thing—to sit with someone of that age and realize not just that this person is about to kill and be killed, but that this person might already be dead.

DE BOER: They haven't had that inner seed recognized.

MEADE: And something has happened that's caused that to seem impossible. I don't know if it's ever completely removed. I would say there's always the possibility of bringing that seed to life. But, seeing the terrorists made me realize they were in the same condition. Their story has stopped, and they want to take everyone to the land where their stories are frozen or dead.

DE BOER: We don't recognize the terrorist in our own youth.

MEADE: Even more seriously, we don't recognize the terror we've visited upon our youth. Someone planning major destruction, including destroying [his or her] own life, has made a suicide pact. I've seen it with kids who shoot at cops. They usually don't even hit very well. What they're doing is trying to get the cops to shoot them. It's a suicide plot. A lot of gang killing is actually mutual suicide. There are many things that a culture does that stops the story of some of its people. That's a form of terrorism.

DE BOER: The work you're doing with the poet Luis Rodriguez and gang youth seems an attempt to provide an antidote through myth and poetry. Has that been successful?

MEADE: There are some areas where success is hard to measure. Culturally, we're always looking for outcomes. Mostly, what people want is a story where, against all odds, someone overcomes the obstacles and turns out "like us."

DE BOER: Sounds a lot like the movies.

MEADE: I understand that level of story. But there's something else going on, an odd thing where at a certain level of culture you have young people who are really not in the culture, in most regards. Two things happen there: You can study what it is to be of the culture, but outside it, and you can see some possibilities beyond the culture.

Often, those who have removed themselves from the culture are capable of rapid change. I've seen more thorough and quicker change in pretty hard-core street kids than you might see in someone working hard to change their life every day.

Because of their lack of engagement or involvement with what's going on around them, they become more capable of change.

DE BOER: Is it, to some extent, their proximity to danger?

MEADE: Yes, and their feeling that their life could be lost any moment. I don't want to overdo the connection because I don't want to glorify what's going on, but there are moments when they're monklike. Because they're outside the culture, they're available to different imaginations and perspectives. They're capable of changing because they're less tied in. I find that intriguing, both as a possibility where good change can occur and also as a place to learn, where a tremendous amount of education can go on.

Let's say you have a good idea. You're quite excited about it. It has to do with ecology. Then you find a group of young people who have never heard that idea, and may not even know what you mean by ecology, and don't necessarily even have any interest in you. If you present that idea to them, and they get it, you've got a truly good idea. It's a tremendous place to test your knowledge or inspiration because they're not tied in or invested. They don't have to accept anything you say.

What happens when Luis and I are working with gangs is that if they don't hear something authentic, they walk out. No discussion, no apology, not even any rancor. They've been walking out of the culture, so they can walk out on anything. You have to say something authentic or the conversation is over. It throws you back on yourself. Being authentic is an immediate, momentary thing. What was authentic yesterday is not so today. So you really have to get into the moment. In that sense, it's a great place to learn. What can be applied there can be applied anywhere. All the new ideas I've seen are growing on the edges and margins of culture, like new species of plants.

At Mosaic, we do events called Voices of Youth. There was a young girl in it. She had so many scars on her body from cutting herself and being beaten on the street by other people, it was amazing that she was alive. No one knew why she was there. She would not talk. We started to write poetry. She wrote a poem and at some point decided to read it. It was an anguished poem, but also beautiful.

When she finally decided to speak, out came this poetic story of what had happened to her. You heard something of the raw expression of a voice trying to get into the world, and behind its pain, some kind of still-hoping life. From that, you learn something about the basic ground of human life because a lot of the people who are outside the culture [have] fallen to the ground that is sometimes the deeper earth where life learns itself.

DE BOER: Fire is an image you've used in stories. One is an image of the elder at some distance tending the fire for a youth. The other image that seems to correlate with that is tending the fire of the inner "daimon," or genius. This seems an image of the elder who has the capacity to heal.

MEADE: I often call it "tending the fire of god." Pick your god. It can be the god of nature, of the heavens, of knowledge, whatever kind of god a person is aimed at. In that story, "The Fire on the Mountain," the young person is on the peak of the mountain, totally exposed to wind and cold, in order to find liberation or freedom. At some point, that's the condition and position of every young person. The elder is distant, on a flat rock not as high as the peak of youth, but not as low as the flatland of daily life. That tells you about the position of the elder, that a person needs to learn to build a fire in between. In sight of the peak, yet at a level where they can sustain a flame.

Youth are on fire. That's the big problem of culture. Culture has a huge problem with every generation: What do you do with them? Now, we give them electronic games so they burn off their energy. What are they doing in those games? Moving as fast as possible, hand-eye coordination, killing things, exploding things. It has to be bright and fast. That's because youth themselves are on fire.

In the story, the elder keeps the fire and the youth sees it. Both are burning, fire to fire, there's a connection. As the story progresses, it's no longer the heat of the fire the youth experiences, but the illumination caused by it. What I take from the story is that a person becomes an elder in their life when and where they get more of the illumination and not so much of the heat.

If you take ecology as a movement, it needs the heat of youth and the more steady illumination of elders. Anything that's going to change a culture requires this connection between youth and elders. They're the two pivotal elements in any culture. Children are beautiful, but need protection and support. They can't change a culture, but they can be changed by a culture, for better or worse. Mature people, when they're doing their mature thing, are so busy paying the mortgage and sustaining the status quo, or trying to move slightly up or down within the status quo, that they rarely change culture essentially.

The two groups that never quite fit in, however, are the youth and the elders. Both are strangers on the threshold of culture. Between the two of them, there is a flame that is both heat and illumination. In that twin flame, culture reinvents itself. When the old folks have something genuinely illuminating to say to youth, the future changes. When youth can aim their reckless heat in a meaningful direction, the culture changes.

We saw some of it in the 1960s. Not enough. Why? We had plenty of the fire, but not the illumination. The group that grew up in the '60s now becomes the elders, like it or not. If those of us who qualify, just by being born at a certain time, can illuminate our own struggles and what we see around us, meaningful change can occur. If it occurs, it will affect nature and culture, which, I think are intertwined, not separate as Western theory tries to have it.

DE BOER: It seems like change is so difficult, even for well-meaning individuals. Do you think September 11 has the potential for shaking us out of the comfort zone sufficiently to bring real change?

MEADE: All in all, no. I think the hardest thing about change is sustaining it. Change is right there. September 11th is a historical moment and more than that. It also lives outside of history, burned into the imagination. People are still talking about it, still trying to feel it, move it, get rid of it, understand it better. It hangs in the air as a possibility.

At the time, I tried to say, "Don't give up the actual feeling of what happened. Don't give up the shock and the mourning." To me what was so important was the way people were trying to come together in their various communities, as if people were stumbling toward an unseen center that everybody longs for anyway. Now, everyone had a reason to go there. Meanwhile, you can watch the media. They're on the job making stories, repeating stories, telling lies. It's all storytelling. Then they start to see it slip away, because they're reporting it at the wrong level. Then, the announcement: People have to go back to work. The president comes out and says, go back to "normal," go to work, go to Disneyland! Go shopping! It shows how the culture quickly dissociates from anything real.

For a few moments though, people were out in the street. They didn't always know where to go. They went to churches, community centers, vigils of many kinds. I know from talking to people that they went for different reasons, and that's good. That means that it became a symbolic moment. But, what's already happening is the deconstruction of the moment: The reduction of the moment, the glorification of heroes, the loss of the shock and grieving, the justification of the next war. The moment of change passes by.

DE BOER: But there was that moment of community.

MEADE: To me, it wasn't "united we stand." [It was] more like "united we fall into the sorrow of the world, united we mourn, united we recognize loss." Part of what unites peoples is shared loss that keeps being denied as they try to hold up the Dow Jones average. What got lost was the loss itself. That's typical of America. Yet, loss and descent are natural parts of life, as they are for the tree that's dropping its seed or withering through winter. When we deny loss, we're headed for a bigger version of it. We're headed for bigger tragedies and dramas of loss.

DE BOER: Let's talk about mentoring. What's the difference between a mentor and a teacher, parent, or elder?

MEADE: Mentoring is a way to refer to a particular connection, what I call genius to genius. Real mentoring occurs when a young person sees in an older person—not always biologically older, but older in knowledge—someone who has a similar genius to their own. They see a flame of life in that person which reminds them of the flame burning in themselves. These two flames relate. When that happens, the younger person can get their flame blessed. And the older person can move deeper into their own knowledge. Real teaching comes out of that. It's based on that kind of relationship.

Teaching is about the genius of both the teacher and the student. Mentoring is a way of finding and refining that. It's significant to me that the word mentor comes from *The Odyssey*. Mentor is an old sailor who comes upon Telemachus, the son of Ulysses, while he's weeping about the loss of the realm.

DE BOER: A little like the situation in which we find ourselves today in this country.

MEADE: Yes. Mentor steps in at this moment of extreme loss and says to Telemachus, the young son of the realm; "You have to find your voice and go speak in public." It's very beautiful because the story says that Athena, the goddess of wisdom, is actually speaking through Mentor.

DE BOER: This brings in the feminine.

MEADE: The feminine appears. It reminds one of Sophia and that wisdom has a feminine style, a feminine tone. It also says that when mentoring occurs, there is a divine inspiration because Athena or Sophia is present. So, what happens between a mentor and a student is a sacred moment. Both feel some sense of their own sacred nature and that presence moves both along in life. I think that's what we're trying to rediscover—the sacred relationship with the genius. It's the exact opposite of standardized testing.

Being a mentor or elder is not a consistent experience. People have moments of mentoring. To become a full-fledged elder, one has to do some mentoring and teaching. If a person isn't working with someone coming along behind them, they get stuck on their own road. The younger ones push the older ones further along because of the extreme nature of their anguish and longing, their fiery desire and imagination.

DE BOER: One example of a "younger" elder is Julia Butterfly Hill. It seems her experience in the tree, Luna, her trouble being up there in storms, facing the head of Pacific Lumber and Maxxam, created a powerful elder moment that seems to be reverberating throughout the culture.

MEADE: It's a very beautiful image, someone living in the top of a tree. I have to look at it mythically. There are many traditions throughout the world of youth going through initiation by being in trees. There's a form of vision quest where they make a platform in a tree. The young person goes up and sits in the tree until they have a vision about the quest in their life.

There's another tradition, amongst the Irish, best known as "Sweeney Astray." Sweeney can't fit into the culture for various reasons. He begins to live in trees. Once in a while, he pays a visit to the king and delivers strange, compelling messages.

DE BOER: Like Julia to Charles Hurwitz or the culture at large.

MEADE: Think of it as a shamanic journey . . . straight up. People climb up in the tree to get closer to god. There's a shamanic level to it where the tree person receives images from above. Mythically, each tree is the World Tree. The roots of it are down in the underworld, where the ancestors stay. The branches reach into the world above, the world of deities, the spiritual world. The tree is also the pillar that connects the three worlds—the middle level we live in, the level of everything below, and the level of everything above us. Someone climbs a tree and begins a transformative journey, or initiation, the purpose of which is to receive messages from the deities above and bring them back to Earth. The other reason a person might do it is to retrieve their own soul.

The name Butterfly is interesting because a main mythic image of the soul is a butterfly. She created a storm-blown cocoon up there from which she could grow herself. It's a modern initiation. As such, it changes both the individual and the culture.

One other connection could be that in many cultures, the initiation of a girl into a woman occurs in a tree. Sometimes they go into the hollow of the tree in order to be born from the tree, from nature. What she was doing was so beautiful and powerful. It was clear in its ecological perspective. It was also clear in the idea of a young woman telling a culture, "You're making a huge mistake." That kind of knowledge is what burns in young people. To live that out is fantastic, real, and mythic at the same time. Many stories come from that.

DE BOER: Her story keeps opening and opening . . .

MEADE: Initiation means to begin, to take the step. It first happens in youth, but it also is the birth of the elder in them. What's born is not the young person; the young person is already there. What's born is an old knowledge in them, the elder hidden in the younger. Julia certainly went through that initiation. And she gained authority, which is what elders have. It's a great story and one that gives life to ecology.

DE BOER: We're back to eldering and trees. I think back to the banana tree story and the throwing of seed. I wonder if we could end with a discussion of a poem you've used.

"Throw Yourself like Seed"
Shake off this sadness, and recover your spirit,
sluggish you will never see the wheel of fate
that brushes your heel as it turns by,
the man who wants to live is the man in whom life is abundant.

Now you are only giving food to that final pain
which is slowly winding you in the nets of death,
but to live is to work, and the only thing which lasts
is the work; start then to turn to the work.

Throw yourself like seed as you walk, and into your own field,
don't turn your face for that would be to turn it to death,
and do not let the past weigh down your motion.

Leave what's alive in the furrow, what's dead in yourself,
for life does not move in the same way as a group of clouds;
from your work you will be able one day to gather yourself.
                                        —Miguel de Unamuno

MEADE: It's a poem by the poet and philosopher Miguel de Unamuno. Part of what this poem says is that certain things have to be turned away from or we are just winding ourselves in the nets of death. I don't think that means that you don't look at death and understand that it's in the world. Rather, that you don't allow yourself to get caught in the net of a meaningless death. I don't know if he knew Blake's work, but he seems to be referring to Blake's garden, where everyone who comes into this world is already seeded. Our job is to throw the seeds of ourselves "into our own field." What field of the world is your field? Once you know that, you know where to throw your seeds. It's a major accomplishment in life to be working and playing in the right field.

DE BOER: It's finding your own ground. I love the way the poem starts: "Shake off this sadness, and recover your spirit." You just have to do the great work of change in the world. You can't be in the sadness all of the time.

MEAD: It doesn't mean a rejection of sadness. Yet, every emotion has motion—that's what I think the word means. The emotion of sorrow is to release and let go. At a certain point, the sorrow of a given situation has run its course. The person has dealt with it, then it's time to release it, to shake off the sluggishness that is natural to sorrow—and recover your spirit. It's a brilliant way to begin a poem.

The poet makes a distinction: The person whose life is abundant is "the person in whom life is abundant." We come to this life already seeded and aimed. When we find those seeds, we have the permission to cast them into the world. Imagine someone who's tossing seeds with the idea that some of the seeds will fall and make new life and the world will become abundant and full and remain beautiful. If a person can stay in that motion, that's called work. It's a giving, a repeated gathering and throwing of oneself into life, which I think is real work, yet also real play.

"Throw Yourself like Seed" ends [with], "from your work, you will be able one day to gather yourself." This casting of our seeds, this natural altruism, a giving of what is of second nature to us, allows us to gather ourselves. We find ourselves by giving away what we are at the core, by revealing ourselves, and throwing the revelation into the world. That's a hard thing to keep telling yourself.

As people get older, there's the problem of thinking they can't do it anymore. That's why mentoring is so important because the young people come along and say, "You've got to do it; otherwise what am I going to do?" Then, you have what I call the stream of knowledge—everybody lined up walking along the timeless stream of knowledge, casting everything they can into the field and forest around them. In that way, we continue the creation of life, we participate in creation of both nature and culture.

DE BOER: Interesting how the youth encourages the elder. You usually think about it the other way around. It's like "encourage," drawing the courage out of the elder to continue.

MEADE: That's exactly what happens. It's a real experience. I've seen youth struggle and find courage in their lives. And I've been in situations where I wasn't sure what to do, running scared, not going with my instincts, and starting to freeze up a little bit. Then, the image of one of them comes to mind and says, "I need you to go ahead. I need that from you." It's almost like you borrow their courage to go further into your own life. That's the beauty of that exchange. It's the mutual story, where each is pulling and pushing the other one along.

DE BOER: We're very grateful for your courage and work. Any final words?

MEADE: I really hope that people can find ways to weave together myth and ecology, the spiritual and ecological, because otherwise, separated, everything gets defeated.

5

Teachers: The Heart of Education

Sam M. Intrator

Sam M. Intrator is assistant professor of education and child study at Smith College. The son of two retired New York City public school teachers, he was a high-school teacher and administrator in Brooklyn, New York, Vermont, and California. He was awarded a W. K. Kellogg National Leadership Fellowship and was named a Distinguished Teacher by the White Commission on Presidential Scholars. He is the author of Tuned in and Fired Up: How Teaching Can Inspire Real Learning in the Classroom *(2003) and editor of* Stories of the Courage to Teach: Honoring the Teacher's Heart *(2002) and* Teaching with Fire: Poetry That Sustains the Courage to Teach *(2003).*

Several years ago, I interviewed a veteran teacher from South Carolina about her work. She struck me as the embodiment of the very best teachers I've known. She spoke reverentially of the mystery and complexity of learning and how she struggled to understand the "rivers of her students' minds." She spoke with concern and respect about her colleagues and how she learns so much when she has time to talk and work with them. She spoke wryly of the "thrill ride" of teaching and how her everyday work is filled with moments of glory and despair. She talked with sadness about the heavy pressure that pervaded her school because of the fascination with scores on standardized tests.

At the end of our conversation, I asked her if she had anything else she wanted to add. She paused and then said, "One more thing. Maybe the most important thing. . . . Like the old saying, 'If Momma ain't happy, ain't nobody happy.' If you get a teacher in the classroom who's not happy—then look out little children."

In this one remarkable homespun image, I believe this veteran of many years in the classroom captures an essential first principle of teaching and learning: We cannot teach children well if our teachers are unwell. In fact, it is worth lingering on its cold inverse: If our teachers are unwell and demoralized, then our children will suffer.

My premise is simple: The classroom teacher is the pivot on which all else turns, and if schools are to be places that promote academic, social, and personal development for students, everything hinges on the presence of intelligent, passionate, caring teachers working day after day in our nation's classrooms. Demoralized, depleted, and disconnected teachers cannot achieve the triumphs of the mind and heart that characterize true and enduring education.

This common-sense truism is not just "kitchen table" wisdom: A spate of high-profile, blue-ribbon reports synthesizing a corpus of new and significant research on improving student achievement affirms this position. The report *What Matters Most: Teaching for America's Future* (1996) asserts, "What teachers know and can do is the most important influence on what students learn"(1996, 10). The American Council on Education arrives at a similar conclusion in its report, *To Touch the Future* (1999). The success of the student depends most of all on the quality of the teacher. We know from empirical data what our intuition has always told us: Teachers make a difference. We now know that teachers make *the* difference."[1] In fact, the presence of a thoughtful, skilled, and knowledgeable teacher is the most important in-school factor for improving student achievement.

This evidence compels all of us who are concerned with the quality of education received by children in this country to turn our attention to recruiting high-quality people into the profession and then providing the support that allows them to become more expert and accomplished as teachers. This approach to educational improvement may seem obvious; however, there is a long history of educational reform initiatives that overlook the essential role of the teacher. These agendas treat educational problems as technical equations in need of rational solutions. Solutions that dictate what should be taught in the curriculum, prescribe the methods of instruction to be used in all classrooms, restructure the organization of the school, employ new technologies that seem to promise more efficient learning, or institute more comprehensive accountability measures designed to raise the stakes of success and failure. The heart, discretion, and spirit of the essential variable, the teacher, is routinely ignored by these approaches.

Stanford researcher Jim Collins offers a powerful way to understand why we must attend to how the men and women who teach our children are doing both personally as well as professionally. His research asks why some organizations make the leap from good to great and other companies trudge along as mediocre or merely good.

Collins began his research with the assumption that what would explain an organization's rise from good to great would be the discovery of an innovative approach, a new method, or a novel technology. Instead, he found something quite the opposite. He discovered that leaders who ignited transformations from good to great were not innovative geniuses, but good judges of talent who were able to assemble teams of people who could work together. Success had little to do with innovation of products or process. His key finding: begin with the *who* rather than the *what.*

Great vision by a charismatic leader is not enough. A leader needs the right people to execute that vision. According to Collins's research, once the right people are assembled, "[T]he problem of how to motivate and manage people largely goes away. The right people don't need to be tightly managed or fired up; they will be self-motivated by the inner drive to produce the best results and be part of creating something great" (2001, 42).

Translated to education: If we want great schools, we have to invite talented, intelligent, passionate people into the profession. But that is not enough. We, that is, teachers, educational leaders, and engaged citizens, must shape an agenda that takes seriously the reality that teaching is demanding emotional, spiritual, and intellectual labor and that teachers need to be cared for by the institution of school in ways that keep them alive for their students, attentive to their colleagues, and excited by the subject matter they teach.

In envisioning a profession where teachers flourish, two dimensions emerge as worthy of attention. First, teachers should be encouraged to attend to their inner life and explore their ever-emerging relationship to their vocation. Second, teachers should be provided opportunity to work in authentic companionship with colleagues around the essential questions of teaching.

TURNING INWARD TO ENGAGE QUESTIONS OF VOCATION

In reflecting on her life as a poet, May Sarton writes: "I, in my normal life, am alone all the time. I work alone. Therefore, when someone comes for tea, and it's the only person I see all day, that is precious too, because solitude without society would be meager and would, in the end, make for a dwindling of personality, perhaps. You can't eat yourself all day and all night. There has to be something that brings life-food from the outside" (1994, 34).

The message for teachers is the mirror message: *We, in our normal teaching life, are mostly with and for others.* We work in complex and demanding settings. Our classrooms are crowded and our work demands us to be interactive, reciprocal, and responsive to a ceaseless stream of face-to-face decisions. The busy and public nature of teaching invites a small play on Sarton's words: Society and action without solitude would be meager and in the end make for a dwindling personality, perhaps. You can't eat with others and for others all day and night. There has to be something that brings life-food from the inside.

Teachers need nourishment from the *inside.* In my experience as a teacher, high-school administrator, and researcher, I have heard teachers give voice to their visceral need to think, muse, and reflect on what teaching does to them. They hunger to live an examined life; however, the crushing immediacy of teaching leaves little time and opportunity to attend to the emotions, thoughts, and dreams of their lives.

This is not a loony plea to encourage navel gazing, but a reasoned invitation to provide the time and encouragement for teachers to think deeply about their values, beliefs, and personal habits as teachers. As Michael Fullan and Andy Hargreaves assert in their book, *What's Worth Fighting for in Your School?* (1996), inviting teachers to locate, listen to, and articulate their inner voice is a first principle for creating successful educational settings. They write that: "Teachers must want to reflect and reflect deeply. They must believe that it is important to get in touch with their feelings and purposes. And [they] must be prepared to put other things, even important things, aside to do it. It's a matter of the tortoise and the hare. Sometimes the marking, the bulletin board, or that extra resource should wait, because a little time for reflection will lead to better things in the long run" (1996, 5).

WORKING IN COMPANIONSHIP WITH FELLOW TEACHERS

This work is too hard and too complex to do it alone. Nothing deforms a teacher's heart or contributes to a festering school culture more than the professional isolation of teachers. When teachers fall into patterns of work that force them into lonely, individualistic habits, they lose out on opportunities to form life-giving collegial relationships and engage in critical conversations about their work, their hopes, and the situations of practice. By working cloistered behind closed doors, we deprive ourselves of support, empathy, shared wisdom, and communal expertise.

The truth is, teachers rarely come together to probe and prod a problem of practice or perform their work in the presence of colleagues. I'd been teaching for two years before anyone who wasn't evaluating my work ever came into my room to watch me. My supervisor was a smart, experienced, savvy assistant principal—but every time she walked into the classroom, I was gripped by anxiety akin to stage fright. Teaching in her presence felt like driving on the interstate next to a police cruiser.

The culture of most schools and the cellular structure of the institution rarely provide opportunities for us to come together for the appointed purpose of talking honestly and openly about our teaching and the deep questions about our lives as teachers. I know of no better way to keep heart and continue to grow in my role as a teacher than to collect companions with whom I journey. I am most alive and creative as a teacher when I am connected to others who affirm me, share my passion for this work, and provide a stream of ideas and questions that challenge me to continue learning about what it means to be a better teacher.

Pulled apart, the word *companion* derives from *com* (with) and *pan* (bread). Etymologically, a companion is the person with whom you share bread on a journey; a companion is a messmate, a comrade, and a fellow sojourner. In my own journey as a teacher, I cherish those people and resources that help me do my best and most inspired work. Their presence in my life helps beat back the forces that would otherwise exhaust me, deplete me, or leave me feeling too lonely to be fully present for my students.

The companions in my own journey as a teacher share their lives with me. They don't preach; they don't proselytize—they know better than to offer glib and simplistic advice because they trudge in this world with me. They share the triumphs and challenges of work and allow me access to their teaching, planning, and relationships with students. I have always believed that those who share both their life and work with me have undertaken an act of special generosity and courage. In the private culture of teaching, they buck the default position and offer me a perspective that gives me strength and inspiration and what I need to get better at this work.

I am, as are most teachers I have met, not a born teacher. I have grown and developed over time and become better at this complex work through association with mentors, models, colleagues, and companions. My practice is an amalgam of ideas, lesson plans, methods, techniques, and philosophies that I have picked up, in large part, through interactions with companions.

While companions can offer much, initiating a constructive, life-giving professional relationship must begin with a decision each teacher makes. Like many teachers, the notion of opening my classroom and curriculum to the scrutiny of others leaves me feeling anxious. The idea of shutting my classroom door and toiling solo without interference and without that feeling of vulnerability that comes from the judgment of others sounds pretty good sometimes. I was inducted into the profession in a big, comprehensive high school where the norms of individualism had deep roots. I learned to close my door and to speak about practice in guarded generalities. Over the years, I've worked hard at shucking off those habits learned in the early years of my teaching.

One image that has helped inspire me to reach out and discover companions in this work of teaching was offered by Frederick Buechner, who, in writing about the punishing consequences of isolation, offers those in our profession a guiding principle. He writes: "You conceal your sense of inadequacy behind a defensive bravado. And so on and so forth. The inner state you end up with is a castle-like affair of keep, inner wall, outer wall, moat, which you erect originally to be a fortress to keep the enemy out but which turns into a prison where you become the jailer and thus your own enemy. It is a wretched and lonely place. . . . People can't see through all that masonry to who you truly are and half the time you can not see who you truly are yourself, you've been walled up so long" (1992, 65–66).

We must not become sealed in. We must learn to break asunder those habits that would sentence us to work in isolation and leave us deprived of the support, love, and renewal necessary to be the best teachers possible. As individuals, we can do this by reaching out, listening to our colleagues with abiding respect, and by asking for help when we need it. As an institution, we need to reorganize the work processes so that we can consider accommodations around scheduling, curriculum work, and resource deployment that will facilitate schools that are supportive and sustaining of the adults.

This logic returns us to the words of the wise teacher from South Carolina. She surmised that if our teachers feel disheartened, and if they do their work cloaked in isolation, they will "not be well" and our children will suffer. To keep our teachers well, we must attend not merely to their pedagogical skills, but to their heart, emotions, and intellectual development.

NOTE

1. American Council on Education. *To Touch the Future: Transforming the Way Teachers Are Taught.* Washington D.C.: American Council on Education, 1999, p. 5.

REFERENCES

Buechner, Frederick. 1992. *Whistling in the Dark: A Doubter's Dictionary.* San Francisco: HarperCollins.

Collins, James C. 2001. *Good to Great: Why Some Companies Make the Leap—and Others Don't,* 1st ed. New York, N.Y.: HarperBusiness.

Fullan, Michael, and Andy Hargreaves. 1996. *What's Worth Fighting for in Your School?* New York: Teacher's College Press.

National Commission on Teaching and America's Future. 1996. *What Matters Most: Teaching for America's Future.* Washington, D.C.

Sarton, May. 1994. *From May Sarton's Well: Writings of May Sarton.* Edited by Edith Royce Schade. Watsonville, Calif.: Papier-Mâché Press.

Downside Up:
Getting Education Right

Ronald G. Veronda

Trust the dreams, for in them is hidden the gate to eternity.—Kahlil Gibran

Ronald G. Veronda is an educator of children, teens, and adults with over three decades of experience. He is the author of No More Turning Away, A Revolution in Education, Solutions for a Violent World *and cofounder of the Children's Consulting Center, a nationally recognized educational center. Over the past ten years, he has been asked to travel across the United States and throughout Europe, working with educators, parents, and concerned community members to offer ways of using education to create a healthier world.*

It happened slowly. There was no single breakthrough or event. But after twenty years of teaching children, youth, and adults in public and private schools, I came to realize the design of education we inherited is upside down. Of course, coming to this radical conclusion was one thing, but as an educator I had to do something about it. I had to turn it downside up!

The educational design we follow came from our fathers' fathers, but the world has changed. The failure, dropout rates, violence, and alienation of our children and youth demand that we question this design. Recommending that we reverse our educational approach may initially sound outrageous, but that is in fact what we must do. To do so is common sense. To do so gives hope.

Education looks quite different through a reverse-angle lens, and we get our first clue in the definition of education itself. The Latin predecessor of the English word *educate* is *educare*. *Educare* comes from the same root as the word *educe*, which means "bring out." Our educational system is built on the premise that educators put *in* data. They determine what is to be learned, how it will be learned, and how the success of the learning will be measured. This is backward on all points. The system, for the most part, ignores the learner, who should be the beginning and prime focus of all educational steps.

Reading, writing, and arithmetic are the "meat and potatoes" of our current educational system. They are the points of measurement used to assess the success of education. This is ironic because reading, writing, and arithmetic are not "education" at all. They are *tools* for education, tools to be used in the pursuit of something else. It appears that as a society we have forgotten the "something else."

This something else is our dreams and the mystery of life itself. It is understanding who we are and what the world is all about. It is the greater context we call the "bigger picture." As teachers, we were taught to teach curricula separately rather than teach children in their totality. The three Rs are critical tools, and curricula are supportive components, of our current learning design. But by teaching reading, writing, and arithmetic outside of the context of students' lives, we have never been able to attain our desired level of performance.

Have you ever wondered why school districts purchase new curricula every four years or so? Is it to feed a multimillion-dollar industry? If so, the intention is misguided, and the results will reflect this. Is it because the teaching of a curriculum, rather than the teaching of a child, is an incomplete approach? Whenever you pursue something with conviction and are off target, the pursuit can be never ending. Do you realize how many millions of hours and billions of dollars are spent seeking, evaluating, purchasing, and selling these programs and texts to teachers, parents, and school districts each year? What are the results? You'd think we would simply get good at what we do and repeat the process. I agree with Michelle Karns, an educational activist, who says, "You will never teach a child to read with a curriculum, but you will never fail to teach a child to read when he or she is in [a] relationship with an adult who truly wishes them to read." People and relationships, not things, make education work.

Most parents and educators today would probably agree that we go to school to get a good job. There is irony in this. The concept of "job" is only as old as the current design of education. They go hand in hand because they both came out of the Industrial Age. The job of the school system was to prepare the populace to work in factories. The idea of going somewhere and working for money at something that has little personal meaning may be fine for a while; but is it a wise use of one's life? A job may be very important to us during a particular period in our lives or as a way of getting money to do what we truly love or need to do, but at no time are we to confuse a job with life. We do not become educated simply to get a job; we become educated to live fully and understand the world around us. If we were to gather a large representative group of our society to design a way of fully educating our children, how many people do you believe would choose a factory design?

CRITIQUING THE CURRENT DESIGN

Let's consider more closely our current educational design and then step back and look at it in reverse. Currently, our philosophy of education begins with a number of basic premises: All children learn the same way; they progress through their education by age, year by year; learning is a function of the brain; and education (teaching) is dispensed by the teacher to the student. We provide basically the same information to all children (what we have been told they are to learn) and assess how well they can give back information from memory. We grade students on how well they perform this process and use grades to motivate them.

Let's look at the first premise of the design we inherited: All children learn the same way. We know better than that. In every classroom and school some children fit the learning design well, some sort of fit, and some do not fit at all. We accept this because that is the way it has been. But people are not objects on an assembly line. Each of us is beautifully unique, and trying to fit various shaped pegs into round holes hurts; causing alienation, depression, or even violence in the long term. We see this in our children and youth—and in society as a whole.

With our linear way of thinking, we can't get past a simple numerical way of grouping. Setting up classrooms or teaching groups by age or grade level is superficial and ineffective, but it is part of the design we were handed—so even though we know better, we continue to try to ride a dead horse. There is a huge variance—a delightful variance—among six-year-olds, or eighty-year-olds. Let's appreciate and use this difference instead of trying to squash it. We can group children by similar interests or dreams. Or better yet, let's set up families of life-long learners, whose ages span all generations. Older children thrive when given responsibilities with younger children; younger children thrive when put under the tutelage of an older child. Within limits, we can allow children to choose their projects and assist them by teaching tools (curricula) to use in their pursuit. This method pulls *out* of the child and has *desire* inherent in the choice. Internal desire promotes learning, whereas external motivation is a hit-or-miss proposition.

We also know better than to believe learning is purely a function of the brain. The brain and nervous system are transducers of thought; neither of them is the thinker. People are far more than organs and tissue. Does anyone for a moment believe our emotions are held in the organ we call the heart?

Ignoring a person's desires, dreams, and spirit does not make sense. The greatest block to cognitive learning is an emotional need that has not been recognized, acknowledged, or addressed. Not addressing emotions guarantees less academic growth. Do you want to increase student performance in a school? Don't focus entirely, or even initially, on the brain! First and foremost, focus on each child's dream. Give emotions healthful expression, then—and only then—dive into the cognitive process and the accompanying academics. Test scores, then, go off the chart. We have come to believe that emotions are a subset of the mind. The reverse is actually more accurate. Emotions open and close the mind. All learning begins with the desire of the learner—from internal desire outward to other sources. Without desire, there is no learning.

Our current educational system focuses heavily on knowledge recall. In most cases, the teacher gives out factual knowledge; the learner takes in the knowledge and then gives it back to the teacher, demonstrating that they have absorbed the learning. According to Benjamin Bloom's taxonomy of educational objectives this is level one, the lowest level of learning. Forty years ago, Bloom found that 95 percent of test questions in schools were at level one. Some movement on this front has been made over the last two decades, but improvement is not advancing to the degree we might expect. Knowledge recall fits the old industrial model, and systems are resistant to change.

Grading is also a stalwart part of our current structure. Although we are never happy with how it makes us feel, we continue to grade—judge—our children. We change the symbols used to judge, but not the concept itself. We ignore the re-searched fact that for many people grading actually *stops* motivation. If we reverse the process and have the student assess their own accomplishments, displaying their ac-complishments in journals or projects, without judgment, an internal system of motivation is put in motion. The power of nonjudgment cannot be overemphasized. Judgment, built into our current educational system, stops learning.

There is another key point of the current paradigm of education that looks silly, if not sad, from the other side. Our educational design puts the responsibility for learning on the child. If the educational approach, which was designed by some-one else, doesn't work and the child is unsuccessful, we consider it the child's fault. As an educator, I know that it is my task to meet the child and not the child's task to meet me.

The current design of education comes out of a paradigm of thought that is limited. Its view is focused on preparing students for the material, measurable world only. Anything that begins with such limitation can only hope for limited success. What is recommended here is to teach the full miracle that is the child. By beginning with the miracle of the child, the success cannot be anything less than miraculous.

A COMMON-SENSE DESIGN

Let's consider a philosophy of education that says children learn in different ways, are interested in different things, and need to be prepared for different lives. Each child's needs and interests determine what is taught and how it is taught. The teacher and parents find out what the child loves, where his or her strengths lie, and then use this information to move the child into lessons to help prepare for the life for which he or she longs. Instead of seeking what the child doesn't know, the teacher emphasizes what he or she does know. Instead of looking for disorder in the child, the teacher seeks to see the order through the eyes of the child. Life education becomes the milieu for teaching, and the individual curricula are taught in relation to the life needs and dreams of the student. Strategy will change many times along the way. Instead of seeing education as a linear, finite process that seeks answers, education becomes an infinite *process* of learning. Education explores the metaphors of life. This broad interplay is done naturally through play. In this sense, play may be more important than study. The teacher and student, side by side, seek truths, knowing these "truths" may change.

If the lessons are not successful, the teacher and child will learn from that challenge. Techniques will be changed to meet the student, and delight will be found in success. The child, with the teacher's help, will accumulate examples of his or her activities and accomplishments. Projects demonstrating the child's progress will be proudly displayed, and the adulation the child receives will be a prime motivator.

We do not need to reinvent education or throw out what we currently have. We need to change our way of seeing education and do what we already know is healthy and effective. As Carolyn Myss says, "The answers are around us always. It is not so much the learning of something new as it is a peeling away of what has been keeping us from seeing."

THE GARDEN OF CHILDREN

There is one sure way to learn a healthy and effective educational design, and that is from the children themselves. When parents come to me, frustrated by their child's school experience, I sometimes use this technique. I ask them to follow me for a moment, and we walk over to one of the kindergarten classrooms. I open the door and step aside, letting the parents peer inside. Something happens each and every time I have done this. Both parents, almost instantly, get a smile on their face, their eyes start to twinkle, and both become silent. The smile, twinkle, and silence will last the whole time they are at the door. What I have just done is taken them to holy ground. The miracle of the child is there in full view—unencumbered by the societal paradigm. The children are free to squiggle and wiggle, ask questions, talk a mile a minute, laugh, cry, and dream dreams beyond words. There are no bad kids in a kindergarten class. No one is disordered. No one needs to try to become perfect; they are already more than that. It is a healthy place for learning—not just for them, but for us too. Traditionally, the societal design doesn't enter our educational system until first grade. The kindergarten design is right-side up. What we need to do to make our schools more effective is extend the kindergarten concepts—and honor the physical, psychological, emotional, and spiritual aspects of our children. As Robert Fulghum recommends in his essay, *All I Really Need to Know I Learned In Kindergarten,* children need to "learn some and think some and draw and paint and sing and dance and play and work every day some."

I refer to the educational paradigm that we inherited as the *bodymi* because it focuses only on the material *body* and the measurable part of the *mi*nd. As has already been mentioned, the mysterious mind, the heart, and the spirit are not included. To answer this educational challenge, we must return the missing parts to our educational design, to our schools and classrooms. To do so, we need to return them in the order of their magnitude—first spirit, then heart, then the full mind, and finally, the miraculous body.

THE RETURN OF DREAMS

Spirit lies within our dreams, and there are a number of ways to pull out a dream, whether from a child, teenager, or adult. For teenagers and adults, their dreams are often buried, but I have found that the kindergartner within them never really goes away.

The following is one technique I have used to pull out a dream. In this case, Mike is a high-school student, but I have used this same technique with five-year-olds and eighty-year-olds with only slight variations. Before I begin with anyone, I have to have their trust or they won't participate. It all begins with a loving, nonjudgmental relationship.

This interchange was in front of a Next Step audience with the dedicated founders of the Challenge Day program, Yvonne and Rich St. John-Dutra. The audience included teenagers, teachers, school administrators, and a mixed bag of community activists and other adults. Similar results can happen in a classroom or one-on-one. In a classroom, I have the other students participate in the metaphorical interplay, and every student gets a turn.

"Mike, how old are you?" I ask. Speaking quietly into the microphone, Mike answers, "Seventeen."

"If I came back to see you in ten years, and you could be anything at all . . . you do know you can be anything you want to be, don't you?" I pause and look confidently into his eyes. Many children and teens do not believe this anymore. My confidence suggests otherwise.

"If I come back to see you in five to ten years and nothing can stop you, what will you be doing? Now remember, grades can't stop you. Money can't stop you. Your parents, teachers, and even your principal can't stop you. If nothing can stop you, what will you be doing?"

Mike smiles at me a little nervously and finally says quietly, "I'm going to be a welder. A union welder on ships." I show I am impressed. I think for a moment about what he has said to me and then explain a little of what I am doing.

"Mike, I'm kind of weird. Jobs don't mean a whole lot to me, and I can't seem to take words literally. I try to think of the broader meaning or metaphor of words. I try to get a larger picture, one that's bigger than a job." I pause.

"So what I am hearing you say, in my way, is, you want to create." I think for a moment and then say, "Goodness. Let's see. You don't want to make something out of paper. And you don't want to glue something or make it out of clay. You want to use steel and meld it with fire!" The audience starts to murmur.

"Union must mean you want to be in an organization, a family, make good pay, have security, or maybe be like your father." I look to see his face registering agreement.

"And you want to fix things or create, big time . . . with fire!" I say. As I speak, Mike begins to stand taller and becomes noticeably more confident. He probably hesitated earlier because he wasn't going to say what most high-school teachers and principals want to hear. He wasn't going to say he was going to college. Now, Mike looks at me with a proud set to his jaw and adds with confidence, "Underwater."

The audience lets loose with small cheers and expressions of pleasant surprise. "Whew," I exclaim. "If I have this right, what you are telling me you'll be doing in ten years is . . . you'll be a man . . . you'll be a member of a family . . .you'll create by melding metal with fire . . . and *nothing* will stop you!" Mike is now standing ten feet tall. And I have Mike's dream!

The audience saw how to pull out a youth's dream, not simply a job, and look at it, without judgment, from a bigger place. As an educator, I retrieved the information I needed to create lessons for success for this young man. If I were his parent, I would understand where my child dreams of going. The job may change many times over, but the metaphor won't. I just got a glimpse of his core. I just tapped his desire—the place where all learning begins.

NOTE

Portions of this chapter are excerpted from the following book: Veronda, Ron. 2001. *No More Turning Away: A Revolution in Education/Solutions for a Violent World.* Pink Floyd Music Publishers. Copyright © 2001 by Ron Veronda. Used with permission.

7

How Schools Can Empower Our Children

An Interview with Deborah Meier by Mike Seymour

Few educators have inspired progressive education as much as Deborah Meier. When I met her at her home in Hillsdale, New York, fresh from a swim in the pond on her property, Deborah's grandmotherly nature belied her having been the visionary behind Central Park East Elementary, and later, secondary schools—and that's part of her success. In 1974, Central Park East Elementary School (CPE) in East Harlem opened its doors with a mission to provide inner city children with the finest educators and pedagogy available. Instead of saying that the old neighborhood had to be torn down and students more rigidly tracked, the reformers dared to ask: What would happen if we gave inner-city students the best education the country has to offer? The results of this bottom-up reform were astounding. To this day, Central Park East and its later secondary school are known as one of the most academically enriching schools in the United States. Meier's work has given inspiration to literally hundreds of academically rigorous, progressive schools around the country. Her books: The Power of Their Ideas: Lessons from America from a Small School in Harlem; In Schools We Trust: Creating Communities of Learning in an Era of Testing; *and* Standardization and Will Standards Save Public Education *are a must-read for those involved in meaningful school reform. She is now principal of Mission Hill School in Roxbury, Massachusetts.*

MIKE SEYMOUR: School could help children experience their own uniqueness and giftedness, but schools emphasize comparison and competition and tend to hold up an ideal. Most of us are approximations to the ideal, which means that most people tend to feel that they're not measuring up in some way. What are your thoughts on this?

DEBORAH MEIER: I think you're right, although I'm sure we both agree that part of what a good education does is offer other perspectives, widens our view of possibilities. In doing so, it also makes possible precisely what you are worrying about—the ability to compare ourselves to others. We tend too often to look at children—and ourselves—as though we can be set along some single rank order, comparing ourselves to someone else or to an ideal. It's so hard for us to shift the way we think and take pleasure in our own special qualities along, of course, with our difficulties and complexities. So, naturally, we do the same with our children. I'm not sure what the trade-offs would be if we moved away from this habit of ranking of traits—always seeing some as better or worse, with a single ideal toward which we all must seek. Some societies are much less oriented toward an ideal model. What do they give up in the process?

One problem we have today which bears on this discussion is that parents know their children less well compared to, say, a century ago. Children are in the hands of impersonal institutions for a larger portion of their waking hours than they ever were before. This means they are less known and their caretakers are less able to advocate for a child because they don't really know who [he or] she is themselves. Someone else's judgment about your own child may or may not be right, but it's dangerous if it isn't balanced by the family's intimate and biased knowledge. Many parents are told their child is a "4.2 reader," and thus even if they understand the jargon of "4.2," they may not know their child well enough to dismiss it as inaccurate—which it well may be—or as irrelevant. Some parents, who know their child well, may be able to comfortably retort: "Who cares? My child reads and loves to read." Too many parents today are at the mercy of whoever designed the test to define their own child.

SEYMOUR: When children aren't known, they can't know themselves. It takes a caring adult to help young people see who they are. How are young people drawn out, listened to, and seen for who they are in Central Park East and other schools that you have worked with?

MEIER: What an interesting point: Being known and knowing oneself! First, school has to be a place that is generally interesting to kids. Second, children learn by being in an environment where other people are really interested in them and in what they are doing. You need an interesting space—a place with books of all sorts that intrigue and excite children's interests. A place with materials that invite touching, building, inventing, and constructing. Then children need the time to follow their interests, like going into the woods or making up stories. We have so little time like this with kids today. Even before- and after-school activities tend to be programmed.

The grown-ups whom children spend their time with should have a range of expertise and character. This helps kids see how they are alike or different from a range of other people and provides a natural way of choosing who you want to model yourself after. We learn from somebody else's fascinations—avocations, hobbies, obsessions. Finally, the whole thing has to be within the context of a caring community. School is held together not only by supporting individual interest but also by the pleasure of being part of a safe community.

SEYMOUR: Parents hope schools will help their children in a variety of ways. Are parents really interested in the giftedness of their children or is the special quality of a child a nebulous idea that gets overridden by the societal pressures for success and achievement?

MEIER: I think many parents are aware of, and treasure, that "something special" in their child but also see school as a place for getting ahead—to become socialized; to become more like everyone else. There is a tension here. Parents are uncertain about their child's uniqueness and are anxious about not failing children as parents, so they sometimes push more for achievement along accepted lines. For some kids, this can be very painful. Parents naturally want to be sure that the school isn't underestimating their child's abilities, and they are often anxious about a school that may not appear concerned about preparing kids for what they've been told is "the real world." They fear that the real, rank-ordered world may not appreciate their children for who they are—for their uniqueness.

SEYMOUR: Many adults, if we bother to think about it, didn't really benefit much from school apart from graduating on to the next level, learning to socialize, and so on. So much of what we learned was quickly forgotten. Why do we make our kids go through the same regimen that in many ways didn't work for us?

MEIER: Interesting issue. In fact, some parents think school did work for them, or if it didn't work for them, it was only because it wasn't tough enough. I often ask parents in a family conference to tell me about themselves as a student, how teachers helped, and what the school could have done better. Some say they should have been meaner even though they realize the punishments didn't really work. Maybe more [punishment] would have been better? On the other hand, I think there are more parents who, when asked to stop and recall their school years, are open to rethinking it. After all, school didn't really succeed the way it was done for them, so maybe it's time for a change?

SEYMOUR: I wonder how the emphasis on achievement, standards, and testing is being fueled today by the growing lack of public trust in schools and the withdrawal of community support.

MEIER: There are sometimes good reasons for a lack of trust, but it often needlessly stands in the way of positive change. More people today buy the media's message about the need for more rigid forms of accountability because they think schools are getting away with something. So, much of this mistrust is artificially created. The public has been sold the idea that you've got to threaten teachers' jobs and you've got to test more to make sure the job gets done. They see teachers as part of a self-interest group out to protect itself, that needs to be checked up on. The same for kids! That's where testing comes in.

There has always been a certain inevitable tension between school and family. This was, for most, the first public world you were letting your child go into without you. You knew the school wouldn't love your kids the way you did. So parents are judging teachers: Are they good enough and loving enough for *my* child? This is natural in a culture in which families and schools are more separated and do not know each other well. But we have now made a public policy that a parent is an idiot not to mistrust his child's school—a bad parent according to many columnists and policymakers. The view is that parents who trust have been fooled into thinking the school is better than it is. One reason we need test scores: To prove to the parents that the school is not as good as they think it is.

So the press and policymakers have built a consensus viewpoint that, to improve the quality of American education, we've got to encourage parents to mistrust school and suggest to people that trust in school is dangerous to reform. Only a distrustful public can drive reform forward, say such reform leaders. Instead of changing schools so they can build healthy trust, we leave the schools as they are and invent accountability schemes that we hope will control teachers and kids—and make them better.

SEYMOUR: You indicate that liberating the gifts of mind and the hearts of kids requires unsettling our accepted organization of schooling and the unacknowledged agreements about the purposes of school. What are these unacknowledged agreements? One I can think of is the school as a babysitting function, which we don't address directly in our planning or mission statements.

MEIER: I think you're right about the babysitting function. A second function is getting the kids credentials that they need in order to get the next credential. These are both facts of life. Parents work and need sitters and these credentials determine how much money, freedom, and security their kids will have when they grow up. So they [kids] have to go through all of these hoops to get there—even if they learn nothing useful in the process. Some people feel one of the primary purposes of school is to teach obedience to authority. Some would argue that school helps young people see where they fit into the real world—by sorting them out by ability and motivation.

Being obedient is, of course, sometimes necessary, although one hardly needs twelve years of schooling to learn that. And the social agenda is, of course, critical— if not quite the way I just described it. Understanding the pecking order is probably useful—but should schools be the place it is taught? I used to believe that young people would learn something about being a member of society by being with kids who were different and thus having to learn to get along with them. Two things have changed my mind about this.

A book by Vivian Paley reminded me of how horrendous the social life can be for kids in schools, with peer pressures whose impact we often ignore. It was also watching the home-schooled kids who came to our school—in the late elementary grade—that led me to look again at the "socializing" that goes on in school. I think the home-schoolers are some of the best-adjusted kids socially, with much higher self-esteem; they are more comfortable with being different than their schooled peers and more comfortable with adults. My sample, of course, is pretty small!

SEYMOUR: A democratic environment at school encourages involvement, personal responsibility, and empowerment and can help strengthen community. What is your approach to involving teachers, students, and parents in decision making at school?

MEIER: Making schools places which honor democratic decision making is a great idea, but you only have so many hours in the day for making group decisions. That's one of my dilemmas every time someone comes up with a wonderful idea for our school. I listen and think "that is marvelous, but does it require another meeting?" Doing some things well is better than doing all things in a mediocre way. So there are trade-offs. What do we give up when kids or teachers spend enormous amounts of their limited time in meetings, some of which seem to go on endlessly, whereas the time might have been "better" spent on other kinds of learning? It's why teachers and schools need considerable autonomy, and why we sometimes delegate authority.

We try to strike a balance at our school. In a good discussion we listen enough to the kids, family, and staff to usually reach a consensus. But it's dangerous when teachers reach a false consensus—just to get the meeting over! Some people are sick of the topic and they know the principal is going to win at the end anyway. Or, they don't feel enough of a part of this school, so they withdraw and don't want to spend any more time worrying or pretending that they care about the school as a whole. Finding the right balance means figuring out some division of labor, some way to use time well, keeping in mind that it's not undemocratic for the staff to decide to delegate certain responsibilities to the principal, or to parents or kids! Therefore: small schools. This makes it easier for people to communicate and get things done—but still not easy.

When it comes to kids' experience of democracy, my conviction is that what makes families or teachers good at preparing strong citizens is not whether they take a vote on everything but whether they listen carefully so that children know they have been heard. . . . They know they and their ideas are being treated with respect. If they get mad and rebel, that's part of democracy too. And it sends a message that we ponder with care.

With respect to school, I suspect that some schools that call themselves democratic actually survive because there is a very charismatic leader who is setting the tone for the decisions that the school, and even the kids, think they are making. That's risky when the leader leaves. Real democracy is full of perils; but worth it if we don't assume it's all about voting on everything, and we remember that adults do possess some expertise and wisdom.

SEYMOUR: There is this split in public thinking between what I call the three Rs aim of education versus the whole child. The first is focused on skills and the other on character and who the kid is. The cultivation of self and subject really can and need to go together. How would you address this subject?

MEIER: As my colleague Dennis Littky of The Met School in Rhode Island says about kids—educate them "one kid at a time." Similarly, [we should educate] each community at a time. And each will reach somewhat different conclusions about how to sort out these dilemmas. Not the same way for each kid or each school. One school might decide that to have a school without music is unthinkable; that for such a community, music is fundamental. Each community must decide its own priorities and what kind of different choices should be available to its children. But [these communities] need to make their priorities explicit and be accountable for the choices they have made.

There is no one single answer either as to how many choices there should be or what those choices should be. Should it be okay for there to be schools that, for example, make math an option after reaching basic fifth-grade arithmetic skills? There are enormous losses in not learning more art and music in schools, or cutting out foreign languages, cooking, and carpentry, for example, which happens everywhere these days—while we add on more and more math and science. Who should decide such matters?

SEYMOUR: You often speak of certain habits of mind you would want to see young people develop and that these are signs of a good school. Could you go into this a bit?

MEIER: One habit I want kids to develop is the habit of assuming that the world should be fair and that their voice should be heard—just because they are all human beings. At Mission Hill School in Boston, where I now am principal, it pleases me that the kids assume they have a right to use the Xerox machine. Some of the students think the phones and the Xerox machine are part of our common property. I think they are right. Another basic is that they should assume that there is a reason for decisions that are made and that someone should have an obligation to explain those decisions to them. I want these ways of thinking to be such a habitual part of who the kids are that, by the time they grow up, they won't put up easily with someone who would say, "Well, this is just the way it is." Schools should encourage this kind of attitude; it should be natural for a thinking person who respects [himself or] herself.

I want to see students used to reflecting on themselves and the world around them. They should be accustomed to wondering why things are the way they are; why yesterday something worked but didn't today.

We celebrate five specific habits of mind. First, we want kids to ask questions like: I wonder why that person would have done something like that? What were they thinking when they did that? We call this the habit of seeing things from other viewpoints. It's akin to the golden rule—stepping into the shoes of others. I would want this kind of thinking to be extended to other countries and cultures, asking questions like: I wonder why that culture is that way. How could somebody be Muslim? Why would people want to bomb us? Why did Hitler have such a point of view?

Second, there's the habit of looking for and weighing evidence: How do we know what we know? Then, third, the habit of making connections, looking for a pattern: Have I seen something like this before? Fourth, the habit of wondering:

Could it have been different? And finally, we want kids to be in the habit of asking: So what? Who cares?

With these kinds of habits of mind, students don't have to be afraid to listen to views they don't agree with. We want kids to learn that they don't have to be afraid that by understanding beliefs different from their own they will become like someone else. In the end, we hope that they are in charge of who they are, and what they believe—they willingly accept responsibility for their own ideas and their own behaviors.

SEYMOUR: In addition to these habits of mind, what other features would you like to see in schools?

MEIER: Schools can help widen the places where your voice counts. We want our kids to experience membership in a variety of different kinds of community other than their personal social clique. We'd like them to know what it is like to feel patriotic about their school, to identify with people who have a passion for something that seems strange to them—like a love of history or snails. I mean, not every kid will have the same experience, but each can voluntarily—however temporarily—step into a different community that will expand their world and their own sense of possibilities.

We want students to see the inner working of the schools so that they are continuously aware of how people go about making decisions and how they handle disagreements. Even decisions we sometimes cannot easily change—like the state-mandated MCAS tests. They know, for example, what our views are but they also know we will administer them [the tests] and why. In other words, students need to know how the grown-ups arrived at decisions so they don't feel mystified about the process.

SEYMOUR: Where do you see the signs of hope in education today when there is so much pessimism?

MEIER: Change always happens. Nothing ever stays the same. That is my essential hopefulness. There are little things. For example, when I talk to people their words resonate with the kind of things we're talking about. So that is a source of hope. I've seen positive changes in the last twenty or thirty years that make progressive ideas seem less far out. In the 1960s, in New York City, there wasn't a single public school that was thoroughly progressive. Today there are several hundred. The same is true in Boston, Chicago, and many other cities. Some of the pedagogical curriculum ideas that now seem commonplace came from the work of ordinary teachers meeting together to develop new approaches to children's work.

I don't think there's ever been a time in the last half-century when the idea of smaller classes and even smaller schools has been so prominent. Surely it's the first time that anyone took seriously that schools should be judged by how well they do by their most vulnerable, poorest, and hardest-to-educate child. We're not taking any of these ideas seriously enough—but they are out there. We're still building, for example, huge schools for thousands of kids while we talk about small schools. And as we slide back into more conforming and standardizing trends, as distrust becomes again the reigning idea, I remember that the pendulum will swing back. And we surely show by how we spend our money how serious we are about the hardest-to-educate children.

In the meantime we need to resist, look for openings, cracks in the façade where our ideas may flourish and grow, share what we do, and listen and learn so our own work improves.

PART III

Educating for Authentic Community: Holding Space for the Heart

Mike Seymour

John Donne's oft-quoted phrase, "No man is an island," reminds us of the ultimately relational nature of human beings. Being close to others and having a sense of belonging is about as fundamental as any human need we can think of.

Most people—perhaps, most of all, teachers and parents—would say, therefore, that relationships and community should play an important role in school. But that is not the case in too many schools today. The gulf between students' and teachers' needs for community versus the reality of relationships is painfully broad in many schools, and the positive influence authentic community can play in true learning is as often lost.

Community is a matter of the heart. When people report that such-and-such a school or group feels like a community, they are referring to an emotional environment that is readily perceived but harder to define. A social environment that has community simply "feels good." This communal feeling is made possible by many small, visible things—the way people walk and talk, the look on their faces, the quality of eye contact, the way they discuss what is important to them and observe mutual agreements.

At its core, community springs from the deepest level of collective inner life, sustained through an invisible web of positive emotions and thoughts people in the community hold about the community itself. These emotional bonds are strengthened through sharing common values, history, memories, stories, and ceremonies that, over time, can imbue community with an almost otherworldly strength and resilience.

Underlying all community building is a conscious desire and capacity to make and hold space for the heart. What do I mean by make and hold space for the heart? First, heart in a group deals with how we come to understand who we are, what has value to us—what we are all about. This is the heart a group has in common. Space-holders for heart are able to speak about community vision in a variety of ways and with a conviction that helps all to come back to the source of meaning—binding everyone together. Second, space-holders model emotional openness and receptivity, often by being vulnerable—talking about their own thoughts and feelings which, in more formal settings, could be labeled "getting personal," but which is a prized essential in a true community. Third, community is sustained through a myriad of demonstrations of caring and thoughtfulness and a willingness to be scrupulous about looking at practices, policies, or behaviors that do not fully live up to a group's idea of caring. Most of all, space-holders for community hold the space for themselves and their own inner lives by being deeply connected to their own purpose and heart.

So, community without grows from the seed of community within. We commune first with ourselves; we are then able to make space for heart between ourselves and others—deep talking to deep.

SHOWING UP AND A CULTURE OF CARING

Anthropologist and author Angeles Arrien explains the importance of "showing up" as the first part of the Four-Fold Way, a program of human potential that inspires the highest good for the individual and group. Symbolized by the archetype of the warrior or leader, showing up means being present mentally and emotionally, and accessing our personal power through presence, clear communication, and skilled timing. When we show up, the leader in us acts on behalf of our highest good. This is the first in a series of four ways of being, without which the journey cannot begin.

How many kids or teachers do not really show up at school? How many people do not fully show up to life itself? Too many, I would suggest. This is, in part, a failure of the system to provide a sense of community and emotional safety that invites people to be who they are and to show up in spirit and emotion, as well as in body and mind.

Schools that are more formal and less family-like discourage openness and community. This is part of a larger societal habit of disconnection that has come to be seen as normal by most people, although many don't like it.

We've gotten accustomed to the societal norm of not showing up to ourselves or one another. "How are you today?" person *A* asks of person *B*. "Fine," says person *B* mechanically. Even though *B* may not be fine, *B* doesn't want to burden person *A*, feel self-conscious about exposing him- or herself, or just doesn't want to get into it at the moment—or so goes the inner rationalization. So we justify this social convention of shading the truth to others (and to ourselves) and opt instead for a stock, formal response. Formal, less personal, and inauthentic ways of relating are common ways people don't show up. Formality of this kind is a common way in which we avoid having community with others.

Community takes commitment, care, and time, but it is the only way kids and teachers will be encouraged to show up at school and bring a whole person to the learning process. Conversely, showing up is the first step toward community. At school, it would mean that when students come to class, the teachers don't just overlook what is happening in their own or their children's lives in order to get on with the lesson. Many teachers begin every class day (or each new week) with some form of greeting circle, check-in, or other process as a caring invitation to be present. They stop and attend to the human story with a conviction that what's going on in their students' lives and in themselves must be attended to in some way if everyone is to going show up and be ready for learning. Without emotional presence, without being engaged fully, school is just a game. We all know that—none better than the kids themselves.

Making space for the heart is not a skill to be done mechanically, as in: "OK, kids, let's have circle this morning." Teachers who "do" circles or any other practice because it's in style or because it has been asked of them, but who haven't truly found it in themselves, play at community, but never really connect. This is part of the game in school when community and relationships are talked about—sometimes even with emotion—but are rarely lived out in ways that match the talk. In this case, it is better not to talk about community at all. Espousing one thing and doing another just sows distrust and cynicism among youth, staff, and parents who rightfully turn away in disgust or disappointment at slogans that aren't real and are simply seen as being politically correct.

EXCLUSIVITY AND THE HEROIC WIN-LOSE SYSTEM

We cannot have authentic community in school when some people are in and others out—when there are structures, practices, policies, or coalitions that divide, exclude, and extol in ways that suggest some people are fundamentally better and more worthy than others, or that continue privilege for a few at the expense of the many. We cannot have authentic community in school when kids—because of color, gender, sexual preference, age, grades, or any other matter—don't enjoy the educational resources of the more advantaged in our society. We cannot have community when kids are systematically relegated to inferior status by not being seen and celebrated for who they are because of skin color, accent, dress style, physical ability, level of "academic achievement"—in short, because they're "not like us"—meaning the White, Anglo-Saxon, Protestant male, whole body, "successful," heroic model which we hold up as a cultural standard in just about all aspects of American life.

Even as a young kid, I had problems with heroic culture in which an ideal is celebrated and held up as the way to be, leaving everyone else vulnerable to feeling "less than." Heroic culture has a built-in inferiority complex that leaves everyone anxiously scrambling for the limelight, elbowing their way to the front of the class or to the top of the corporate pile. Young hands reaching for the ceiling in classrooms to be recognized with the right answer begins this competitive quest in which, as noted author and critic, Alfie Kohn says, everyone is a loser in the race to win.

The ones who get to the finish line second or third—we can readily understand how they feel like losers in a culture that pits one against another. But the winners? They can be even bigger losers because they don't know that they, too, have lost. The bright light of winning—having the reward of the "good life"—can lead to a smugness, a false sense of security of having arrived and, therefore, of having the answer and "being right." This can insulate so-called winners from others and make them uncritically protective of their way of life. After all, winners often have to defend their territory! Most of all, we fail to see that cultural heroism can take one away from true self, as the hero can become more defined by external social ideals and expectations than by their own inner guidance. To the extent that the rest of us are trying to keep up in the race, we, too, can be distracted from being who we are.

I believe modern society has inherited a dangerous win-lose game from thousands of years ago when humans evolved the heroic archetype and hero-based cultures. The heroic culture is based on a zero sum game in which it is impossible for everyone to win. The hero did not get to be a hero by being a nice guy, but by defeating monsters or tricking goblins and witches. One becomes a hero because of someone else's loss.

Heroic cultures make very clear who is in the game and who is not, and how people must be in order to be accepted. Social norms, ethics, and rules are essential to social order, harmony, and security. Yet it makes all the difference in the world—the terms and assumptions under which rules, norms, and ethics are evolved. Heroic cultures hold up a narrow picture of what is ideal and tend to be exclusive and not inclusive, hierarchical versus participatory, and certain that external control is needed to maintain order. They are characterized by a sense of insufficiency, leading to a false sense of scarcity and always lacking. The drive engine behind the heroic culture is a root fear of anything "Other," the shadow side of humanity's unexplored psyche that gets projected outward. In fact, noted psychiatrist, Ernest Becker, writes in *The Denial of Death* that heroic cultures evolved in response to the fear of death. We fear the unknown—darkness without and within—which means Other is seen through colored lenses. Women, children, people in other cultures who don't "look like us" are seen through the lens of heroic culture as "less than." They are routinely repressed and marginalized in ways that put them on the losing end in the win-lose game.

INCLUSIVITY—CULTURES OF CARING AND COMPASSION

Modern society and education are so permeated with the thinking, norms, assumptions, and policies of heroic culture that it hardly seems possible to imagine a different kind of school, one that is not based on competition, tracking, ability grouping, grading, heavy focus on academic success, celebration of winners, reward/punishment systems in "classroom management," texts, curricula, and practices that don't honor people of color, and so on—all of which make some people winners and others losers. They do exist, however, and bear powerful testimony to the fact that a better way is possible and is a matter of choice—that the win-lose culture in many schools is not inevitable.

First, a community ideal must be walked and talked and not shoved into the background by the press of so-called more important business. This means that becoming a caring community is a significant part of school purpose and not simply a way to get student compliance, reduce violence, or improve academic achievement. When these intermediate rationales are put forward as "reasons for" community, the ethic of community is diminished by being made subordinate to something else. Community should be sought because it is the human thing to do and has value enough in itself apart from any benefits it brings to learning.

Second, community should be built on unity through diversity. Schools that work hard to celebrate the calling and giftedness in each child make every child an honored student, as opposed to the heroic model, in which only a few are honors students and everyone else is second best. This giftedness clearly involves the cultural roots unique to each young person and an honoring of the beauty and distinctiveness in each culture. Culture fairs, family history projects, culturally diverse literature, field trips to explore different cultures, and culturally diverse classroom guests are all used successfully to convey the message that the community is not based on assimilation and toning down one's cultural identity, but on celebrating the joy in our cultural richness.

Third, multicultural education ultimately deals with issues of access and equity—as Sonia Nieto makes clear in my interview with her (this volume). Here, we address the racism and inequity embedded in the system itself, in things like adoption of texts, hiring practices, key committee selection, and bias in testing instruments. The Eurocentric bias (which is a heroic bias) in our school practices and policies must be open to critical dialogue for alternative community voices to be heard.

Fourth, the development of empathy, caring, and compassion must be seen as the heart of community and as a part of each child's nature. These virtues bring community to life and can be read about, discussed, role played, and practiced in daily interactions in the lives of our young people and their teachers. This means moving away from the false assumption of heroic culture that some kids are inherently good while others are inherently bad (successful versus unsuccessful). I have met many kids who were angry, did mean things, or were violent to other students. Yet in all my years of working with the most troubled children and teens, I can say I have not met one truly "bad" child. Community is built on faith in the goodness in each person's nature and the principle that kids—when given the right opportunity and context—would rather be caring and compassionate than mean and violent.

Fifth, impressive amounts of research favors small, human-scale schools that make authentic community more easily achieved. These include schools-within-schools, choice schools, and charter schools—all of which are growing rapidly as reform options across the country. In addition to improved achievement and cost-effectiveness, small schools tend to be more equitable across racial, ethnic, and income groups; they are safer, more personalized communities where everybody—kids, teachers and parents—come to know and depend on each other far more than is possible in a large school. Because they clearly offer a better way to educate our children, I trust a time may come when the wisdom of small schools will prevail as a standard.

Sixth, and last, I sincerely hope we can get off this juggernaut of achievement and success and ask more often what we are striving for and if that has worth. I am a strong supporter of kids working hard, pushing their limits, and discovering potentials within themselves that might not otherwise rise to the surface without that extra bit of resolve and effort. On the other hand, I worry that we question too little the meaning of what we are doing and pass that mindlessness onto our children. The regime in school today is too much like the treadmill that life can become, where what is done now is simply to get to the next level and is not appreciated for any intrinsic worth.

Importantly, we demean the role of childhood in society with an excessive focus on our young people "getting somewhere." More and more, children in our society are valued for the adults they will become and not for the people they are now. We act as if the school years are training for better years to come. When we treat childhood as a stage to get through—and children as nothing more than adults-in-the-making—we cause children to mistrust or undervalue the playful, intuitive, and often prophetic perspective they bring to our culture. In undervaluing childhood, culture loses its childlike resilience, wisdom, and vision.

CIVIC ENGAGEMENT AND SERVICE LEARNING

The decline in volunteerism and engagement in political and civic life, especially among young people, is one (among many) signs of an eroding sense of community in American life. This shows up in the form of less trust and willingness to invest in anything public, and has affected people's willingness to support and trust our public educators. Likewise, this presents a direct threat to democracy, which relies on people's good will to participate in public life for the common good and to work out differences in a fair way and not retreat (as we have seen in recent decades) into partisan squabbles where factions talk *at* and not *with* one another.

Education's answer to this dilemma of social capital is service learning. Service learning involves young people in learning important academic content and skills through community-based projects that provide a social benefit while connecting youth to their local community. A community-service project that is well designed and managed allows students hands-on learning, a meaningful connection between what they are studying and real life, and a sense of the importance of the place where they live. Kids learn that there are lives and issues beyond their own that are worth caring about, and they experience empowerment in actually being able to make a difference.

Schools in which service learning is part of a larger commitment to authentic community give young people the chance to experience their own caring within a context that gives caring importance. In this sense, a community of caring in school helps to liberate young people's altruistic nature from self-interest and single-minded individualism. I can think of no finer gift to a growing mind than to know from direct experience that one's own sense of fulfillment cannot be achieved by only seeking self-gain, but that true well-being comes through compassion and service to others.

THE GLOBAL VILLAGE AND
THE MULTICULTURAL CITIZEN

Feelings of connection with—and obligation to—diverse people the world over is an economic, political, and ecological necessity. Increasing numbers of people also recognize in our global interdependence a spiritual necessity—that our moral health is related to how we respond to the larger community of need around the world.

This is linked directly to how our citizenship education defines sphere of obligation in an increasingly global, multicultural world. Not only does the growing interdependence of nations make rigid national identification problematic but the increasing cultural diversity of many nations makes citizenship models around singular cultural norms unworkable for students of diverse ethnic, cultural, and religious backgrounds, and for society as a whole.

Here, the purposes of social justice within nations and among nations coincide. The message of educating for authentic community is that we need a vision of ourselves as one people, both at home and abroad.

REFERENCE

Becker, Ernest. 1973. *The Denial of Death.* New York: Free Press Paperbacks.

Caring as a Foundation for Learning

An Interview with Nel Noddings by Mike Seymour

When I met Nel Noddings at her home in Ocean Grove, New Jersey, I was struck by her warm and engaging manner and her impressive vegetable garden—her zest for the earthly was a nice balance to her considerable intellect. Ever since reading her book, The Challenge to Care in Schools: An Alternative Approach to Education, *I knew I had found a kindred spirit in this leading figure in the field of educational philosophy, feminist ethics, and moral education. She has been professor of philosophy and education at Teachers College, Columbia University, and Lee L. Jacks Professor of Child Education Emerita at Stanford University. She is author or co-author of numerous books, including* Justice and Caring: The Search for Common Ground in Education, *and* Awakening the Inner Eye: Intuition in Education.

MIKE SEYMOUR: I speak about the need to educate for self, community, Earth, and spirit, and this closely parallels your own thought that education might be organized around centers of care. You speak of care for self, for intimate others, for associates and acquaintances, for distant others, for nonhuman animals, for plants, and the physical environment for the human-made world of objects and instruments. In your own words, and at the risk of belaboring the obvious, what suggests that caring should be the essential purpose of education?

NEL NODDINGS: Life itself suggests this. When you look at what is important to people—what really matters to them—all the things that you just mentioned are things that really matter to people. Without acknowledging that, without having care at the center of our lives, I think life becomes superficial, hectic, a continual pursuit of an elusive something in which people's lives lose meaning. We can do better than that and can help kids to connect with themselves. My book on happiness emphasizes self-understanding because self-understanding is essential to happiness. If we don't know what makes us happy—and I think a lot of people don't know what makes them happy—then it is unlikely that we will be happy.

SEYMOUR: I agree with everything you have said, but I realize that some parents, educators, and policymakers say that helping children to be happy is not the work of schools but of families and civil society. There's a complaint that schools are already too burdened and that they are having so many problems academically because of too many things to do. How would you answer that?

NODDINGS: When you ask whose job it is to raise moral people: It is everybody's job. It can't be just the job of the family or just the job of the school. We can't compartmentalize functions like this and expect society to work, not if we want to raise whole people. It has to be everybody's work. You can't assign something like that to one institution and think that it is going to work. It doesn't because then kids feel compartmentalized. This happens also when teachers know only one subject. We ask high-school kids to master, say, five major subjects. But if they ask their algebra teacher for help in interpreting *Moby Dick,* for example, she says, "Oh no, that is not my field." Or if students ask the English teacher for help with their algebra homework, the English teacher can't do it. So what are kids supposed to think when they are asked to learn five subjects but their teachers, who are models of educated persons, know only one subject and sometimes that not very well? So you have to get out of that frame of mind where you suppose that a big important task can be assigned to only one agency in society.

The second answer is that, initially, U.S. schools were not founded with academic purposes. They were founded for moral purposes to produce good people and good citizens. Academics were used to prompt those purposes, which is something we've forgotten. People today think that the only purpose of the school is academic. This never was the case, and I hope it never will be the case because there are more important purposes to education.

SEYMOUR: I think the compartmentalizing you speak about stems from our society's overemphasis and valuing of individuality and autonomy to the extent that families feel they must be self-contained and that it's not acceptable, therefore, to need a village to raise a child.

NODDINGS: That's right, and the nuclear family is not the only model of family or raising children. In most homes today, both parents work outside the home, and as a feminist, I celebrate that. Both men and women have to care in the home and, second, schools have to pick up much of what used to be done in the family when more mothers stayed home. It is just futile for teachers to say, "Well, if the parents did their job, I could do mine." That day is gone. Of course we want parents to do their job, but we have to help them do their job. Jane Roland Martin says school today has to be more like the best homes, and I don't know of any way to avoid that if we want to raise whole, moral people.

SEYMOUR: Teachers will say they weren't hired to do that and that the institution doesn't support the concept of taking a village to raise a child. We are not funding smaller classrooms nor making conditions possible that create a community feeling or a sense of mutual support.

NODDINGS: That's right, and I would say that I think we now are on very hard times in education. The current school reform movement that concentrates entirely on standards and standardized testing is really destroying our schools. I understand the stated reason for it—that now we will do the right thing by our low income and minority students. We are going to insist on high standards so these kids get the education they deserve. But the current reform is a poor technical solution. We have known about the problems in the urban schools for years and we might have tried progressive education philosophy and methods. But in most cases we haven't. Back in the sixties, Herb Kohl, Jonathan Kozol, and Edgar Friedenberg told us about the problems in the urban schools and suggested ways to solve them. So now, to lay a standards movement on all of the schools, thereby destroying the creativity in some of the best of them, is just awful.

SEYMOUR: You mentioned James Comer's comments on the widespread alienation of students from school life. Comer says that the greatest student complaint is that the schools and the people in them don't care. We know that most teachers are caring people, so it must be the institutional culture that restricts caring. What are your thoughts on that?

NODDINGS: You have really underscored what I think is the main contribution of an ethic of care, and that is its relational interpretation. What Comer has described is that kids want to be cared for and teachers want to care. Teachers work hard and care deeply about having their kids succeed, and yet, as students report, there are no caring relations. From the perspective of care theory, to have a caring relation you have to have a "carer" who operates in a certain way, you have to have a "cared-for" who recognizes that and responds to it. Then you've got a caring relation. The absence of a caring relation could be the fault of the carer or the fault of the cared-for, or it might be an institutional problem. More and more, failed teacher–student relations are embedded in institutions that simply do not support relations of care. We must ask how can we change that whole environment so that people who want to care and people who want to be cared for can enter caring relations. That means changing quite a lot in schools.

SEYMOUR: I've heard many teachers complain about administrative admonitions not to touch children for fear of abuse claims and lawsuits. On the one hand, many teachers simply go ahead and hug the kid anyway. But I see too many putting more professional distance between themselves and their students, which they may have been inclined to do in the first place and now have a district argument to support them. What do you suggest to teachers who describe this kind of concern?

NODDINGS: This is another manifestation of the problem of not having the conditions under which caring relations can flourish. One thing you can do is put two adults in a classroom, which is often done in primary classrooms. Because a male teacher ought to be able to hold a child on his lap and read to the child, I have often suggested to young men who want to teach at the elementary school level to find situations in which they would be protected. There should be another adult in a classroom. I worry for young men going in to the profession because their careers and lives are at stake when they are accused of some dreadful thing like this. Another solution to the more general problem of not being able to establish caring relations is continuity (a practice some call "looping") where kids stay with the same teacher for several years. I prefer for teachers and students to stay together by mutual consent so the student has some choice in the matter. You can't order things like this. Wonderful school environments, like Debbie Meier's Central Park East, can't simply be duplicated [in a] cookie-cutter fashion. Choice for teachers and students and parents allows the spirit of a particular community and school to come forth.

SEYMOUR: I wonder how we have gotten so far away from the truth that learning is fundamentally a matter of relationship and that caring relations between teachers and students and among students themselves are essential for open hearts and therefore open minds. Have teachers forgotten this truth, or have they had to push it into the background, because the business-as-usual makes relating so difficult?

NODDINGS: Teachers are so harassed today and [are] pushed to produce higher test scores on standard tests, even though the teachers know that this is not the right thing to do. Sometimes teachers will question me, "How can we really have time for relationships on top of everything else we have to do?" I say that caring is not done on top of everything else, it's just the other way around. Caring is the foundation for teaching and learning. Time spent establishing relations of care and trust is not time wasted. It isn't time taken away from academic studies, because once those relations of care and trust are established, everything else goes better. Kids will do things for people they like and trust. That puts a great responsibility on the teacher to be a model of a good person.

SEYMOUR: We already talked about the complaint from educators and policymakers that schools have too much to do and that this is seen, in part, as [being] responsible for the difficulties schools are having. Besides the moral argument for caring in schools, what other evidence do you cite for making caring a central purpose in education?

NODDINGS: One strong argument is the progress we have made in public education in the last century in terms of student retention. We keep many more kids in school now compared to the first few decades of the twentieth century when only about 10 percent of students got through high school. We are still losing kids now, but nothing like the early 1900s. Some counter with the argument that kids could get good jobs then without finishing high school. That might also be true today except for a public school credential system that limits certain students' work opportunities. We have no proof whatever that the skills students learn in high school are those used later in work. It's a credential thing more than anything else. So the school has to be a place for everyone, and that means the way we define academics has to change. We have to find intelligent ways of approaching many subjects that will be of interest to a wide variety of kids instead of insisting on the same material for all kids, which causes them to lose ground academically and us to lose the student. On this subject, I don't think anybody was more right than John Dewey, who said that any subject that is of interest to people can be taught and learned intelligently and contribute to intellectual growth. Mathematics is not more academic in the sense of developing an intellect than cooking, for example. Either one can be taught and learned stupidly or intelligently.

SEYMOUR: I know you are concerned that our current way of educating is actually doing harm to young people. You quote John Dewey, who I think quoted Rousseau when he said, "After we have wasted our efforts on stunting the true gifts of nature, we see the short-lived and illusory brilliance we have substituted die away, while the natural abilities we have crushed do not revive." Why don't more people see and react to the destructive side of schooling and protest in greater numbers?

NODDINGS: I think that people who have gone through school successfully, possibly even with difficulty, think that school as they know it is the way it has to be, and that accepting the grind is just part of getting on with life and a measure of the person. Also, we're stuck in this artificial hierarchy where people who do well on SATs and GREs and get all As in school are somehow better than the people who aren't interested in that stuff and do well on something else. So, we establish human and social value by sorting kids like this. This is what the tracking system is all about, and what's wrong is the hierarchical ordering in tracking. On the other hand, it would be wonderful if we provided students multiple options in accordance, for example, with Howard Gardner's intelligences, so that kids have choice and are not labeled by the system.

SEYMOUR: Tracking comes from a Eurocentric-biased way of assessment that is prejudicial to students who do not come from the dominant culture. What you speak of is honoring the special interests and talents that each child has, and allowing them to pick what they want to do, understanding that whatever they learned can be done with intellectual rigor. That's the antithesis of the tracking and lack of choice we see in many schools today.

NODDINGS: I speak to this point in my new book on happiness and raise the question: Why [do] educators in a liberal democracy put so little emphasis on choice, when choice is at the very center of our lives in a liberal democracy as adults? When it comes to granting choice to kids, we say they are too young, don't know what they need, or don't even know what they want.

SEYMOUR: Much of that is a system failure, as John Taylor Gatto says—that we're dumbing students down.

NODDINGS: Exactly. I couldn't agree more. We could help students make well-informed choices. I would give tests, interest surveys, and advice to help students get connected with their interests and involved in their education—not assign them to classes chosen by us.

SEYMOUR: The history of genius and achievement really shows that nine-tenths of it is desire and interest. Reports of children who don't read, for example, until fourth grade, suggest that they become avid readers when they find a subject they're curious about, and they quickly get their reading at grade level with peers who were earlier readers.

NODDINGS: Well another point building on what you just said—if you read the biographies of creative people—you find that the majority of them hated school. People like Churchill, Einstein, Edison, and even Dewey, who talks about being bored in school, all had to push against the system in order to maintain their own creativity.

SEYMOUR: Can you help us understand the distinction you draw between character education and your idea of how caring would be developed in school?

NODDINGS: I don't think any decent parent, and certainly no care theorist, would object to a notion of developing good character in kids. Where we part company, at least with some character educators, is that we don't think you can teach virtues the way you teach times tables, for example. Some schools will have a virtue of the week or month, like honesty, and so classrooms concentrate on honesty, then go to loyalty or compassion next. That sounds like a caricature, but it is pretty close to what actually is happening in some schools. You can't teach virtues directly that way as a lesson, but I think we do get a start on teaching virtues in interventions. That is, when something happens, we intervene, using the immediate context for student learning.

I use the example of a small child picking a cat up by the tail. I would tell her not to do that and explain why is it wrong (because it hurts), and then you show the child how to do it right. Today, we're not doing enough teaching in the moment around social and emotional issues, and there is much less of this emphasis than back in the beginning of the twentieth century. For example, we have allowed student-to-student cruelty to grow out of all proportion. We get so busy teaching academics that we don't pay enough of the right kind of attention when negative student situations occur. In school, we need to approach moral development the way a good family would, in an intimate, person-to-person way and not through teaching a lesson on specific virtues. We know from past attempts that this kind of direct approach just doesn't work.

SEYMOUR: So moral education needs to come out of lived experience and also [it is important to] acknowledge the gray areas in moral behavior which elude the black-and-white approach that you tend to get through a direct teaching method.

NODDINGS: Yes, and I have just written a piece for the *Journal of Moral Education*, entitled "Are the Virtues Always Virtuous?" For example, is honesty always a virtue? From the perspective of care theory, it isn't, if it causes harm and unnecessarily hurts another. Is courage always a virtue? The suicide bombers certainly had courage, but to what end?

SEYMOUR: You ask questions of ultimacy and where is it going. Virtue needs to be considered in the larger context of human good or harm.

NODDINGS: Exactly, and this points out the notion that too much of character education is superficial and doesn't go into the more complex issues, like context, in moral education.

SEYMOUR: Earlier, I touched on the idea that excessive individualism coupled with the abdication of the individual's responsibility to the community has eroded the social commons and civic life. This make ours a less friendly world where going 24/7 after success, or well-meaning moms and dads and kids jetting between one venue and the next leaves little room for simple pleasures—relating being one of the most dear. How do you envision a change in America's outlook on the need to slow down, smell the roses, and start caring about what deserves to be cared for?

NODDINGS: That is a very tough question. I can describe what it would be like if we were to do that, but I have to say that I am not optimistic about positive change. Likewise, I am not as optimistic as I would like to be about the future of public education. I think we may be living in the last days of public education as we have known it. On that pessimistic note, I think we have to change the conversation. We have to get educators and parents talking again about the aims of education. We have to show people that the result of the kind of change we are talking about is a happier life, and then we need to show that it is possible to have schools that are really there for teachers and kids.

SEYMOUR: We need to remind people of the fact that there are real joys in having a more humane environment at school and that true learning can happen and be fun at the same time.

NODDINGS: Take it out of the realm of duty and more into the realm of pleasure. Fundamentally, there should be a joy to learning. There has to be hard work, too. But people are willing to struggle through the hard work if there is some intrinsic reward. Whitehead talked about the first stage of learning as the stage of romance; that has to be the way we get started. Something speaks to you, something calls you, something interests you, and once you are grabbed by it, then you can put up with the hard work required to produce an end result.

SEYMOUR: There are many schools like those inspired by Central Park East elementary and secondary schools, the Coalition of Essential Schools, the small schools funded by the Gates Foundation, the expeditionary school of movement, and now almost 3,000 charter schools that are part of a very promising movement in school choice. Do you see cause for hope in these trends?

NODDINGS: Sure I do, but the problem is that the picture is very mixed. Some of the schools you mentioned are reminiscent of some of the best schools in the sixties and early seventies . . . the alternative schools, the "storefront" schools. That era of open, democratic education is reflected in some of the schools today. But there are other schools that parents have chosen for their kids which emphasize academics narrowly, push kids to think only of high grades, and do not truly value caring relationships and student-centered education.

So along with the good, you've got a mixed bag. You've also got a choice forced on the kids, so that in some cases the sort of happy classroom that you and I would like to see is not what the parents have chosen for their kids. They have chosen the nose-to-the-grindstone sort of model for their kids. Ultimately, those kids will grow up thinking that that's the way things should be. Swiss psychologist Alice Miller has described something called "poisonous pedagogy," where education is punitive but is rationalized as being "for the child's good." Children in that system grow up thinking that there is something wrong with them, and without really examining that system, they turn right around and use that sort of poisonous pedagogy on their own kids.

Yes, we need more choice in schools, and emphasis on caring and creative ways to get parents committed to education like the contracts many schools have parents sign before admitting their child. The worry is that if the public schools don't respond with revisions like this, then we are going to hear an even greater clamor for the privatization of education.

SEYMOUR: What parting words would you like to leave us with?

NODDINGS: The most important thing I think is to deepen and broaden the conversation about what school should be for. Parents and educators need to talk about the things that really matter in life and try to get those things incorporated into what we do in schools.

9

Creating a School Community

Eric Schaps

Eric Schaps is founder and president of the Developmental Studies Center in Oakland, California. Established in 1980, DSC specializes in designing educational programs and evaluating their effects on children's academic, ethical, social, and emotional development. The center has a full time staff of sixty; its work has been supported by forty philanthropic foundations and governmental agencies; its in-school and after-school programs have been recognized as exemplary in a number of governmental and other program effectiveness reviews. Dr. Schaps is the author of three books and over sixty book chapters and articles on school change, character education, and preventing problem behaviors. He serves on several boards, including the education advisory board of Boys & Girls Clubs of America.

Imagine that you are a student entering a new school for the first time. Picture the scene. What would be on your mind? You might be wondering: Will I make friends here? Will I be popular? Will my teachers like me? Will they care about me? Will I be able to do the work here? Will I be smart enough? Or, in all too many cases: Will I be safe here? Will I be teased, shunned, humiliated? Or even: Will I be ripped off or beaten up?

These questions reveal our basic psychological needs—for emotional and physical safety; for close, supportive relationships—a sense of "connectedness" (Resnick et al. 1997) or "belongingness" (Baumeister and Leary 1995); for autonomy, or a say in what happens to us; and for a sense of competence—a belief that we are capable people and able to learn. These fundamental needs shape human motivation and have major implications for learning and development. We are willing to work very hard to preserve our sense of safety, belonging, autonomy, and competence (Deci and Ryan 1985).

We also bond with the people and institutions that help us satisfy our needs, which makes the creation of caring, inclusive, participatory communities for our students especially important (Watson, Battistich, and Solomon 1997). When a school meets students' basic psychological needs, students become increasingly committed to the school's norms, values, and goals. And by enlisting students in maintaining that sense of community, the school provides opportunities for students to learn skills and develop habits that will benefit them throughout their lives.

A growing body of research confirms the benefits of building a sense of community in school. Students in schools with a strong sense of community are more likely to be academically motivated (Solomon et al. 2000); to act ethically and altruistically (Watson, Battistich, and Solomon 1997); to develop social and emotional competencies (Solomon et al. 2000); and to avoid a number of problem behaviors, including drug use and violence (Resnick et al. 1997).

These benefits are often lasting. Researchers have found that the positive effects of certain community-building programs for elementary schools persist through middle and high school. During middle school, for example, students from elementary schools that had implemented the Child Development Project (created by the Developmental Studies Center)—a program that emphasizes community building— were found to outperform middle-school students from comparison elementary schools on academic outcomes (higher grade-point averages and achievement test scores); teacher ratings of behavior (better academic engagement, respectful behavior, and social skills); and self-reported misbehavior (less misconduct in school and fewer delinquent acts) (Battistich 2001). A study that assessed the enduring effects of the Seattle Social Development Project—another elementary school program—on former participants at age eighteen found lower rates of violent behavior, heavy drinking, and sexual activity, as well as higher academic motivation and achievement, for program participants relative to comparison group students (Hawkins et al. 1999).

Schools can readily assess the degree to which students experience community in school by asking students how much they agree or disagree with such statements as:

- My class is like a family.
- Students in my class help one another learn.
- I believe that I can talk to the teachers in this school about things that are bothering me.
- Students in my class can get a rule changed if they think that it is unfair.

An annual survey of this sort can help assess a school's overall effectiveness and how well specific community-building efforts are working.

Unfortunately, schools with a strong sense of community are fairly rare. In fact, most schools that survey students' perceptions of community wind up with mediocre mean scores. Of further concern is the fact that low-income students and students of color usually report a lower level of community in school than do affluent or white students. Many schools are ill-equipped to provide community for the students who may need it most (Battistich et al. 1995).

COMMUNITY-BUILDING APPROACHES

Fortunately, research also suggests that schools can strengthen students' sense of community by adopting feasible, commonsense approaches. Four approaches are particularly beneficial.

Actively Cultivate Respectful, Supportive Relationships among Students, Teachers, and Parents

Supportive relationships are the heart of community. They enable students from diverse backgrounds to bring their personal thoughts, feelings, and experiences into the classroom. Supportive relationships help parents, especially those who would otherwise feel vulnerable or uncomfortable, take active roles in the school and in their children's education.

Emphasize Common Purposes and Ideals

Along with academic achievement, schools with a strong sense of community stress the development of qualities essential to good character and citizenship, such as fairness, concern for others, and personal responsibility. Everyone shares an understanding of the school's values, which then shape daily interactions.

Provide Regular Opportunities for Service and Cooperation

Students learn the skills of collaboration, develop wider and richer relationships, and experience the many satisfactions of contributing to the welfare of others.

Provide Developmentally Appropriate Opportunities for Autonomy and Influence

Having a say in establishing the agenda and climate for the classroom is intrinsically satisfying and helps prepare students for the complexities of citizenship in a democracy.

Several leading program developers have focused on using one or more of these approaches to build community. The more prominent programs include James Comer's School Development Program,[1] Eunice Shriver's Community of Caring Program,[2] the Northeast Foundation for Children's Responsive Classroom,[3] David Hawkins's Seattle Social Development Project,[4] and the Developmental Studies

Center's Child Development Project.[5] The Child Development Project, for example, focuses on the regular use of several key activities:

- Class meetings are useful for setting goals and norms, planning activities, and identifying and solving problems. They are essential for building peer relationships and fostering shared goals in the classroom. Class meetings at the beginning of the year, for example, include a few "unity builders." Students may bring a favorite toy or memento and discuss it with a partner, who then presents it to the entire class. Later, the class may collaboratively establish goals for the year (such as "to make our room a safe place for everyone"), shared values (such as "to treat one another with respect"), or shared norms (such as "to make decisions by consensus whenever we can").
- A buddies program pairs whole classes of older and younger students for academic and recreational activities. Every older student gets a younger buddy for the year. They get acquainted by interviewing each other, charting ways in which they are both alike and different, and sharing their classroom portfolios. During the year, they may read or play math games together, visit museums, work together for a cause, or create a joint journal of their activities. At the year's end, they show their mutual appreciation by exchanging thank-you notes or gifts that they have made. Buddies programs help create powerful cross-age relationships, teach important social skills, and create a caring ethos in the school.
- "Homeside" activities are short conversation activities for students and parents or other caregivers to do at home once or twice a month. These conversations, mostly interviews conducted by students with their parents, link school learning with home experiences and perspectives. For fourth-grade state history units, for example, students interview their parents about how their family or ancestors first came to their state. Whether family members have lived in the state for 100 years or 100 days, the story of how and why they came to settle there is part of state history and serves to personalize learning for students.
- Schoolwide community-building activities link students, parents, and teachers; help foster new school traditions; and promote helpfulness, inclusiveness, and responsibility. They can be as undemanding as family film nights, invitations to the entire family to view a feature-length movie at school and perhaps discuss a question related to it within the family. Or the activities can be as challenging as creating a family heritage museum, for which students and their caregivers prepare displays of information and artifacts that tell something about their family heritage. The school then features the displays for a week or two and organizes an evening event so that parents and children can view them together.

These activities help educators make significant changes in the norms, practices, routines, and policies that often prevail in a school's hidden curriculum. They provide tools for promoting all stakeholders' experience of community. Some of them—class meetings, especially—may involve new skills that teachers need to learn through additional staff development. Other activities require little or no additional training for implementation.

MAKE COMMUNITY A PRIORITY

U.S. policymakers are calling for schools to adopt "evidence-based programs," and we know now that the evidence for the importance of building caring school communities is clear and compelling. One promising development is the recent recognition by the federal Safe and Drug-Free Schools program of the importance of community building; its August 2002 national technical assistance meeting in Washington, D.C., gave community building center stage as an effective violence prevention strategy. Community building should become—at a minimum—a strong complement to the prevailing focus on academic achievement.

NOTES

This chapter first appeared as "Creating a School Community" by Eric Schaps, in *Educational Leadership*, March 2003, Volume 60, No. 6, pp. 31–33. Alexandria, VA: Association for Supervision and Curriculum Development. Copyright © 2003 ASCD. Reprintd by permission All rights reserved.

1. For more information on James Comer's School Development Program, visit http://info.med.yale.edu/comer/index.html.

2. For more information on Eunice Shriver's Community of Caring Program, visit www.communityofcaring.org.

3. For more information on the Northeast Foundation for Children's Responsive Classroom, visit www.responsiveclassroom.org.

4. For more information on David Hawkins's Seattle Social Development Project, visit http://depts.washington.edu/ssdp.

5. For more information on the Developmental Studies Center's Child Development Project, visit www.devstu.org.

REFERENCES

Battistich, V. 2001. Effects of an Elementary School Intervention on Students' "Connectedness" to School and Social Adjustment during Middle School. Paper presented at the meeting of the American Educational Research Association. Seattle, Wash.

Battistich, V., D. Solomon, D. Kim, M. Watson, and E. Schaps. 1995. "Schools as Communities, Poverty Levels of Student Populations, and Students' Attitudes, Motives, and Performance: A Multilevel Analysis." *American Educational Research Journal* 32: 627–58.

Baumeister, R., and M. Leary. 1995. "The Need to Belong: Desire for Interpersonal Attachments as a Fundamental Human Motivation." *Psychological Bulletin* 117: 497–529.

Deci, E. L., and R. M. Ryan. 1985. *Intrinsic Motivation and Self-Determination in Human*

Behavior. New York: Plenum.

Hawkins, J. D., R. F. Catalano, R. Kosterman, R. Abbot, and K. G. Hill. 1999. "Preventing Adolescent Health-Risk Behaviors by Strengthening Protection during Childhood." *Archives of Pediatric and Adolescent Medicine* 153: 226–34.

Resnick, M. D. et al. 1997. "Protecting Adolescents from Harm: Findings from the National Longitudinal Study on Adolescent Health." *Journal of the American Medical Association* 278: 823–32.

Schaps, E., V. Battistich, and D. Solomon. 1997. "School as a Caring Community: A Key to Character Education." In A. Molnar, ed., *The Construction of Children's Character, Part II: 96th Yearbook of the National Society for the Study of Education.* University of Chicago Press: Chicago.

Solomon, D., V. Battistich, M. Watson, E. Schaps, and C. Lewis. 2000. "A Six-District Study of Educational Change: Direct and Mediated Effects of the Child Development Project." *Social Psychology of Education* 4: 3–51.

Watson, M., V. Battistich, and D. Solomon. 1997. "Enhancing Students' Social and Ethical Development in Schools: An Intervention Program and Its Effects." *International Journal of Educational Research* 27: 571–86.

10

Community in School

An Interview with Thomas Sergiovanni by Mike Seymour

Thomas J. Sergiovanni is Lillian Radford Professor of education and administration and senior fellow at the Center for Educational Leadership at Trinity University in San Antonio. Prior to joining the Trinity faculty he was professor of educational administration and supervision at the University of Illinois for eighteen years. Dr. Sergiovanni serves on the editorial boards of The Journal of Personnel Evaluation in Education *and* Catholic Education: A Journal of Inquiry and Practice. *He has broad interests in the areas of school leadership and the supervision and evaluation of teaching. Among his recent publications are* Moral Leadership: Getting to the Heart of School Improvement *(1992),* Building Community in Schools *(1994),* Leadership for the School House: How Is It Different? Why Is It Important? *(1996),* The Lifeworld of Leadership: Creating Culture, Community, and Personal Meaning in Our Schools *(2000),* The Principalship: A Reflective Practice Perspective, Fourth Edition *(2001),* Leadership: What's in It for Schools? *(2001), and* Supervision: A Redefinition *(2002).*

MIKE SEYMOUR: What is your understanding of community as an aspect of school culture and its role in healthy schools?

THOMAS SERGIOVANNI: There are formal organizations and social organizations. Literature on school reform and leadership assume that what we are trying to improve are formal organizations. Some schools may very well be formal organizations, but that is part of the problem. We need to understand that a school works best when understood as a social organization or community, which are about people relationships. Communities as social organizations are much more like families, neighborhoods, and friendship groups, whereas the formal organization is like General Motors or most businesses. Reform efforts that don't see schools as communities are out of step with the human reality of education.

SEYMOUR: Accountability and performance seem more natural to the formal organization. Can we have these and still maintain a sense of community in school?

SERGIOVANNI: Perhaps for school the word "accountability" is not appropriate because it sounds so formal and intimidating. It seems to me the more community-like the enterprise, the more family-like should be the talk, so responsibility may be a better word in schools. In that sense, yes, accountability is important. When schools become authentic communities, they also become communities of responsibility. There is something special about the relationships that exist among people in communities. It includes their identification with traditions or purposes that people feel obliged to embody in their behavior. That is what families are about. Responsibility is natural when we take the stance that we are obligated to meet our commitments based on shared values and agreements. Responsibility provides a heck of a lot more powerful sense of what accountability is than to give someone a test, although there is nothing inherently wrong with tests.

SEYMOUR: Explain how the crisis in schools can be understood as a crisis of community and the lack of quality relationships or norms.

SERGIOVANNI: The major problem we are facing, in my view, is a lack of connections. All of us need to be connected to ourselves, to others who are important to us, to our work, and our responsibilities. Schools are, unfortunately, not in the connections business, and without connections they have difficulty achieving their goals. Since kids have to be connected somehow, they are left to find their own connection, which is what gangs are all about.

It seems to me that successful schools create their own culture in which different cultures merge. To be connected, our attitudes and perspectives need to change somewhat. Also, people are connected to things they feel a part of and have some say in creating. Catholic and other religious schools and some secular private schools do a better job of providing connections because people share common ideas and values that pull them together. The best we can do in most public schools is to have a pep rally where the squad comes out and everyone goes, "Rah, rah, rah." This is a feeble attempt to try to connect people because it is about less important things. People have to be connected in a meaningful way.

If you want a school to be a community of responsibility where kids feel obligated to fulfill their roles and their responsibilities, then students need to have a say in what goes on. Throughout the whole standards debate we've overlooked what students have to say. We know from Deborah Meier's [school] (Central Park East) and other schools that this kind of involvement works.

SEYMOUR: A school that has norms and stands for something harmonizes all the subcultures and creates a new culture for young people to identify with. Could you talk more on this?

SERGIOVANNI: When I go to a school that really bowls me over, I generally find an idea structure, some of it tacit but often visible as well. An idea structure is comprised of expectations, purposes, values, and norms that define what is important, what people's roles are and what is expected of them. For example, you can't teach a kid the importance of respect without that being adopted as a value by everybody in the school—adults included. This is not just for the students, but what we are obliged to do as a whole community in order to meet our commitments to ourselves and to what we are about.

There are so many places where this is going on, like Stevenson High in Lincolnshire, Illinois, a huge school of 4,000 students broken up into four smaller schools. This is a school that has an idea structure. One idea that they really practice is that every youngster can learn if we can figure out a way to provide the proper support. For example, they give a common exam to all eighth grade students (who are on their way to Stevenson) and invite those that need help to attend summer school funded and put on by Stevenson. The summer school not only deals with some of the academic problems but helps kids understand the Stevenson culture, which is important for them to do well. There are a dozen other steps like mentoring and advisories that are available if needed—so these are good examples of putting your money where your mouth is.

Stevenson also values the intellectual capital of the staff, and you can't do that unless people work collaboratively. Working collaboratively is something that everybody in the school knows and accepts. One simple and unique thing that they did was to organize faculty teams around the courses they teach and not so much in terms of traditional departments. All of the faculty that teach Biology 101, for example, are a learning community, and those who teach American History are another, and so on. These people share their lesson plans, come up with curriculum, identify the standards they want to meet, examine one another's work, come up with ideas, and visit one another's classrooms. This collaboration works because teachers become connected sharing that course and being more successful as a result. Those collaborative teams have a tremendous amount of responsibility. Teachers are not told to teach the same way, but there are certain things that have to be embodied in their teaching, no matter how they decide to teach. This is a different stance in teaching today—to make room for a teacher's uniqueness within a shared framework.

SEYMOUR: The word community seems fuzzy to some, and is associated with something that just feels good. But you speak more precisely of community, like the caring community or the learning community as well as the community of responsibility, which we've already talked about. Could you talk more on that?

SERGIOVANNI: I think it's important to be precise and to have a clear picture of the various aspects of community. A caring community emerges from dialogue and commitment to notions of how we want to live our lives together, who we are, and how we relate to one another. Being caring, respectful, and inviting become part of the obligations in such a school. So if I'm wandering around a caring school looking lost, I shouldn't be surprised if a number of kids ask me if I need help.

A learning community is another thing. One aspect of a learning community is that kids accept the idea that they are all responsible for each other's learning. If a youngster is having problems in geometry, his or her peers feel a sense of responsibility to help. There is a sort of "we are all going to pull each other up by our boot straps." That is a lot different from the typical high school where the name of the game is competition and everybody is fending for themselves. After all, we too often find that a student's class rank depends in part on that student's success *and* in part on the failure of other students.

SEYMOUR: Robert Bellah, (author of *Habits of the Heart: Individualism and Commitment in American Life*), whom you cite, talks about rampant individualism and the erosion of communal ideals. How does this show up in schools?

SERGIOVANNI: Most schools encourage individualism, which I don't think is natural—the natural tendency is for kids to want connection. This happens through grading, comparison, competition, and tracking, all of which have unintended consequences of creating an individualist culture. Apart from that, kids are left to make communities for themselves that are often exclusive and not communal. They may not have norms consistent with the school nor bridge well with other groups. In a high school, a good question is how to build bridges between student groups so that connections are broader and you avoid the negative effects of cliques.

SEYMOUR: Could you explain the idea of "community of mind" and how that is important to the health of a school?

SERGIOVANNI: For people to be bonded together they have to be bound to something. People just don't walk into a room and connect—they connect as a result of finding common interests in other people. When you find out that someone else shares your general view of the world, then that is the person you are likely to sit next to when it is time to go to dinner. So, a critical part of community is shared mental models, to use a term by Peter Senge. This commonality of thought is a prerequisite for community, whether it is a community whose purpose we like or don't like.

If you are going to honor diversity and build bridges from one mindset to another, the content of that community of mind needs to be more like a framework than a script. I tried to suggest that about Stevenson High School. Stevenson certainly has common expectations for teaching, but they still have an enormous amount of discretion, and so a teacher's individuality is not compromised. One teacher can be student-centered while another may be more teacher-centered, with both embodying common principles and standards. This is much more liberating than working from a script where everyone is expected to do it the same way.

We get closer to the community of responsibility ideal when common mental models make room for individual expression. In this culture, people are inclined to do things not because the rules say so or because they are going to get rewarded or punished, but because they feel obliged to do it. The reason this sense of shared obligation is so important is that virtually every other way needs calculated involvement, like rewarding people, but when there is no reward, where's the incentive? There are some things that we need to do in this society that are not much fun, which is where a community of responsibility comes in. It is great if a kid finds a lesson intrinsically satisfying; on the other hand, he may find other lessons that aren't, but still is obliged to do it. A mother or father doesn't love changing their kid's diapers, but they feel, as parents, they've got a moral responsibility to do it. So as an example, mutual responsibility is an idea, a basis of community of mind, worth talking about with our kids and our teachers and [worth] using as a kind of a metaphor for how we might work together.

SEYMOUR: Given the importance of shared mental models in developing community, have people thought enough about their values to really converse about them with others?

SERGIOVANNI: Most parents are absorbed with other thoughts and may find it difficult to come up with an idea of the kind of school they want for their child unless a school presents both a framework and a philosophy for comparison to another school. Parents may not have been part of the conversation that formed a school, but if they make the effort, they may find a school that fits their thinking.

For this reason, successful schools work hard to understand and present what is unique about them, their values, and what they believe. There has to be some reason why people select them over another school. It's good for schools to come to grips with what they are, and this becomes a source of authority for what they do. A distinct identity and standing for something are the first steps by which a school becomes a responsible, learning community.

11

The Bridges to Civility: Empathy, Ethics, Civics, and Service

Sheldon Berman

I had the pleasure of meeting Sheldon Berman (known as Shelley to his colleagues) when I spent four days visiting Hudson public schools where he has been superintendent for the last ten years. Under Berman's dedicated and inspiring leadership, and with a team of outstanding administrators and teachers, Hudson has proven to be a showcase of authentic school improvement based on the development of community, caring, and social responsibility discussed in this chapter. Shelley is one of the founders and a former president of Educators for Social Responsibility and a former president of the Massachusetts Association of School Superintendents. He is the coeditor of Promising Practices in Teaching Social Responsibility *and author of* Children's Social Consciousness. *In 2003, he was selected as Massachusetts Superintendent of the Year.*

In 1979, social psychologist Urie Bronfenbrenner wrote: "It is now possible for a person eighteen years of age to graduate from high school without ever having had to do a piece of work on which somebody else truly depended . . . without ever having cared for, or even held, a baby; without ever having looked after someone who was old, ill, or lonely; or without ever having comforted or assisted another human being who really needed help. . . . No society can long sustain itself unless its members have learned the sensitivities, motivations, and skills involved in assisting and caring for other human beings" (1979, 53). In the absence of a sense of both community and family, many young people lose the connectedness that gives them these sensitivities, motivations, and skills. In part, the incivility and apathy of youth result from the break in their sense of connection to others as well as from their lack of confidence that they can make a difference to others and to the world as a whole.

Young people's disengagement with the social and political world has become increasingly more serious over the past thirty years. In January 1998, the Higher Education Research Institute (HERI) reported the results of its 1997 survey of 348,000 college freshmen at 464 different institutions. HERI reported that the nation's college freshmen are less connected to politics than any entering class in the thirty-two-year history of the study. The report indicated that college freshmen were less likely to believe that "keeping up to date with political affairs," "becoming involved in programs to clean up the environment," and "helping to promote racial understanding" are important life goals. They had less of a desire to influence the political structure, participate in a community action program, influence social values, or even discuss politics. A 2003 Carnegie Corporation report on the research on youth civic engagement entitled, *The Civic Mission of Schools,* echoed these findings. Although researchers reported that young people were becoming more involved in community service and volunteering and more tolerant of and committed to free speech, they found many measures of youth civic engagement showing disturbing declines. Young people's voter participation rates have declined substantially. Young people are less interested in public affairs than they once were. And young people's political and civic knowledge is inadequate. These results are consistent with the evaluation of civic achievement conducted by National Assessment of Education Progress that has shown consistently poor performance in the area of civic competence.

Our democratic culture and our social well-being depend on the renewing energy of young people who have the sensitivities and vision to help create a better world. The very fabric of our national community depends on the degree to which we care about each other and we treat each other with respect and civility. Nurturing a democratic culture and a civil society was, in fact, the central mission of public education at its inception. Although we often pay lip service to this goal, we have not invested the energy, thoughtfulness, or financial support to ensure its effective implementation. Unlike our investment in the teaching of math, science, and technology, we do not have the equivalent of the National Science Foundation to support basic research into the development of social consciousness among young people or to support the development of exemplary curriculum materials. Schools have tended to relegate these issues to the social studies curriculum, where democratic participation is generally taught through lecture and text rather than by engaging young people in active participation of contributing to the well-being of others and society.

CHILDREN'S SOCIAL CONSCIOUSNESS

The research in character education, moral development, prosocial development, and citizenship education is rich with data on the factors that motivate participation and commitment and the instructional strategies that nurture this commitment (Berman 1997). This research indicates that prosocial behavior and activism are stimulated not so much by the traditional constructs of efficacy and locus of control, but by much deeper sources—the unity of one's sense of self and one's morality, the sense of connectedness to others, and the sense of meaning that derives from contributing to something larger than oneself. Young people are continually negotiating a sense of meaning, place, and commitment. In often subtle and internal ways they ask: Are there larger purposes that my actions can serve? Do I have a meaningful place in the social and political world? Are there values that I can make a commitment to and people I can stand with? Am I capable of contributing something useful to others and will they welcome and appreciate it? Will my efforts actually make a difference? Do I have the courage to act without guarantees of success?

A sense of self connected to one's morality and to the world at large emerges over time and through ongoing dialogue with others. Family and important role models play a critical role in this development; direct experience with human suffering or injustice helps crystallize it. Often, action comes before there are clear answers to these questions and serves as a vehicle for finding answers.

Throughout their childhood and adolescence, young people are formulating a theory of how their society works and negotiating their relationship with society. This relationship often remains implicit, visible only in offhand comments expressing their attitudes and judgments about the world around them. Children, in essence, feel their way into the world. The degree of connectedness that they experience determines their sense of efficacy and their interest in participation. In spite of the stereotype of children as egocentric, children care about the welfare of others and care about issues of fairness on both a personal and social level. Social consciousness and social responsibility are not behaviors we need to instill in young people but rather behaviors we need to recognize as emerging in them.

Therefore, restoring civility, nurturing character, or developing civic commitment in young people means reconnecting them with their community, providing them with the basic social skills to negotiate their differences with others, and teaching them they can make a difference. This does not occur as a result of a set of lessons on specific character traits, customs and manners, or civic responsibility. It occurs when we take the issues of care, connection, and civic action seriously and make them core components of the culture and school curriculum. It occurs when we look deeply into the ways young people see society operating and help them struggle with how they can make a commitment to a larger sense of meaning for their lives. It occurs when we apply what we know about learning in general to character and civic education—that we learn best by doing rather than by being told.

For the past ten years, the Hudson public schools have pursued, in incremental steps, the teaching of civility, character, and social responsibility through instructional strategies focused on the themes of empathy, ethics, civics, and service. We have sought to embed these into the fabric of each child's school experience from kindergarten to twelfth grade. We have not completed our journey but we have taken a sufficient step forward for our efforts to help others on the road to fostering social responsibility among young people.

EMPATHY

Often, adult reaction to incivility and challenging behavior in children is to rewrite and tighten the school's behavior codes. Although this might be a small part of the solution, the problematic behavior of young people is a communication to adults that they do not know how to react with compassion, empathy, and sensitivity to the needs of others or to conflict. The skill that is most critical to the development of social responsibility is that of taking the perspective of others and the most productive instructional strategy to develop that skill is to teach young people skills in empathy and conflict resolution.

Social understanding and social responsibility are built on children's desire to understand and feel effective in the social world, to initiate and maintain connection with others, and to reach out to those in distress. Research on the social development of children has revealed that children's awareness of the social and political world emerges far earlier, and their social and moral sensibilities are far more advanced than we previously thought. Martin Hoffman, Judith Dunn, and other researchers place the first signs of empathy during infancy. Empathy may, in fact, be an innate human attribute that is either nurtured or inhibited by the child's environment. Empathy can be developed by helping children become sensitive observers of the states of feeling of others and by helping them understand the causes of these feelings. Norma Haan and her colleagues, in studying the development of empathy and moral behavior, found that children could think in profoundly empathic and moral terms. However, their behavior did not reflect this because they lacked skill in handling moral conflict. Thus, the key to teaching empathy and moral behavior is training and practice in those skills—perspective-taking, conflict resolution, assertiveness—that enable us to maintain clarity in conflicting and stressful situations. Whether through role-playing, analysis of children's literature, or dealing with actual classroom situations, we can help young children begin to understand and appreciate how another may feel and how they may experience a situation differently.

There are many curriculum materials available in this area and numerous programs that schools can adopt. Hudson has combined several programs to teach basic social skills and to create a sense of community in the classroom. At the preschool level, we use the "Adventures in Peacemaking" curriculum produced by Educators for Social Responsibility. This engaging set of activities provides a solid foundation for our preschool population. At the elementary level, we use an empathy development and anger management program produced by the Committee for Children entitled "Second Step" supplemented with conflict resolution material from Educators for Social Responsibility. This thirty-lesson per grade program begins in kindergarten and involves students in role-playing and discussions that identify the feeling states of those involved and helps students reflect on and practice various ways of appropriately responding to the situations. "Second Step" includes a parent component as well, so these skills can be supported at home. A study of this program funded by the Center for Disease Control and Prevention found that it was successful in decreasing physical and verbal aggression and increasing prosocial behavior (Grossman et al. 1997).

Finally, to create a classroom environment that models these skills on a daily basis, almost all of our elementary and middle-school teachers have been trained in the "Responsive Classroom" program developed by the Northeast Foundation for Children. Based on the principles that the social curriculum is as important as the academic curriculum and that a specific set of social skills fosters children's academic and social success, the program enables teachers to effectively use class meetings, rules and their logical consequences, classroom organization, academic choice, and family communication to create a caring classroom environment. The program blends well with the direct social skill instruction provided by the Second Step program.

Although Hudson selected these programs to create the right blend of skill instruction and modeling for our circumstances, there are a number of excellent programs available to schools that are equally effective. Programs such as the Educators for Social Responsibility's "Resolving Conflict Creatively Program," the Stone Center of Wellesley College's "Open Circle," and the Developmental Studies Center's "Caring School Communities" are all effective avenues for teaching these skills. In each of these programs, not only are students given direct instruction in basic social and emotional skills but the whole school becomes involved in creating a caring community that models respectful and empathetic behavior. The Collaborative for Academic, Social, and Emotional Learning (CASEL) has published a valuable review of these programs entitled *Safe and Sound: An Educational Leaders Guide to Evidence-Based Social and Emotional Learning Programs,* which identifies a number of exemplary programs that have demonstrated their effectiveness through evidenced-based results. It is an excellent resource for schools interested in the social and emotional development of young people. Through the school's curriculum and culture, students gain behavioral experience in ways that are sensitive to and considerate of the feelings and needs of others while at the same time learning that there are ways to deal with differences other than avoidance or fighting.

ETHICS

Although teaching skills in empathy and conflict resolution are important, they are not sufficient. Young people need to find a moral center in themselves and learn how to manage moral conflicts. This does not mean preaching a particular set of values to children. In fact, there is little evidence to show that "moralizing" children, or giving didactic instruction in moral principles, has a positive impact. What seems to work best is considered dialogue about moral dilemmas, practice in situations of moral conflict, and role modeling by adults. The work of Lawrence Kohlberg, Carol Gilligan, and others has had a profound impact on our understanding of the nurturing of such ethical principles as justice and care. Their research has shown that ethical discussion can enhance moral reasoning and that placing young people in situations where they must work with real moral dilemmas within the context of a democratic community is effective in nurturing moral action. In essence, internalization and ownership of ethical principles develops through a noncoercive, open-minded approach that invites discussion, exchange, dissent, and understanding rather than demanding agreement and adherence.

Consideration of ethics is an area that becomes contentious for schools, with some individuals wishing to promote particular religious principles within the curriculum and others advocating for value neutrality. There is a middle path that schools can follow that will help students reflect on the values we hold collectively as a society. The great contribution that the Character Education Partnership and the character education movement has made to this debate is to help adults see that we can come to agreement on such collectively held values as trustworthiness, respect, responsibility, justice, fairness, caring, and citizenship. The middle path of affirming these values while engaging students in dialogue about moral issues provides an opportunity for schools to nurture moral and prosocial behavior.

Good curricula in the area of ethical development are harder to find than in the areas of empathy or conflict resolution. Hudson has selected material from an elementary literature program developed by the Developmental Studies Center in which students read good literature that portrays prosocial themes. We have added to this program literature that shows people making a difference through service or social activism. In addition, we have created a core ninth grade English–social studies civics course whose essential question is: What is an individual's responsibility in creating a just society? A central part of this course is the "Facing History and Ourselves" curriculum. This curriculum engages students in the study of the roots of two twentieth-century occurrences of genocide—the Holocaust and the Armenian genocide. The curriculum confronts young people with the human potential for passivity, complicity, and destructiveness by asking how genocide can become state policy. It raises significant ethical questions and sensitizes them to injustice, inhumanity, suffering, and the abuse of power. At the same time, it is academically challenging and helps complicate students' thinking so that they do not accept simple answers to complex problems. In the process of studying both a historic period and the personal and social forces that produce genocide, students confront their own potential for passivity and complicity, their own prejudices and intolerance, and their own moral commitments. The curriculum develops students' perspective-taking and social reasoning abilities and students emerge with a greater sense of moral responsibility and a greater commitment to participate in making a difference. The only drawback is that there aren't more such curricula that are appropriate for other grade levels.

We live in a complex time. There are few simple answers to the complicated issues we face. Children become aware of the trauma in the world around them at a far earlier age than we would like, and they lack the skills to deal with its complexity. In our efforts to preserve their childhood, we often allow important ethical issues to go undiscussed and attitudes of cynicism, hopelessness, and powerlessness to develop. This need not be the case. Social, political, and ethical reflection build character by peeling back the layers that underlie our values and helping young people find within themselves the strengths and commitments to make a difference for themselves, others, and the planet as a whole.

TEACHING EMPATHY AND ETHICS THROUGH CIVIC ENGAGEMENT IN HIGH SCHOOL

A significant number of studies of social development show that creating a sense of community in the classroom and within a school can have a powerful impact on young people's prosocial development. Michael Resnick and a group of researchers studying "protective" factors or influences that would help prevent drug and alcohol abuse, teen pregnancy, violent behavior, and so on, found that there were only two consistent protective factors. These two were a young person's sense of connection to family and his or her connection to school, that is, feeling close to people at school, feeling fairly treated, feeling part of the school community. This study highlighted the importance of young people feeling a sense of connection to others at school and a sense of community within the school.

Eric Schaps and his colleagues at the Developmental Studies Center in Oakland, California, completed a multiyear study of a social skill development program that came to the same conclusion. They found that the sense of community among students favorably impacted the tendency to help others, reasoning about prosocial and moral issues, conflict resolution skill, democratic values, and reading comprehension. Building community, therefore, has become a central goal of our social development efforts in elementary and middle schools. However, building community in a high school of over 1,000 students is far from easy.

In addition to the research on community, the research on student involvement in decision making, and particularly in small "just communities" within high schools, shows that this involvement is highly effective in fostering moral growth (Power, Higgins, and Kohlberg 1989). In the just communities of approximately 100 students that Power, Higgins, and Kohlberg studied, students experienced direct democracy through weekly town meetings where each person, including adults, had one vote. In these meetings, students made meaningful decisions about the management, care, and direction of the school and experienced real conflicts with other students and teachers who had different perspectives on these issues. The experience with real-life moral dilemmas was, in fact, more effective in promoting moral development and moral action because the issues were meaningful to students, and discrepancies between public judgments and actions were apparent and had consequences for the group. In addition, collective decision making and shared responsibility built a sense of community in which members had a personal sense of responsibility to the community.

At the elementary and middle-school level, class meetings and other participatory organizational structures can provide this sense of participation in decision making. However, at the high-school level, there is little time in the curriculum for this kind of participation. It is striking that we have learned that the most effective way to teach math and science is to have students engage in mathematical and scientific investigations. Yet, we try to teach democratic citizenship by lecture in the classroom and by modeling autocratic structures in the organization of the school.

CREATING DEMOCRATIC CLUSTERS

Based on our interest in creating a high-school program that extended our elementary and middle-school efforts in a way that was appropriate to adolescents, we decided to combine the concepts of community and democracy. As a result, we have created small democratic communities to enable students to develop a sense of social responsibility. Fortunately, we have also been able to design this concept into the very architecture of our new high-school building.

Two concepts have been critical to our design and planning for a high school that reflects the principles of democratic community and civic engagement. The first was a cluster model of organization to facilitate closer connections among students and staff within the context of a small, caring community environment. The second was a governance structure that would engage all students in decision making about school issues.

By *clustering*, we mean the reorganization of the high school into units of 100 to 150 students. Hudson high school includes grades eight through twelve. At the eighth and ninth grades, we have teams that include approximately 80 to 100 students. At grades ten through twelve, we have created thematic clusters with approximately 150 students in a cluster. Unlike the eighth and ninth grade teams in which students are organized by grade level, each of the upper-level clusters involves a generally equal number of tenth-, eleventh-, and twelfth-graders. Also, in contrast to the eighth- and ninth-grade teams in which students take all their core courses from teachers in their team, students are able to take courses from any teacher. In many high schools, these clusters are labeled houses. They are often much larger in size than the clusters we have set in place and serve administrative rather than academic or community-building purposes.

There are two primary motivations for moving to clusters of 100 to 150 students. First, it will enable closer contact between teacher and student and a more close-knit student community as the high school gets larger. The data on effective high schools indicate that small schools outperform larger schools and that students feel less anonymous and participate more actively in smaller high schools. There is also a reduced incidence of violence and disruptive behavior in smaller schools. The cluster concept enables us to organize into smaller groups while retaining the curricular and extracurricular benefits of a larger school. It also enables us to effectively integrate into the academic structure cluster-based, advisor-advisee, service learning, and school-to-career programs.

The second reason for moving to clusters is that it facilitates a participatory student governance structure. Representative democracy in a high school, symbolized by the typical student council, is a relatively poor student governance structure.

It involves very few students. The students who end up serving are often the most socially active and popular—the ones who may least need the experience of democratic engagement. A more effective structure is one that engages all students; but that is impossible in a high school of even moderate size. The way to get around this problem is to organize into clusters which average approximately 150 students or less so that all students can fit into one room for a discussion of issues. We have designed our new high school with large group spaces specifically for this purpose. There are a number of basic principles underlying the organization and operation of this model of clustering.

THEMATIC ORGANIZATION

For clusters to achieve their intended goal there must be some common bonds that tie the group together. Therefore, we have organized the clusters thematically, around broad areas of student interest:

1. Communications, Media, and the Arts;
2. Science, the Environment, and Health;
3. Technology, Engineering, and Business; and
4. Social Service, Education, and Social Policy.

The organization of the four clusters was based on career pathways developed by the high school staff. Over a period of three years, we administered career interest surveys to our students based on these pathways. Using the data from the surveys as a way to group the pathways, we created four clusters that divide the student population into four generally equal groups.

The thematic organization of the clusters gives students the opportunity to delve more deeply into areas of interest with other similarly interested students. It also enhances the meaningfulness of the courses they are taking by helping them see the relationship between coursework and work in the larger world. Finally, it gives them some school-to-career experiences that will support their decision making about their future direction.

The thematic organization is not meant to restrict students' exploration of other career or interest areas. It is also not meant to lock students into a career interest. It is simply a vehicle for enrichment and community building that can enhance students' knowledge of and experience with an area of interest.

COMMUNITY BUILDING WITHIN THE CLUSTER

Clusters provide a number of vehicles for building a sense of community. First, the cluster becomes the governance unit in the school with each cluster meeting weekly as a whole group and in small groups to discuss school and cluster issues. This kind of regular participation in decision making gives students a sense of ownership within the school and builds commitment to the school, cluster, and the directions we are pursuing.

Second, the cluster creates a sense of community by offering speakers and presentations around the cluster theme, such as career opportunities or current social issues related to the cluster theme.

Third, the cluster builds a sense of community by students and teachers working together on collaborative service-learning projects that are related to the theme of the cluster. For example, the science, environment, and health cluster can select an environmental project to pursue or the social service, education, and social policy cluster might work on issues of prejudice and appreciating diversity. These projects integrate students from different classes and grades and continue over several years so students have an experience of the depth and continuity of their service.

Fourth, each cluster will, over time, organize small group advisor-advisee meetings to provide students with more support. These advisory meetings can handle anything from discussing college or career planning to teaching conflict resolution skills or holding open discussions of how students are feeling about a particular event in the world such as the September 11 attacks.

Since students generally remain in a cluster for three years, and since they will take some of their courses from cluster teachers, they develop a greater sense of community simply because they get to know a group of both teachers and students well. They will have to address differences of opinion in their cluster meetings and work on projects and issues together. They will have closer relationships with faculty members whom they get to know not only through classes but through service-learning projects, presentations, and cluster discussions. In essence, students will have a more personal, connected, and meaningful high school experience.

CLUSTER MEETINGS AND DEMOCRATIC GOVERNANCE

To enable the clusters to build a sense of community requires that they have time for cluster activities. The principal has created a schedule that provides weekly cluster meeting times of sixty minutes in length. We will be able to accommodate the four teams and the four clusters with each cluster alternating between large group and small group meetings.

One example of a four-week schedule would be:

Week 1: Small group governance meetings in classrooms discussing an issue
Week 2: Whole cluster governance meeting discussing the issue talked about in the small groups the previous week
Week 3: Small group work on service projects in classrooms
Week 4: Large group meeting to hear a speaker

The governance meetings will replicate, in many ways, Kohlberg's just community approach. Students select topics of concern to them. Sometimes these will be topics of particular interest to that cluster, but often they will be topics of interest to all students.

For the past two years, we have been piloting this concept at the high school by engaging the entire student body in small-group, student-led discussions of issues selected by students. The first issue raised by students was the quality and selection of food offered by our food service program at the high school. After a series of whole school discussions on the topic, a committee of students took the lead in working with our food service director to implement some of the students' ideas and improve the program.

The second topic selected by students was the lack of integration of students from other countries into the school culture. Students developed a videotape of interviews with a number of students about their feelings of isolation within the high school. Again in small groups, student facilitators showed the tape and led discussions on how we could create a more inclusive school community. One of the results that evolved from these discussions was a program entitled "Friends," in which students volunteered to buddy with students who had come to us from other countries. The group has had a number of collaborative events to create a bridge between these student cultures.

We have discussed other topics as well, including the democratic clustering model we are now implementing in the high school. We believe that these whole-school conversations have been powerful vehicles for engaging students in the beginnings of democratic participation. As a result of these conversations, we have created a "constitution" that delineates the decision-making rights and responsibilities within the high school and provides students with a clear vehicle for influencing school-related decisions.

The development of the democratic communities within the high school presents an exciting opportunity to build a stronger sense of community within the school, richer relationships between faculty and students, a more meaningful instructional program, a more stimulating professional culture for staff, and a more respectful and responsible student body. But most important, this is an opportunity to create an experience of democratic community that enables young people to enter the adult world with the skills, values, and commitment to actively participate in our civic community.

SERVICE LEARNING AND STUDENT LEADERSHIP

Finally, to truly encourage civility and civic responsibility, we need to get young people involved in taking action that makes a difference to others. They need to be a part of the solution rather than remain passive observers. The understanding they develop through reflection needs to be translated into action whether it is through community service opportunities or direct social or political participation.

The research shows that those who are active early in life, whether in school or the community, are more likely to be active later in life. The studies of programs involving students in active engagement in the social and political arena indicate that this involvement may be an important stepping stone to later participation (Berman

1997). We tend to treat young people as "citizens-in-preparation" rather than active members of their community, and we give them little responsibility for acting on citizenship skills. However, students who are given greater responsibility often develop a greater sense of responsibility.

The Hudson public schools have made a strong commitment to integrating service learning into our curriculum. Approximately 90 percent of our students are involved in service learning each year; our commitment is to reach 100 percent of the students. We are creating a consistent, systemwide approach so that an ethic of service and an ethic of care are sustained at each grade level from kindergarten to graduation. Our goal is to provide students with service-learning experiences marked by continuity, depth, and meaningfulness.

Our service-learning program begins in kindergarten with all kindergartners being involved in several efforts: A handicapped awareness program that extends into a "hap'ning"(event) that raises funds for the March of Dimes; an interdisciplinary quilt project in which students in each kindergarten class create a quilt and a book to donate to a homeless women's shelter; and a holiday toy drive linked to a social studies unit on community. Like our kindergarten, each grade develops its own initiatives. For example, a group of our first-graders have an ongoing relationship with senior citizens at our local senior center that helps teach students basic literacy skills. Our third grades raise money and collect food for our local food pantry. Our fourth grades engage in an environmental field studies program that involves protecting and caring for wetlands and other natural areas near our schools. Our fifth-graders work with classrooms of multiple-handicapped children to develop an awareness of and respect for diversity. Our ninth grade English and social studies teachers ask students to find a way that they can help create a just society through a service-learning experience. All of our clusters will develop service-learning projects that are consistent with the theme of the cluster and enable students to continue their involvement in this service-learning project over a three-year period. In addition, through a collaborative of ten school districts, we have developed a student leadership program that provides our middle- and high-school students with such leadership training experiences as student leadership conferences, summer institutes, and courses. These are only samples of the many projects our teachers implement on an annual basis. A community service committee of teachers and administrators guides our efforts and has created service-learning reference and resource kits for each school library, teacher guidelines for CSL projects, a list of 100 good service-learning ideas, and a resource list of local organizations.

To highlight the importance of service learning in the district, the school board sets aside one of its meetings for a service-learning exposition in which all of our projects are displayed and parents and the community are invited to learn about our students' efforts. In addition, special Superintendent's Awards for Service are awarded to students at each school. These awards are presented to middle and high school recipients at the Hudson high school graduation to highlight their importance.

It is also our belief that service learning is more than older children tutoring younger children and more than students raising money for a local food pantry or entertaining at a retirement home during the holiday season. Although these are a part of the culture of service that must be present, true service learning means helping students make the connections between the subject material they are studying and issues in the larger world. It means engaging students in action and reflection on important community, social, political, and environmental issues. It means thinking of students not as future citizens but as active members of their community.

There are encouraging trends nationally in the area of service learning. Many states and school districts have pursued initiatives with the support of the Corporation for National and Community Service. The Education Commission of the States has formed a K–12 National Center for Learning and Citizenship, involving school superintendents and chief state school officers in an effort to provide national leadership in the areas of both service learning and civic education. Providing a voice for school leaders to advocate for effective programs, the center has significantly advanced the quality and acceptability of service learning as a vehicle for the development of civility, character, and responsibility. In addition, the National Service-Learning Partnership, a professional association of teachers committed to service learning, has been created to support teachers in their classroom efforts and to advocate for service learning on a national level.

A COMMITMENT TO COMMUNITY

Human beings gravitate to simple answers to complex questions. The path to teaching civility and character is strewn with curricula that are no more than our own pleadings for young people to be good. If we are truly concerned with helping young people become good individuals and citizens, we need to look more deeply into what it is that promotes these qualities and to build programs based on these qualities. Our focus on empathy, ethics, civics, and service is an effort to provide students with the skills and experiences that can give meaning to civility for young people.

At a time when many in the public as well as most policymakers are focused on standards, accountability, and testing, it is bold to make the kind of commitment that Hudson has to teaching social and emotional skills. We have not neglected making improvements in our academic program, but we believe that students will benefit both academically and socially from an education that integrates challenging academics with a commitment to nurturing a caring and civil community.

Unless young people experience a sense of community and a connection to others and Earth and see the implications of our actions for the future of our society and the planet, civility will mean little to them. Hudson's focus on empathy, ethics, civics, and service is an effort to help young people experience the sense of community that ties us together. It is through this experience that young people begin to understand the meaning of the common good, appreciate that their actions have consequences for others and the community at large, and develop a sense of relation to and responsibility for the larger human community. Empathy, ethics, civics, and service are the bridges to community, and over this bridge lies a civility that enriches us all.

NOTE

This chapter is an updated version of an article previously published in *The School Administrator,* Vol. 55, no. 5, May 1998. Copyright © 2003 Sheldon Berman. Used with permission.

REFERENCES

The American Freshman. 1998. A report by the Higher Education Research Institute on the results of a 1997 survey of 348,000 college freshman at 464 different institutions.

Berman, S. 1997. *Children's Social Consciousness and the Development of Social Responsibility.* Albany, N.Y.: SUNY Press.

Berman, S., and P. LaFarge, eds. 1993. *Promising Practices in Teaching Social Responsibility.* Albany, N.Y.: SUNY Press.

Bronfenbrenner, U. 1979. *The Ecology of Human Development.* Cambridge, Mass.: Harvard University Press.

The Civic Mission of Schools. 2003. A Report of the Center for Information and Research on Civic Learning and Engagement and the Carnegie Corporation of New York, 437 Madison Ave., New York, N.Y. 10022.

Dunn, J. 1988. *The Beginnings of Social Understanding.* Cambridge, Mass.: Harvard University Press.

Grossman, D. C. et al. 1997. "Effectiveness of a Violence Prevention Curriculum among Children in Elementary School." *Journal of the American Medical Association* 277: 1605–11.

Haan, N., E. Aerts, and B. Cooper. 1985. *On Moral Grounds: The Search for Practical Morality.* New York: New York University Press.

Hoffman, M. L. 1991. "Empathy, Social Cognition, and Moral Action." Pp. 275–301. In K. Kurtines and J. Gewirtz, eds. *Handbook of Moral Behavior and Development, Volume 1: Theory.* Hillsdale, N.J.: Lawrence Erlbaum.

Power, C., A. Higgins, and L. Kohlberg. 1989. *Lawrence Kohlberg's Approach to Moral Education.* New York: Columbia University Press.

Resnick, M. et al. 1997. "Protecting Adolescents from Harm: Findings from the National Longitudinal Study on Adolescents' Health." *Journal of the American Medical Association* 278: 823–32.

Sax, L. J., A. W. Astin, W. S. Korn, and K. M. Mahoney. 1997. "The American Freshman: National Norms for Fall 1997." Higher Education Research Institute, UCLA Graduate School of Education, 3005 Moore Hall, Box 951521, Los Angeles, Calif. 90095-1521.

Schaps, E., V. Battistich, and D. Solomon. (forthcoming). "Community in School as Key to Student Growth: Findings from the Child Development Project." In R. Weissberg, J. Zins, and H. Walberg, eds. *Building School Success on Social and Emotional Learning.* New York: Teachers College Press.

Multicultural Education: Access, Equity, and Social Justice

An Interview with Sonia Nieto by Mike Seymour

I met Sonia Nieto at the University of Massachusetts, Amherst campus, and we talked for what seemed like several hours, as if we had known each other before. She is a passionate and leading spokesperson for multicultural education, born out of her Puerto Rican roots and early career in classroom teaching. She is now professor of education at the University of Massachusetts, where she has taught courses in language, literacy, and culture. She has served on several national advisory boards that focus on educational equity and social justice and she has received many awards for her advocacy and activism, including the 1989 Human and Civil Rights Award from the Massachusetts Teachers Association; the 1995 Drylongso Award for Antiracism Activism from the Community Change in Boston; the 1997 Multicultural Educator of the Year Award from the National Association for Multicultural Education (NAME); and the 1988 New England Educator of the Year Award from Region One of NAME. Her latest book, What Keeps Teachers Going in Spite of Everything, *follows her previous works, including* Through Students' Eyes: Combating Racism in United States Schools; Affirming Diversity: The Sociopolitical Context of Multicultural Education; *and* The Light in Their Eyes: Creating Multicultural Learning Communities.

MIKE SEYMOUR: Let's talk about your book, *The Light in Their Eyes,* which is a wonderful title in that it speaks about the promise in each young person.

SONIA NIETO: I think that's a promise we frequently forget. We need to connect the promise in children to the hope of public education, particularly for the urban and rural poor for whom the promise of public education was never fully realized. I don't think that public education ever reached the ideals that we had for it. At one time there was more faith, but now, the nation is losing faith.

SEYMOUR: We're losing faith in young children. Doesn't that also reflect a loss of faith in ourselves and the community, our civic life, and our faith in "we, the people?"

NIETO: Absolutely. We've lost faith in the collective, but people have faith in themselves, their own power to do better for their own children, which they do more and more by withdrawing them from public schools. But this is not available to everybody.

SEYMOUR: So, this leads me to ask: What is multicultural education?

NIETO: Many people have a hard time with it because they don't realize what it is, and other people have a hard time with it because they *do* realize what it is. The most common error is to understand multicultural education as simply ethnic tidbits, celebrating a few holidays, or Black history month, although these can be an important first step. It's also not just human relations, getting along, and learning to love one another. Kids can learn to love one another, but when they leave the schoolhouse door, they leave to go home to vastly different environments, some with many more resources than others, that affect a young person's life circumstances and opportunities.

Really, multicultural education has to do most of all with access and equity, not just cultural sensitivity or curriculum units that, while important, won't alone change the educational experience for our many underserved children. Here are some good questions to assess the climate for a true multicultural education: Who is learning calculus? Who has access to science labs? Are books shared equally? Who's on the hiring committee? Who's hired? Who wrote the books that the kids are using? Who has a conversation about the curriculum? How are families involved? These are all profoundly multicultural questions because they deal with access, equity, and making sure that all kids have the resources that they need to learn.

SEYMOUR: In that vein, you write that multicultural education is about transformation on a number of levels—individual, collective, and institutional—the major structures affecting what is available, which in turn communicates its own message.

NIETO: I learned that lesson from thinking I could change the world as a teacher and had to wake up, as I write in my newest book, *What Keeps Teachers Going in Spite of Everything*, to the power of the institution to do harm. The collective level is most often neglected. Individual teachers start with lots of enthusiasm, great ideas, and a love for kids; and many [teachers] wind up burned out, blaming the kids and their culture for a failure to learn. That happens because they don't have the institutional support they need and because they feel alone without support from colleagues. Without that kind of support, solidarity, and care for one another, teachers just can't go on. Teachers need deep conversations, critique, affirmation, and to be pushed by their colleagues—and that can only happen when institutions support it.

SEYMOUR: In your book, you talk about the biases of education. Could you elaborate on that in terms of curriculum, teacher attitudes, school policies, and practices that disadvantage students of minority backgrounds?

NIETO: Let me give an example from here in Amherst where the high school selected *West Side Story* as their play. A number of kids were upset by that choice and protested successfully against staging the play, because they felt it presented Puerto Rican people in a negative way, associated with gangs. I do think there is a tendency to present marginalized groups in stereotypical ways, but I think there would have been a benefit in putting the play on if it had been done well. This got a lot of media coverage, with many letters to the press, one from a young woman graduate from Amherst High School, which I particularly remember. She was glad that they were considering not putting on the play because of the biased way in which Puerto Rico was represented when she was in high school. Of the two times Puerto Rico was mentioned, one was when the kids had put on a cabaret and they took some music from *West Side Story* and she saw white kids singing with funny accents. The second was when a teacher informed the class that Puerto Ricans were the second greatest consumers of Cheez Whiz® in the world.

When you have so much neglect of any community, there is bound to be resentment, anger, alienation, and marginalization. This happens with kids from a lot of different backgrounds, and they can't even name what's happening to them because they assume that it's normal that anybody who did anything important didn't look like them.

SEYMOUR: Kids are not able at a young age to put their feelings of alienation and low self-esteem into words. All they know is when they go to school they feel bad and they don't know why that is. They just know that they don't like school because of not feeling good about themselves there.

NIETO: Exactly. They don't feel like they belong. I have one little example when I was a kid in school with the food charts they put up in the classroom. I remember looking at the basic food groups on the chart and seeing nothing there that I ate. My family used to eat beans and rice and different kinds of bread, plantains, and root vegetables. When I didn't see that on the food charts, I didn't assume the chart was wrong, but that something was wrong with our diet at home. So something as seemingly innocent as the food chart became the authority that made me feel bad about myself and my family. And this is just one little example multiplied many times over for children of many different ethnic backgrounds.

These are the kinds of biases that permeate the school culture. It's not necessarily about serving Puerto Rican or Thai or ethnic food in school. It is just about being more honest, comprehensive, and sensitive to the realities in which we live and the invisible ways in which people from nondominant cultures are affected. It's about making the curriculum truly reflective of the diverse, multicultural body of students, and not just those from European backgrounds.

It's about restoring affirmative action in our hiring practices, not to right historical wrongs, but because it's important to have diverse backgrounds and points of view represented around the table. Bringing people into a school from different backgrounds creates some tension and turmoil but also leads to growth and greater wisdom.

SEYMOUR: One of the major issues in schools is the small percentage of teachers from culturally diverse backgrounds compared to the student body. There is evidence that all students benefit from exposure to cultural diversity in their teachers.

NIETO: Certainly, African American children, at some point in their lives, should have an African American teacher, as should, especially, children of European or Asian descent. Everybody should benefit from the diversity in our society, and that is not happening at present.

One study of some Texas schools found that children of color exposed to diverse teachers did better academically than similar kids who were not. The surprise was that white children also did better if they were exposed to teachers of color.

SEYMOUR: Psychologically, the inner landscape becomes impoverished when the outer landscape becomes impoverished, and vice versa. I believe that "we are the world," as the song goes. All cultural minds are potentialities within myself.

NIETO: Yes, we are all multicultural, but we haven't come to terms with that. In that vein, I think the most important thing teachers can do is to start where the kids are. It means that you don't try to erase who they are but that you build on what they bring, recognizing who they are as a gift, a treasure.

SEYMOUR: In your writing you mention the Catholic school effect that reveals how students of color do better in Catholic schools compared to comparable students in public schools. What's going on there?

NIETO: In spite of the fact that Catholic schools don't account for multicultural differences, for example, by having things like special bilingual classes, students of color do better. I think this reflects the high expectations these schools have of all students and the fact that they don't have the variable resources to stratify the curriculum for tracking students. Also, I think it helps that the Catholic school tradition has a historical commitment to social justice.

SEYMOUR: High expectations coupled with compassion convey a profound, even transformative, belief in the ability of a child. The message to reach high says, "I believe you can do this," which affirms belief in who the child is. This brings us to the idea you discuss—that learning is affected by cultural context and does not just reflect individual or psychological phenomena. Too many in education assume that if the student is not learning, it's got to be [his or her] fault.

NIETO: I think the whole issue of context has been extremely powerful in my own thinking. Many teachers work, as I did for a while, as if education were context-free. I came to understand that the social, economic, and political contexts of the dominant culture have a tremendous impact on kids, how and what they learn. We must recognize the child as a complete human being with lots of talents and vulnerabilities and honor what gifts they bring as opposed to looking at them mostly as deficient in some way.

SEYMOUR: The fact that a culturally responsive, critical pedagogy examines institutional bias and issues of social justice would make many teachers uncomfortable. I have heard complaints about politicizing education. How would you answer this kind of complaint?

NIETO: I think that schools are sometimes very scary places and [are] full of fear, which can be immobilizing; so we need to understand that fear and then move through it. Also, schools are populated by many women, and as women, we are trained to be nice and not to make waves. I suggest to teachers to do what they can do today and do a little bit more tomorrow. There is a lot of injustice in our world and our schools, and the way to make change is to confront that injustice bit by bit, working in collaboration with others.

I know a teacher who decided to do a project on gay and lesbian issues in schools and went to her principal who was extremely supportive. That year, she, the principal, and a few other teachers marched in the gay pride parade in Northampton with a banner from the school. That was a very big step to take. But she did it because she knew that some kids who had two moms or two dads felt invisible in school because their parents' lives were "hush-hush" —something to be kept secret. Today that school has a picture on the bulletin board of every single family from that school—families with two parents, with one parent, with two moms or with two dads, with grandparents, with many kids, with one kid. Every configuration that you could imagine was up on the bulletin board lining the entrance as you go into the school. Very beautifully and very graphically saying, "This is your school and you are welcome here." But things like that don't just happen. They happen because people respond to their conscience and decide to do something. Teachers shouldn't have to do that by themselves, but should be able to have the support of others in the system.

SEYMOUR: You talk about the teacher's role as cultural accommodator. What does that look like in practice?

NIETO: In one of the classes that I teach, called "Teaching about the Puerto Rican Experience," we work with various scenarios to help teachers make culturally appropriate decisions in various situations. For example, a girl student comes to school late every morning and explains she has to walk her little brother to school. We then ask the students, "What do you do?" In this situation, some students will say that we should call the parents, and others that there is little that can be done about family responsibility. I encourage my students not to see these situations as either/or. All similar scenarios involve cultural accommodation and sensitive problem solving.

Teachers are cultural accommodators when they build respectfully on the family's hopes and dreams and discuss with them whatever issue needs to be addressed. Schools, in contrast, too often are organized to accommodate their own needs more so than those of the student.

SEYMOUR: In understanding multicultural education as about equity and access, some people might assume incorrectly that it is only about the minority student and, of course, it is not. Multicultural education benefits all students.

NIETO: All children are deprived of an equitable education when they misperceive their role and their importance in the world. White students may end up with a distorted sense of the world from seeing mostly European, white people in their texts. We also realize the great benefit from learning another language and visiting other cultures. Language carries all sorts of cultural meanings and perspectives. I feel very lucky that I also speak Spanish and that I understand what it is to see the world in different ways. I would be very sad if I didn't speak English, because English is the language I learned at the age of six when I started school and is the language of my academic career. On the other hand, I can't speak to babies in English because my natural instinct is to speak in Spanish.

SEYMOUR: What do you feel are the most important purposes of education?

NIETO: I think that education needs to be about leaving a better world behind for all. As I have become a mother, and later, a grandmother, that has become paramount in my mind. What is this world that we are leaving behind going to look like for those who are going to pick up after us? What are the values that we are leaving for them? What are we saying is worth struggling for? And I hope that education will give young people the desire to carry on, the understanding that the world is bigger than they are, and that the best that we can do is work for the common good.

13

Educating Global Citizens in a Diverse World

James A. Banks

James A. Banks is professor of curriculum and instruction and director of the Center for Multicultural Education at the University of Washington. He is a leader in teaching and the research fields of social studies education and multicultural education. His publications include Teaching Strategies for the Social Studies *(5th edition, 1999),* Educating Citizens in a Multicultural Society *(1997), and the* Handbook of Research on Multicultural Education *(1995). He received the AERA Research Review Award in 1994, the National Association of Multicultural Education Book Award in 1997, and the Teachers of English to Speakers of Other Languages, Inc. (TESOL) 1998 President's Award. I had the pleasure of first hearing Dr. Banks's passionate speaking at the 2001 Fall Forum of the Coalition of Essential Schools.*

Cultural, ethnic, racial, language, and religious diversity exist in most nations in the world. One of the challenges to diverse democratic nation-states is to provide opportunities for different groups to maintain aspects of their community cultures while, at the same time, building a nation in which these groups are structurally included and to which they feel allegiance. A delicate balance of diversity and unity should be an essential goal of democratic nation-states and of teaching and learning in a democratic society.

    The challenge of balancing diversity and unity is intensifying as democratic nation-states such as the United States, Canada, Australia, the United Kingdom, and

Japan become more diversified and as racial and ethnic groups within these nations try to attain cultural, political, and economic rights. The democratic ideologies within these major nations and the wide gap between these ideals and realities were major factors that resulted in the rise of movements for cultural and economic rights during the last four decades.

These nations share a democratic ideal, a major tenet of which is that the state should protect human rights and promote equality and the inclusion of diverse groups into the mainstream society. These nations are also characterized by widespread inequality and by racial, ethnic, and class stratification. The discrepancies among democratic ideals and societal realities and the rising expectations of marginalized racial, ethnic, language, and social-class groups created protest and revival movements within the Western democratic nations. These movements began with the civil-rights movements in the United States during the 1960s and 1970s. The U.S. civil-rights movement echoed throughout the world.

INCREASING DIVERSITY AND GLOBAL CITIZENSHIP EDUCATION

Because of growing ethnic, cultural, racial, language, and religious diversity throughout the world, citizenship education needs to be changed in substantial ways to prepare students to function effectively in the twenty-first century. Citizens in this century need the knowledge, attitudes, and skills required to function in their cultural communities and beyond their cultural borders. They should also be able and willing to participate in the construction of a national civic culture that is a moral and just community. The national community should embody democratic ideals and values, such as those articulated in the Universal Declaration of Human Rights, the Declaration of Independence, the U.S. Constitution, and the Bill of Rights. Students also need to acquire the knowledge and skills required to be effective citizens in the global community.

Citizenship education in the past, in the United States as well as in many other nations, embraced an ideology of assimilation. In the United States, its aim was to educate students so they would fit into a mythical Anglo-Saxon Protestant conception of the "good citizen." Anglo conformity was the goal of citizenship education. One of its aims was to eradicate the community cultures and languages of students from diverse groups. One consequence of this conception of citizenship education was that many students lost their first cultures, languages, and ethnic identities. Some students also became alienated from family and community. Another consequence was that many students became socially and politically alienated from the national civic culture.

Members of identifiable racial groups often became marginalized in both their community cultures and in the national civic culture because they could function effectively in neither. When they acquired the language and culture of the Anglo mainstream, they were often denied structural inclusion and full participation into the civic culture because of their racial characteristics.

Citizenship education must be transformed in the twenty-first century. Several worldwide developments make a new conception of citizenship education an imperative. They include the deepening ethnic texture of nations such as Australia, Canada, Germany, Japan, the United States, and the United Kingdom. The large influx of immigrants who are now settling in nations throughout the world, the continuing existence of institutional racism and discrimination in various nations, and the widening gap between rich and poor nations also make the reform of citizenship education imperative.

BALANCING UNITY AND DIVERSITY

Citizens in a diverse democratic society should be able to maintain attachments to their cultural communities as well as participate effectively in the shared national culture. Unity without diversity results in cultural repression and hegemony. Diversity without unity leads to Balkanization and the fracturing of the nation-state. In a democratic multicultural nation-state, diversity and unity should coexist in a delicate balance. The attainment of the balance that is needed between diversity and unity is an ongoing process and ideal, one that is never fully reached. It is essential that both mainstream and marginalized groups participate in the formulation of societal goals related to diversity and unity. Both groups should also participate in action required to attain these goals. Deliberation and the sharing of power by mainstream and marginalized groups are essential for the construction and perpetuation of a just, moral, and participatory democratic nation-state in a culturally diverse society.

THE DEVELOPMENT OF CULTURAL, NATIONAL, AND GLOBAL IDENTIFICATIONS

A new kind of citizenship is needed for the twenty-first century, which Will Kymlicka calls "multicultural citizenship" (1995). It recognizes and legitimizes the right and need of citizens to maintain commitments both to their cultural communities and to the national civic culture. Only when the national civic culture is transformed in ways that reflect and give voice to the diverse ethnic, racial, language, and religious communities that constitute it will it be viewed as legitimate by all of its citizens. Only then can they develop clarified commitments to the nation-state and its ideals.

Citizenship education should help students to develop thoughtful and clarified identifications with their cultural communities and their nation-states. It should also help them to develop clarified global identifications and deep understandings of their roles in the world community. Students need to understand how life in their cultural communities and nations influences other nations, in addition to the cogent influence that international events have on their daily lives. Global education should have, as its major goals, helping students to develop understandings of the interdependence among nations in the world today, clarified attitudes toward other nations, and reflective identifications with the world community.

Nonreflective and unexamined cultural attachments may prevent the development of a cohesive nation with clearly defined national goals and policies. Although we need to help students develop reflective and clarified cultural identifications, they must also be helped to clarify their identifications with their nation-states. However, blind nationalism will prevent students from developing reflective and positive global identifications. In most nations, nationalism and national attachments are strong and tenacious. Important aims of citizenship education should be to help students develop global identifications and a deep understanding of the need to take action, as citizens of the global community, to help solve the world's difficult global problems such as conflict and war, the AIDS/HIV epidemic, global warming, and world poverty. Cultural, national, and global experiences and identifications are interactive and interrelated in a dynamic way.

Students should develop a delicate balance of cultural, national, and global identifications. A nation-state that alienates and does not structurally include all cultural groups into the national culture runs the risk of alienating its citizens and causing *cultural* groups to focus on specific concerns and issues rather than on the overarching goals and policies of the nation-state. To develop reflective cultural, national, and global identifications, students must acquire the knowledge, attitudes, and skills needed to function both within and across diverse racial, ethnic, cultural, language, and religious groups.

THE BELLAGIO DIVERSITY AND CITIZENSHIP EDUCATION CONFERENCE

Nation-states throughout the world are faced with the problem of how to reflect the racial, ethnic, cultural, and religious diversity within their societies while maintaining national unity. Increasing globalization throughout the world is also challenging nationalism and the nation-state. The Center for Multicultural Education at the University of Washington sponsored an international conference so citizenship scholars and educators from different nations could share perspectives, research, and findings about how citizenship education programs can be reformed to reflect diversity and unity. The conference, Ethnic Diversity and Citizenship Education in Multicultural Nation-States, was held at the Rockefeller Foundation's Study and Conference Center in Bellagio, Italy, June 17–21, 2002. The conference was attended by participants from eleven nations: Brazil, Canada, China, Germany, India, Israel (including Palestine), Japan, Russia, South Africa, the United Kingdom, and the United States.

In *Diversity and Citizenship Education: Global Perspectives*—the book based on the conference—scholars and citizenship educators from the above nations present

132   James A. Banks

their perspectives on how citizenship education courses, programs, and curricula in multicultural nation-states can balance unity and diversity and respond to globalization. The authors also discuss how citizenship education can be reformed so that it will advance democracy as well as respond to the needs of cultural, ethnic, immigrant, language, and religious groups. The authors present historical and philosophical analyses of citizenship education programs, research, and curriculum guidelines to guide action and school reform. The final chapter of the book, written by Walter C. Parker, discusses the curriculum implications of the theories and findings in the previous chapters.

NOTE

This article is adapted from: James A. Banks. 2003. "Introduction: Democratic Citizenship Education in Multicultural Societies." In James A. Banks, ed. *Diversity and Citizenship Education: Global Perspectives.* San Francisco: Jossey-Bass. Copyright © 2003 Jossey-Bass. This material is used by permission of John Wiley & Sons, Inc. This chapter first appeared on New Horizons for Learning website: www.newhorizons.org.

RECOMMENDED READINGS

Banks, James A. 1997. *Educating Citizens in a Multicultural Society.* New York: Teachers College Press.

———, ed. 2003. *Diversity and Citizenship Education: Global Perspectives.* San Francisco: Jossey-Bass.

Banks, James A., et al. 2001. *Diversity within Unity: Essential Principles for Teaching and Learning in a Multicultural Society.* Seattle: Center for Multicultural Education, University of Washington.

Castles, Stephen, and Alastair Davidson. 2000. *Citizenship and Migration: Globalization and the Politics of Belonging.* New York: The Guilford Press.

Kymlicka, Will. 1995. *Multicultural Citizenship: A Liberal Theory of Minority Rights.* New York: Oxford University Press.

Parker, W. C. 2003. *Teaching Democracy: Unity and Diversity in Public Life.* New York: Teachers College Press.

PART IV

Educating for Earth: Future Generations and All of Life

Mike Seymour

What we have called the "environmental crisis" is the most significant challenge humanity as a whole has faced in its recorded history. How we understand and frame this crisis—and how we summon the political courage to change—will determine the extent to which we are able to continue existence on Earth in a way that is worth living.

The enormous significance of this issue demands that it come to the forefront of our thinking in all spheres (political, religious, commercial, and legal) and at all levels (individual, family, community, national, and global)—especially within education. How and why humans are undermining their ecological support—and what can be done about that—make a vital, complex, interdisciplinary area for inquiry at all levels of education. Not to educate with the earth and future generations in mind would be an unimaginable moral folly, much like saying we would rather continue to party on the Titanic's foredeck while refusing to deal with the upcoming iceberg which is in full view.

First, we must understand that the crisis we are talking about is more appropriately understood as a cultural crisis and, specifically, a spiritual crisis. What is happening to the environment is a symptom of something fundamentally awry with the

133

way humans think of themselves and their relationship to Earth—this place which is our home, but which we don't think of as such because we see ourselves living in a world made of human imagination and labor. Thinking of environmental destruction as an environmental problem is another form of disassociative, nonsystemic thinking in which we define the symptom (like a child who runs away) as the problem—without considering the larger context in which *we*, ourselves, have a role.

So, we must first recover an integral way of thinking and the courage to accept the responsibility back in our own human lap. When we do this, we are less likely to retreat into simple technological, legal, and other instrumental actions which, while absolutely necessary, tend to get us off the hook from having to make those difficult, searching, inner changes which are the only basis for real transformation to a peaceful, just, and sustainable world.

Years of well-intended environmental education have sensitized us to the problems and the needs for environmental awareness and stewardship. But as we have employed education, science, advocacy, conservation, and laws to save the land, we have been distracted from more clearly seeing the root cultural issues involved. Thus, we have learned and done meaningful things in environmental education, but have not galvanized the broad public and political will for significant cultural change. As evidence, over 80 percent of people in industrialized countries claim to care and be very concerned about the environment, but most of those same people lead a lifestyle that would take, perhaps, three earth-type planets to sustain if the poorest humans lived similar lifestyles.

What we must do now is look at our deeply rooted perceptions, beliefs, values, institutions, and ways of living that have contributed to a separation from the earth community and our resulting destructive impact on life. We must challenge our assumptions about what has value and dethrone the human as supreme in the order of things, along with the notion that the human economy and its ethic of making and having more is both unquestionably good and inevitable.

RETHINKING WHAT EDUCATION IS FOR

Understanding our role in nature differently will call for the most fundamental and radical transformations in the way we think of, and practice, education. This begins with our notions of ontology and epistemology, from which our assumptions about education and learning are drawn.

Prevailing ideas on the nature of being and the essential properties and relationships between things (ontology) must reveal the integral nature of reality not only as scientific fact, but also as the empirical mandate for an ethic of care. Only seeing the world as made of separate objects will never locate humans in a reality of mutual obligation with nature. We must have a system of knowledge that nurtures obligation to that which is known in revealing the interdependence between all things. Equally, with an integral view of life, we must counterbalance the myth of objectivism as path to the highest truth and reclaim the power of subjective, symbolic, and intuitive ways of knowing.

For eons, these participatory ways of knowing sustained indigenous peoples in a web of mutual obligation with their surroundings. These societies experienced animals and nature as kin and part of larger web of life to which they owed great debt. Today, we know the world without feeling a part of it—and that is inhuman. This disconnected way of knowing has led the most educated people to visit unimaginable atrocities upon fellow humans and other life. Without participatory ways of knowing and being, knowledge too easily falls prey to human arrogance, power, and rationalization unchecked by the moral restraint inherent in the experience and ethic of interdependence.

Moreover, we can no longer pursue knowledge and technology for their own sakes, as if the unending possibilities of human imagination deserve to be reified and not held accountable to larger considerations supporting the whole community of life. Not everything we can think of or invent should be made a reality. E.F. Schumacher (*Small Is Beautiful: Economics as if People Mattered*) argued persuasively, for example, on behalf of earth- and human-friendly, intermediate technologies that a small farmer might use, as opposed to the massive technology that might disenfranchise sustainable living. We must grow out of our adolescent enchantment with innovation, growth, and progress, and mature into the wisdom of self-restraint.

In this vein, we must rethink what body of knowledge we canonize as worthy of study. This will call on keen insight into the studies and perspectives that do (or do not) contribute to the continuance of life, as opposed to perspectives that feed the tendency to exceed our human boundaries and to reinforce a system of philosophies, human ethics, and laws that are blindly human-centered, at the expense of the larger whole. For example, most history books that present an uncritical picture of human exploration and territorial conquest would be considered antithetical to a social and ecological justice commitment—and immoral as well.

LOSING OUR ONENESS WITH NATURE

Beneath the cultural crisis lies a spiritual crisis that might be described as a loss of attunement with, and respect of, nature.

Indigenous cultures reveal how early human societies experienced themselves *as part of* the natural world, not as owners of it. At one time, humans realized they belong to nature—and not the other way around—as has been the case with our own Native American cultures. Streams, rocks, trees, and animals were felt to be alive with spirit in a world that was often fearsome and unpredictable, but not beyond human capacity to propitiate, communicate with, and hold sacred within a delicate partnership of care that kept everything going.

Cultural anthropologists, historians, and ecopsychologists may differ in their explanations of why humankind became psychically disconnected from its fragile kinship and communication with other animate and inanimate life. Perhaps it was the inevitable result of human evolution from medullary to cortical man, in which humans lost a participation mystique—which Levy-Bruhl defines as "embeddedness of human consciousness in nature"—through the process of becoming self-conscious.

Genesis and other creation stories would certainly support this picture of a fall from unity with the advent of self-awareness.

On the other hand, for long periods of time, indigenous societies maintained their reciprocal, familial relationship with nature, a way of living and being that remained until the growth of agrarian cultures, cities, territoriality, and the conversion of the "forest" from a place where we once lived into something remote and the subject of our fearful or romantic imaginings (Harrison 1993).

With this recession of nature into human imagination and a loss of our relationship of necessity with nature, perhaps it was a root human fear that propelled humans to seek a once-and-for-all advantage over nature. To answer the anxious unpredictability of nature and to be forever secure in our human-made world would be a triumph of great proportions. Thus, the monster-slaying hero was born in the human psyche as the conqueror of natural forces (now depicted as evil) and as the ideal for a human-centered culture in which norms made by and for humans replace those derived in reference to nature.

Resolving human ambivalence within the precarious relationship with nature came at both great gain and cost. The Promethean energies of inventiveness (symbolized by fire, which Prometheus stole from Zeus and gave to humans) and technology were unleashed, which allowed humans to harness nature and master technology to levels as boundless as the human imagination. But, as we know from the story of Prometheus, the gift of fire to mankind brought with it Pandora's curse. This was a way to counterbalance the arrogance and hubris of heroic culture, much in the same way that God's wisdom in Eden, once stolen, required toil and suffering to bring Adam and Eve down to Earth, humble and "human" after tasting powers beyond their capacity to use wisely.

With the ascendancy of human creative fire and expanded dominion over Earth also grew civilization's shadow of suffering, despair, war, and chaos in the subjugation of all things (nature, women, the feminine, children, others not like us) that were of lower order in the heroic culture. Thus, we have the basis of the ecofeminist argument that the subjugation of the feminine and nature are of one whole cloth when seen in terms of the larger symbolic patterns in heroic, male-dominated societies. This has inevitably led to our modern, technoscientific civilization in which we are (literally) burning up with an excess of Promethean energy, being cut off from both feminine and Earth wisdom. Like Icarus, who flew too close to the sun and fell into the ocean, our burning is once more calling forth the floodwaters.

But where is the ark?

THE REUNIFICATION OF HUMANS WITHIN THE NATURAL ORDER

The ark to bridge the troubled waters of our time will only come with a transformation to integral consciousness in which humans are reunited in heart and mind with nature. Therefore, questions we must ponder seriously include: How can we regain a felt communion with the natural world? How can this be done in a way that needless harm to any one part of nature is felt personally? How can we educate so that the fruitfulness of Earth elicits a sense of gratefulness and an ethic of responsibility to preserve the abundance of Earth for future generations? The emerging dialogue around this kind of inquiry is an evolutionary process that is as much about questions as it is answers.

In that spirit, I would like to propose several broad areas of inquiry that exemplify what would be at the heart of an ecologically sound form of education.

1. A new myth and worldview that make meaning of life *within* the natural world, as opposed to *transcending* Earth;
2. A reverence for life arising from a perception of the sacred "otherness" in all things;
3. The essential role of nature in the reenchantment of life and the human capacity for aesthetic appreciation and beauty;
4. Reinhabiting a richly storied, simpler life with less distraction, fewer "things," and more meaning so that we can experience the reality of "less is best";
5. Breaking the myth of materialism, progress, and its latest incarnation—a culture and economy of globalization—and moving toward earth-friendly practices and technologies that enable a sustainable world;
6. Social justice (covered previously); and
7. Sense of place and ecological literacy.

A NEW MYTH—AN ECOLOGY OF HEAVEN AND EARTH

We need a new worldview in which the spiritual and material are brought together— an ecology of heaven and Earth, so to speak.

In *The Dream of Earth,* Thomas Berry has written:

It is all a question of story, we are in trouble just now because we do not have a good story. We are in between stories. The old story, the account of how the world came to be and how we fit into it, is no longer effective. Yet we have not yet learned the new story. Our traditional story of the Universe sustained us for a long period of time. It shaped our emotional attitudes, provided us with life purpose and energized action. It consecrated suffering and integrated knowledge. We awoke in the morning and knew where we were. We could answer the questions of our children. We could identify crime, punish transgressors. Everything was taken care of because the story was there. It did not necessarily make people good, nor did it take away the pains and stupidities of life or make for unfailing warmth in human associations. It did provide a context in which life could function in a meaningful manner.

Prior to the scientific revolution, people in the West lived by the Christian view of the "great chain of being" in which plants, animals, and man were understood as part of a great, interconnected hierarchy culminating in the ultimate perfection of God.

This story made sense of man and nature within a larger picture, but gave way during the scientific revolution that required only one cosmological level, the physical, and detached human activity from its higher, moral purpose.

Today, a significant movement on several fronts seeks to rejoin material and spiritual outlooks in order to forge a new ecologically sound belief system and ethic. One such effort is supported by Harvard and Bucknell Universities and is called The Forum on Religion and Ecology—an inter-religious, multicultural, interdisciplinary initiative engaging in scholarly dialogue on the environment. The Forum recognizes the role of religious traditions in fostering worldviews, moral frameworks, and narratives regarding the relationship between humans and the natural environment.

Parallel to this work is the new paradigm from twentieth century science that reveals an interconnected world similar to that portrayed in religions and wisdom traditions. A promising story to emerge in this vein is that of the universe itself, as rendered with depth by Brian Swimme and Thomas Berry in *The Universe Story.*

The Universe Story revisits what we know about all of life, from the "big bang" through billions of years of evolution, but it does so in a way that enchants the heart and mind. Bringing together the viewpoints of poet, saint, and scientist, Berry and Swimme help us to understand that the becoming process, the genesis process, the evolutionary process, is spiritual/psychic as well as material/physical. *The Universe Story* helps us view these two aspects of life as inseparable, and to see that our living is drawn out of the universe itself, which is primary. In Swimme and Berry's hands, what might otherwise be a purely scientific account of life becomes a cosmic drama charged with awe and mystery. Such rendering lies at the heart of great storytelling that elicits a depth of experience far beyond the literal narrative.

Their storytelling elicits a reverence for life.

A REVERENCE FOR LIFE

> If I am a thinking being, I must regard life other than my own with equal reverence, for I shall know that it longs for fullness and development as deeply as I do myself. (Schweitzer 1987)

> Ethics consist in my experiencing the compulsion to show to all [with the] will-to-live the same reverence as I do [for] my own [life]. A man is truly ethical only when he obeys the compulsion to help all life which he is able to assist, and shrinks from injuring anything that lives. (Schweitzer 1936)

Reverence is defined as a feeling of profound awe and respect, often love or veneration, which is precisely the magic elicited by Berry and Swimme's mode of narrative in *The Universe Story.* It was the keen insight of Dr. Albert Schweitzer that fathomed that the world's suffering and inhumanity could be reversed if only each person had a "reverence for life," a feeling of respect so profound for other living beings that an intrinsic ethic of nonharm and joy in life would flourish.

Experiencing a reverence for life requires seeing and feeling beyond ordinary physical reality into its hidden mystery and beauty. It entails an experience of a sacred otherness in all life and a profound sense of moral obligation to give respect and care to that Other. Contemplative modes of observation, seeing the larger patterns in reality, and imaginative and intuitive perception open awe-inspiring worlds closed to the literal mind. Let me provide an example from my own experience.

Looking at my garden from the deck of our house, I noticed that a leaf from a tulip in a far corner was wavering intermittently. I became aware that every other plant or shrub in the immediate vicinity was absolutely still, suggesting an absence of air current. My curiosity was now peaked to the point that I looked at the tops of all the surrounding Douglas firs and Western red cedars and found that none were moving even the slightest bit. Upon returning to the still-moving leaf, a most profound and certain conviction emerged spontaneously in my mind: It's waving at me! At that point, I broke into tears and felt a distinctly enhanced sense of affinity and communication with everything around me, including so-called inanimate things such as rocks, mountains, dirt, water, and so forth.

The profound effect this perception had on me is far more significant than any question about whether or not the leaf was actually waving at me. The former absolutely did happen; the latter is hard to explain with traditional science. However, we do know from Dorothy McClean's work with plants and vegetables in the Findhorn community in Scotland (and much earlier work with measuring plant reactions to human behavior via electronic sensing devices)—that all matter does have some capacity to sense other presences. This is a knowledge humans once had, but which has been lost in the modern world.

THE REENCHANTMENT OF LIFE

The eyes of wisdom and the heart of compassion experience nature as a source of joy and numinous revelation. This brings us into the whole dimension of imaginal and aesthetic ways of knowing. Here, we enter into an enchanted world and leave behind the disconnected, ordinary world of everyday, literal reality. The difference lies in our way of seeing and capacity for openness and being moved.

In *Care of the Soul*, author Thomas Moore writes (*The Reenchantment of Everyday Life*) of nature as the quintessential opening to spirit and a sense of connectedness. The beauty and majesty of mountains, rivers, flowers, the wondrous complexity of living systems, the incredible intricacy of cell structures, the fascination of quantum physics can—when fully apprehended—bring a sense of awe, spirit, and the largeness in life.

"Nature is not only a source of spirit: It also has soul. Spiritually, nature directs our attention toward eternity, but at the same time, it contains us and creates an intimacy with our own personal lives that nurtures the soul. The individuality of a tree or rock or pool of water is another sign of nature's soul. These intriguing natural beings not only point toward infinity; more intimately, they also befriend us. It's easy to love groves of trees or mountain ridges, to feel related to them as though by blood, and to be secure in their familial protection" (Moore 1997, 5).

The awe and beauty in nature speaks to us, for we are constituted of the same stuff, the same soul. We can speak of an ecology of mind wherein the human soul resonates with the world soul from which we came. Ecopsychologist Theodore Roszak writes: "[E]copsychology proceeds from the assumption that at its deepest level the psyche remains sympathetically bonded to the Earth that mothered us into existence (1995, 5). . . . [T]he psyche is rooted inside a greater intelligence known as the anima mundi, the psyche of Earth herself that has been nurturing life in the cosmos for billions of years through its drama of complexification" (1995, 16).

Harvard biologist E. O. Wilson parallels these thoughts with the notion of biophilia, an inherent human love of life and the innate tendency to focus on life and lifelike processes. This is likewise echoed in Howard Gardner's eighth intelligence—the naturalist intelligence. Naturalist intelligence designates the human ability to discriminate among living things (plants, animals) as well as sensitivity to other features of the natural world (clouds, rock configurations).

Thus, we have been deeply tuned into the matrix of nature from which we grew. Nature is an inspiration for language formation, our source of mathematical sense, and our capacity to imagine and think. Nature casts her spell on us all from the youngest age. We are wise to nurture our children's inherent curiosity and love of nature and to regard Earth as first among our teachers in teaching us a reverence for all of life.

SIMPLICITY: LIVING IN A STORIED WORLD

I have taken this route to the subject of simple living because a simpler, sustainable world is possible only with the kinds of inner mental, emotional, and spiritual transformations I have just described. The rich inner life arises in a world whose story makes sense at a personal level and whose daily experience is full of enchantment. When we are full of authentic life, the things of a materialistic, man-made culture seem paltry by comparison and quickly lose their power over us.

A life of fullness and meaning forms the heart of what is now known as the voluntary simplicity movement. Frugality, human-scale living, a view of work as service to others, and a strong communal ethic have always existed in American life. But such simple, ethical living has been declining steadily for centuries—at no time more disturbingly and precipitously than in the present era of our megahomes, flashy cars, and shallow, advertising-saturated culture.

But people are fighting back. All over the United States and in other parts of the world, people are eliminating debt, leaving stressful jobs, getting rid of excess things, and moving into more modest (sometimes communal) housing in efforts to become grounded in something real and alive. This is not new. Thoreau inspired many in the current environmental and simplicity movements when he wrote about his life at Walden Pond:

I went to the woods because I wished to live deliberately, to front only the essential facts of life, and see if I could not learn what it had to teach, and not, when I came to die, discover that I had not lived. . . . I wanted to live deep and suck out all the marrow of life, to live so sturdily and Spartan-like as to put to rout all that was not life, to cut a broad swath and shave close, to drive life into a corner. (1971 [1854], 91)

We now have a broad, grassroots movement through such organizations as the Simple Living Network and The New Roadmap Foundation, whose books, videos, workshops, and informal discussion groups are empowering young and old to live simply, not just for ourselves but also as a commitment to social justice—realizing Gandhi's admonition to "live simply that others may simply live."

When we are freed of being possessed by that which we possess, a whole new relationship with things, man-made and natural, is possible. We can now contemplate and cultivate the significance of the things about us carefully and deliberately. We can begin to live in a storied world in which the boulder in the yard, the beat-up dresser we restored, our mother's favorite necklace, smooth stones collected from some solitary beach, and pictures of people we admire now inhabit our consciousness and homes as loved familiars. We now become makers of life's enchantments and not just recipients of nature's enchantments—assuming that we have learned well nature's lesson in how to perceive and grow beauty.

We see this lesson lived most fully in indigenous cultures, where everything people have resonates with its own unique meaning and story. Martín Prechtl, Native American and former Mayan shaman, emphasized how making something as simple as a knife caused a great debt to the "holy" from which all things come, and, therefore, required equally great ceremonies, thanksgiving, and other love offerings to fill the void left by what had been taken. The making of every gourd, bowl, knife, or piece of rope involved a vast love relationship with the forces supporting the world of man and nature, and bestowed on each thing its own numinous story.

What do we know of the things we own in modern society? Very little. For the most part, our homes and lives are littered with dead things with little life and story. They are things that come from far away, made by people we don't know and who were disconnected from their handiwork. We live in a "wasteland" which has been defacing our souls long before T. S. Eliot made this word famous. And it was Eliot's particular genius to see how the trashing of inner life and outer landscape are of one whole cloth.

Care for things and for nature is also care for self, and vice versa. Let's begin with the dictum "less is best" and live the storied, simple life of depth in our homes and schools! Let's see our obsession with curriculum coverage as part of our broader addiction to quantity and not quality. Let's slow down and go deep in our curriculum, make and collect things with our kids that are memorable and worthy of being cherished. Let's learn to see the beauty in little things that the world may disregard; for these are echoes of the vulnerable little places of essence within ourselves.

DECONSTRUCTING THE MYTH OF PROGRESS: TOWARD A JUST AND SUSTAINABLE WORLD

Along with inner transformation to a more meaningful life, moving into a more just and sustainable world requires that we deconstruct the unquestioned acceptance of social progress through our current market-based, economic model. The United States and the industrialized world has exported much good in the ideals of democracy, rights for women and children, and public education as pathways toward a more humane world. Parading behind these humanitarian ideals, however, greed and power have corrupted our corporate-dominated economic systems and have resulted in economic and social injustices around the world. To the least privileged in developing nations, globalization is simply another face of rampant colonialism.

Worldwide antiglobalization protests and a burgeoning literature on the downside of corporate hegemony (*When Corporations Rule the World,* David Korten) have recently made it fashionable—even among the world's financial elites—to critique the economic policies exacted on developing nations by the Bretton Woods institutions (IMF, World Bank, GATT, now the World Trade Organization). There is a good reason why millions of people have taken to the streets in Argentina, Australia, Bolivia, Brazil, Canada, France, Germany, India, Indonesia, Italy, Kenya, the Philippines, Mexico, the United Kingdom, the United States, Venezuela, and many other nations of the world. The current economically based model of social improvement is not working, even according to its own criteria. Globalization, its corporate practices and policies, have led to a growing disparity between the rich and poor, the dislocation of indigenous, sustainable livelihoods, flight of the dispossessed to overcrowded cities, corporate piracy of natural resources through patenting native seed and plant technologies, environmental deterioration—a list of ills longer than I can recite here.

With the spread of social, economic, and environmental injustices, the choices are becoming clearer each day that our world is either about fear, greed, and money or it is about humanity—about what brings death or what gives life. If we continue to educate for economic being, that is, for jobs (as we do in schools today), then we side with the forces of oppression that rob us of our own lives as they spread havoc among the community of life around the world. If we do no more than prepare kids to participate uncritically in a system that can strip them of their dignity, then we are handmaidens of injustice.

Teaching for sustainability, then, must take on a top priority at all levels of education. Sustainability involves everything covered in this book: our calling and meaning in life; our sense of community, locally and globally; sensitivity to issues of social justice; knowledge of and love for nature; and commitment to advocacy as well as action to reverse natural and social imbalances. Sustainability is about ourselves, our communities, and the world. It is about souls, soils, and spirit—indivisible locally and globally.

The Earth Charter makes an excellent foundation in terms of ethics, principles, and scope to frame our understanding of a sustainable future for the earth family. The Earth Charter[1] is perhaps the most inclusive, widely consulted, global proclamation of human, economic, and ecological rights ever developed in modern history. It came out of the United Nations Conference on Environment and Development (UNCED) in Rio de Janeiro, Brazil, in 1992, and now serves around the world as a guide to communities, local governments, businesses, and educators who are part of a broad, global movement toward a just, peaceful, and sustainable world.

Along with this most important framework, education can engage young people in the study of earth-friendly, sustainable practices and technologies that are lighting the way toward a brighter future. But first, it is important to give young people realistic cause for hope in order to counter the apathy and resignation that are so pervasive today and which contribute to the continuation of destructive policies. Second, kids deserve to know about the new career opportunities that are arising in response to the current crisis. Many fields are showing progressive innovations—renewable energy (wind, solar, ocean), sustainable agriculture, permaculture and ecological design, ecological and local economics, microcredit and other socially responsible lending, green business development (now talking about the triple bottom line as money, people, and environment)—to name but a few. Possible adaptable curriculums range from organic gardens for young children to hydrogen-powered cars for college-age students.

If we really want to leave no child behind, we need to prepare them for a sustainable future worth living.

SENSE OF PLACE AND NATURE LITERACY

Care for our neighborhoods and local landscapes springs from rootedness and local knowledge. Too few people, young or old, really know enough about the social and natural history of where they live to ground them in a real sense of place. This problem is, perhaps, most pronounced in urban settings, but it is also evident in rural settings, and especially apparent in the young who want to get out of town and into the big city.

Modern culture is more about getting someplace else than about being where we are. This has created a rootless element at all economic levels, from migrant labor to the deracinated elite of the multinational corporation who are homeless, don't belong any place, and, therefore, have not entered into a relationship of mutual obligation that place calls forth in us. Without that obligation, what is there to care enough about that one would want to fight for it?

Rootless people may sigh when the new Wal-Mart paves over a once beloved meadow, but they are not likely to walk in protest, write letters to the editor, or give up something so that they can contribute money to the cause. Putting caring to action arises out of a relationship to place, its people, buildings, and natural landscapes.

I currently direct the Heritage Institute, a continuing education program for K–12 teachers in the Northwest that has offered place-based field studies on the natural and social history of our bioregion since the mid-1970s. Teachers love our classes not just because they are fun, but because they nurture a sense of connection with their local neighborhoods and landscapes that make them come alive. It is this sense of aliveness and meaning that draws teachers to our program—as well as the fact that what they learn is useful in their own classrooms and intriguing to their students.

In recovering a sense of place, we discover an authentic basis for learning. We learn more deeply when we care about something enough to sacrifice, cry, or get angry when what we love is threatened in any way. In contrast, learning about "the environment" in an abstract way, wherein we distance ourselves intellectually from what is learned, creates an emotional disconnection and superficial interest.

I want the kind of education in which the trees, rocks, rivers, historic areas, and words of our ancestors speak to our young people—who, in this listening, will be transformed.

NOTE

1. For more on The Earth Charter, visit its website at www.earthcharter.org.

REFERENCES

Berry, Thomas. 1990. *The Dream of Earth*. San Francisco: Sierra Club.
Harrison, Roger Pogue. 1993. *Forests: The Shadow of Civilization*. Chicago: University of Chicago Press.
Korten, David C. 2001. *When Corporations Rule the World*. San Francisco: Berrett-Koehler Publishers.
Moore, Thomas. 1997. *The Reenchantment of Everyday Life*. Boston: G. K. Hall.
Roszak, Theodore. 1995. "Where Psyche Meets Gaia." Pp. 1–17. In *Ecopsychology: Restoring the Earth, Healing the Mind*. By Mary E. Gomes, Allen D. Kanner, Theodore Roszak. New York: Sierra Club Books.
Schumacher, E. F. 1989. *Small Is Beautiful: Economics as if People Mattered*. Vancouver: Hartley and Marks.
Schweitzer, Albert. 1936. "Ethics for a Reverence for Life." *Christendom* (Winter): 42.
Schweitzer, Albert. 1987. *Philosophy of Civilization: Part I: The Decay and Restoration of Civilization*. New York: Promethean Books.
Swimme, Brian, and Thomas Berry. 1994. *The Universe Story*. New York: HarperCollins.
Thoreau, Henry David. 1971 [1854]. *Walden. The Writings of Henry D. Thoreau*. Princeton: Princeton University Press.

14

Ethics and Ecology

Thomas Berry

I first met Thomas Berry at Camp Chewonki in Wiscasset, Maine, at a conference on Teaching for the Environment in Higher Education, and got a firsthand experience with a true elder and prophet of our time. I would like to quote from Matthew Fox's eloquent observations, made in the summer 1999 volume of EarthLight *magazine.*

Thomas Berry has studied contemporary science with depth and abandon, mind and heart. He has also immersed himself in the ancient wisdom of indigenous peoples and the wisdom of China and the East. Yet he has always stayed true to the path of critical thought and of prophetic consciousness. He speaks with the poetry of his Celtic ancestors, and his scholarship (as distinct from academic ego inflation) is both critical and caring.

Above all, his love of the cosmos and his insistence that all education and all professions are ultimately responsible to the cosmos is his deepest legacy. By calling us to an enduring creation story from the new science he gives us tools for beginning over. He not only deconstructs; he reconstructs. So many priests of his generation are cynical and so many academicians are only committed to deconstructing. What Thomas Berry has that these people lack is a sense of wonder that has not diminished with age. There is a youthfulness in Thomas Berry that is evident in the radical questions he asks as well as in the wonder he elicits. He helps us dream the earth anew, dream our work anew, dream religion and education anew.

Thomas Berry is a true elder. He has been true to his Catholic heritage in the deepest sense of finding and naming, with Teilhard de Chardin's help, the sacramental character of the universe. And, in the tradition of Aquinas, he has "shared the fruits of his contemplation" by his writing, his teaching and lecturing, and by his witness as an elder—gifting other generations with the most precious gift of all: The blessing of creation. You would be well fed if you read no other book this year but Berry's *Dream of Earth.*

In April of the year 1912, the Titanic, on her maiden voyage across the Atlantic, crashed into an iceberg and sank at sea. Long before the crash, those in command had abundant evidence that icebergs lay ahead. The course had been set, however, and no one wished to alter its direction. Confidence in the survival capacity of the ship was unbounded. Already, there was a multitude of concerns in carrying out the normal routine of a voyage. What happened to that "unsinkable" ship is a kind of parable for us, since only in the most dire situation do we have the psychic energy needed to examine our way of acting on the scale that is now required. The daily concerns of the ship and its passengers needed to be set aside for the more urgent concern for the well-being of the ship itself. Microphase concerns needed to give way to a macrophase issue.

Now there is a need to recognize that the planet Earth is threatened in its survival by our industrial economy. Already the well-being and basic functioning of the planet—in its air, its water, its soil, and its basic life systems—have been so disrupted that a biologist as extensively acquainted with the life functioning of the planet as Peter Raven of the Missouri Botanical Gardens has addressed scientific groups under the title "We Are Killing the Earth." Other knowledgeable scientists such as Norman Myers, E. O. Wilson, and Paul Ehrlich have told us the same thing. Recently, over one thousand of the most illustrious scientists have issued *A Warning to Humanity.* The introduction states: "Human Beings and the Natural World are set on a collision course. If not checked, many of our current practices put at serious risk the future that we wish for human society and the plant and animal kingdoms, and may so alter the living world that it will be unable to sustain life in the manner that we know."

Such is the situation in which we find ourselves just now. We have an ethics and a jurisprudence that begin with the human and determine our conduct in our relations with one another and our individual relations with the human community. These are our primary concerns. We work out our patterns of conduct simply by considering our inherent nature as intelligent, compassionate beings. As such, we must govern our actions by our reasoning faculty in relation to our own individual well-being and the well-being of the community, understanding by *community,* I mean the human community.

The natural world surrounding us is simply the context in which human affairs take place. Our relations with this encompassing community are completely different from our relations to the human world. In the presence of the human, the natural world has no rights. We have a moral sense of suicide, homicide, and genocide, but no moral sense of biocide or geocide, the killing of the life systems themselves and even the killing of the earth.

Clearly, there is something strangely wrong with such a position. There is thus no continuity in the ordering principles of the universe. In the medieval period, there was a distinction made between the *lex naturae* and the *lex naturalism*. The law of nature was the physical law governing the nonhuman world. The natural law was the law governing human activities that were guided by reason.

This supposes that there is a radical discontinuity in the governing principles of the universe. It also supposes that the natural world is somehow lacking in a spiritual mode of being, that the human did not emerge out of the normal evolutionary processes of the natural world or that the human is not integral to the natural world. This position does not accept the fact that the universe, in the phenomenal order, is the only self-referent mode of being and that all other modes of phenomenal being are universe-referent, that all beings in the universe constitute a single community of existence—a universe community that is totally coherent with itself throughout its vast extent in space and its sequence of transformations in time.

Since all living beings, including humans, emerge out of this single community, there must have been a biospiritual component of the universe from the beginning. Indeed, we must say that the universe is a communion of subjects rather than a collection of objects. This has been recognized from an early period by the indigenous peoples of the world.

If the universe is, from its beginning, a single universe, then there is a continuity in the inner governance of the universe. However distinctive the various modes of being, their very distinctive qualities are such precisely because of their relation to the larger community of beings. The most obvious thing about the universe is that there is an absolute coherence within its total structure and functioning. While Saint Thomas is not consistent in the larger context of his thinking in this regard, he does give a remarkable presentation of the coherence of the universe in Question 47, Article 1 of the first part of his *Summa Theologica,* where he is concerned with the distinction of things. There he asks: "Why are there so many different modes of being in the universe?" He answers: "[B]ecause the Divine could not image forth itself in any single being, the Divine created the great diversity of things so that the perfection lacking to one would be supplied by the other . . . the whole universe of beings participates in and manifests the Divine more than any single being whatsoever."

Obviously, in this view, the supreme sacred community is the total universe, not any single mode of being in the universe. The purpose of the universe is caught up in the total community and not in any single mode of being. Whether we consider the final cause or the efficient cause, the material cause or the formal cause, we find that the universe is intelligible only in the unity of its being. Although this view of Saint Thomas was not presented with an evolutionary understanding of the universe, it does indicate the coherence of the universe.

The difficulty is that our Western civilization has never taken this unity of the universe seriously because of our anthropocentrism, both in our biblical religious and our Greek humanist traditions. We see the human as a princely resident on a planet that is completely lacking in any inherent rights that must be respected by humans. If there are any rights toward the natural world obliging the human, it is obligations that we owe to ourselves, not to the nonhuman world. The universe as such has no psychic, moral, or spiritual dimension.

We have never felt any sense of the primary sacred community being the universe itself, rather than the human community or some part of the human community. Because of this separation from and exaltation of the human in relation to the other components of the universe and of the planet Earth, our Western civilization has been destitute of any ethical obligations toward the nonhuman world. There has also been an attitude that the natural world owes to the human all the support that the human needs for a certain life fulfillment.

Even beyond all this, there seems to be in the Western psyche a deep, hidden rage against the human condition, an unwillingness to accept life under the conditions that life is granted us, a feeling of oppression by the normal human condition, a feeling that the pains of life (and ultimately death) are something that should not be, something that must be defeated. Although much of this has arisen in more recent centuries, this radical discomfort with earthly existence originates in Saint Paul's invention of original sin and in the millennial promises of transcending the normal human condition contained in the Book of Revelations of Saint John. This discomfort with our existence on this planet is emphasized in our religious prayers, especially the prayers of the Mass, in which we are constantly asking to be relieved from the sorrows of time into the bliss of eternity, our true home. This dissatisfaction with Earth was made bearable by faith and the expectation of things to come in some eternal transearthly mode of existence.

This oppression of the temporal order was enormously intensified by the experience of the Black Plague in the mid-fourteenth century when, in the years between 1347 and 1349, something close to one-third of the European population died. In some cases, such as in Florence, it seems that something close to one-half of the population died within three months. Since there was no knowledge of germs at the time, the most obvious cause seemed to be a moral cause. The world had grown wicked and was being punished. Henceforth, the main problem was to be redeemed out of the world rather than to learn to live creatively within the world. This is when revivalist preaching of death, judgment, heaven, and hell came into being. The morality plays such as *Everyman* were invented; plays based on the principle that the only things truly worthwhile were the things that we could take with us at death, that is, our virtues. Everything else was proportionately devalued. We dealt with the sorrows of time by escape from time into eternity.

Somewhat later, as the first glimmerings of science began to appear over the horizon, Francis Bacon would propose that we deal with the sorrows of life by learning how to control the world about us rather than by escaping from the world through a salvation program. As our modern sciences developed in succeeding centuries, the natural world was seen as purely mechanistic in its functioning. This again led the religious traditions to emphasize the spiritual dimension of the human over and against the nonspiritual mode of nonhuman beings.

Thus when the North American continent was discovered and being colonized, the biblical tradition, the Greek tradition, and the modern intellectual traditions, were in agreement that the human was a special being living on a planet to be used for human benefit. There is little wonder, then, that we had no ethical discipline to guide us in any effective manner in our relation with the wonderful continent before us.

That the natural world was a divine communication was so overridden by the verbal communication of the Bible, by our cultural traditions, and by our recent enlightenment philosophy, that we could not consider that the human constituted a single sacred community within the natural world that would prosper or decline, live or die, be redeemed—or not-redeemed—as a single sacred community. Nor could we consider that the various beings of the natural world had inherent rights to their own proper mode of being that should be recognized by us and incorporated into our ethical teachings.

We were caught up in our commitment to transcendence, to a transcendent personal creative deity, to a transcendent spiritual mode of the human—with a transcendent destiny; then, with Descartes, caught up in a transcendence of mind that left the natural world soulless, since there was only mind and extension; and finally, a transcendent technology that was no longer subject to the basic biological law that every mode of being should have opposed modes of being or conditions, so that no single being or group of beings could overwhelm the entire life community.

Strangest of all, our entire tradition from Western civilization prevented us from recognizing that any damage that we did to the outer world of nature would be a damage to our own inner life. The devastation of the forests, the extinction of species, the poisoning of the waters, the pollution of the air, the blocking out of our vision of the stars; we could not understand that this was something more than damage to our physical being; it was also a soul-damage, a ruin within, a degrading of our imagination, our emotional life, even a diminishing of our intellectual life— for all these phases of our inner life needed to be activated by our experience of the outer world.

All this while, during this twentieth century especially, the two institutions that claim to be our ultimate guides regarding reality and value—the universities and the religious establishments—have offered no adequate ethical guidance. The reason for this is quite simple: Neither had an integral or a functional cosmology. Neither could deal adequately with the place and role of the human in the universe. The pathos of this situation is beyond reckoning.

Now we have a devastated North American continent, even a devastated planet that is finally providing, in the stark reality before us, the critique that has been needed. If we will not learn ourselves, then the universe itself will teach us by the penalties that it is imposing upon us.

These lessons were primordial lessons that the earliest humans learned in the beginning of the human venture, lessons that even today the indigenous peoples of the world can teach us. I would like to quote a passage concerning the Bushmen of Africa that was written some time ago by Laurens van der Post. The passage describes a communication being made by a tribal elder to a young boy, a communication that we might take as a primary lesson in ethics for ourselves.

Remember, Little Cousin, that no matter how awful or insignificant, how ugly or beautiful it might look to you, everything in the bush has its own right to be there. No one can challenge this right unless compelled by some necessity of life itself. Everything has its own dignity, however absurd it might seem to you, and we are all bound to recognize and respect it as we wish our own to be recognized and respected. Life in the bush is necessity, and it understands all forms of necessity. It will always forgive what is imposed upon it out of necessity, but it will never understand and accept anything less than necessity. And remember that, everywhere, it has its own watchers to see whether the law of necessity is being observed. You may often think that deep in the darkness and the density of the bush you are alone and unobserved, but that, Little Cousin, would be an illusion of the most dangerous kind. One is never alone in the bush, one is never unobserved.

In this passage, we can clearly observe that the natural world is experienced not simply as so many objects simply for human manipulation, but rather as a community of subjects, each of which has rights to be revered by humans under some awesome penalty. Every being is seen as having will and power, not the type of will or power precisely as is had by the human, but will and power of an even more pervasive and more powerful modality. We can also observe that there is a pervasive order to be observed, a discipline that includes the entire order of things. The natural world has rights, inherent rights that must be respected by humans under severe penalties, for there are forces that can eventually deal with any assault on these rights.

Indigenous peoples are capable of such statements because they live in a functioning universe, in a cosmos. We no longer live in a universe, we live in cities or nations or civilizations or cultural traditions. We do not live in a significant manner with the wind or the rain or the stars in the sky. We recognize the dawn and sunset and the seasons of the years, yet these are only incidental to the major concerns of life. Our laws are the laws of human or of divine origin; they are not laws primarily of cosmological origin.

The inadequate self-critique in our Western civilization is finally giving way to a more adequate critique presented not by verbal analysis but by that monstrous devastation of the natural world that we witness throughout the planet (but which is nowhere more severe than on the North American continent). As I look back over my own life from the opening year of World War I and wonder at all the desolation of this continent and of the larger devastation throughout the earth wrought by my generation, I am at a loss to explain it.

The difficulty is that the assault on the natural world has been carried out by good people for the best of purposes, the betterment of life for this generation and especially for our children. It was not bad people, it was the good people acting for good purposes within the ethical perspectives of our cultural traditions that brought such ruin on this continent and on the entire planet. At the microphase level, these people were acting admirably. At the macrophase level, these people ruined this continent and a great part of the planet, and no one and none of our social institutions seem able—not exactly—to stop them, or even to provide some ethical judgment on what is happening. Biocide and geocide are not terms within our ethical vocabulary.

My own description of what has happened is that my generation has been autistic. My generation has been so locked into itself that it was totally without any capacity for rapport with the natural world. My generation could not get outside itself and the outer world could not get in. There was a total barrier between the human and the nonhuman. This is what needs to be explained. This autism did not begin with the modern centuries. The support for what has happened existed within that part of our tradition that did not emerge from René Descartes or from Francis Bacon or from Isaac Newton.

The barrier between the Western mode of consciousness and the natural world, and the consequent ethical deficiency in Western conscience, began in some manner with the biblical emphasis on the perception of the divine in historical events rather than within cosmological manifestation. The entire biblical experience could be described as a movement from the cosmological to the historical that began with the Exodus experience. It was further strengthened by the historical redemption experience of Christianity, followed by the emphasis on the human mode of being in the Greek humanist tradition. When, in modern centuries, the scientists gave us a natural world that came into being by purely random processes and without any spiritual meaning, then the alienation of the human from the natural world was complete.

It is not easy for us to move beyond those basic points of reference that have guided us in the past, for these have given us our human identity and directed our religious and cultural traditions over the past millennia. These traditions have determined our language, intellectual insights, spiritual ideals, range of imagination, and our emotional sensitivities. Yet these traditions, the classical traditions of the Eurasian and American worlds, are all proving inadequate in dealing with the disintegrating influence that we are now having on the life systems of the earth, influences that imperil the human community itself. Yet we experience a kind of paralysis in our critical judgment of what is happening and what we need to do at this time to avoid an extensive crash of the biosystems of the planet.

In recent times, as our religious traditions diminish in their influence over our lives, it is the human that dominates the scene. Nothing is superior to individual or community human values. Our legal system fosters a sense of human rights over that of natural beings. Our economics is based on our mechanistic exploitation of the earth in all its geobiological systems. Relatively trivial human rights prevail over urgent rights of natural systems simply for survival. Disengagement from such basic commitments to the human requires an ethical stance and a courage of execution seldom found in the course of human affairs.

All of these considerations acquire heightened significance when we reflect that we are not simply in another period of historical change or cultural modification, such as those that have taken place in past centuries. What is happening now is of a geological and biological order of magnitude. We are upsetting the entire Earth system that, over some billions of years and through an endless sequence of groping, of trials and errors, has produced such a magnificent array of living forms, forms capable of seasonal self-renewal over vast periods of time.

Most amazing is the inability of our religious or educational establishments to provide any effective religious or ethical judgment on what is happening. Yet such judgment is what two of our eminent scientists have proposed in order to cope with the ecological devastation we now face. E. O. Wilson, professor of biology at Harvard, has said: "In the end it will all come down to a decision of ethics, how we value the natural world in which we have evolved and now—increasingly—how we regard our status as individuals." Paul Ehrlich, professor of biological sciences at Stanford, has suggested: "[S]cientific analysis points, curiously, toward the need for a quasi-religious transformation of contemporary cultures."

The religious orientation of Western society has also made us vulnerable to superficial attitudes toward the difficulties that we experience. When in a position of great danger, we are prone to believe that we will be saved by some transearthly intervention within the functioning of the planet. Such intervention will provide a remedy in the present as it has, supposedly, done on so many occasions in the past. The most glowing presentation of such expectation is to be found in the apocalyptic literature with its vision of the millennium wherein the human condition will attain a glorious existence. Sorrow will be eliminated. Justice will reign. Peace will pervade the land.

The means of dealing with this situation over the greater part of human history was through an inner discipline that would enable us to absorb the stress inherent in any earthly existence. Then, we began to envisage the possibility of understanding and controlling the processes of nature and thereby bringing about relief from the human condition through our own efforts. Nature began to be seen as an obstacle to be overcome or a resource to be exploited. The ideal of a transformed society continued to be energized by a vision of the millennium. Only now, the millennial experience was to be sought not through divine intervention but through scientific insight and technological skills.

We know the story of the formation of the modern world, the dominant intellectual framework and its beginnings in the seventeenth century with the publication of Descartes' philosophy and its development in the eighteenth century with Newtonian physics. This mechanistic view of the world encouraged the growth of technological invention and industrial plundering, culminating in the 1880s when the electronic and chemical research centers were established, scientific technologies were advanced, and the modern commercial corporations were formed. The objective was to make human societies as independent as possible from the natural world and to make the natural world as subservient as possible to human decisions. Nothing was to be left in its natural state.

Only now can we appreciate the consequences of this effort to achieve human well-being in a consumer society by subduing the spontaneities of the natural world to human manipulation. We begin to realize that the devastation taking place cannot be critiqued effectively from within the traditional religions or humanist ethics. Nor can it be dealt with from within the perspectives of the industrial society that brought it about.

We find ourselves ethically destitute just when, for the first time, we are faced with ultimately, the irreversible closing down of the earth's functioning in its major life systems. Our ethical traditions know how to deal with suicide, homicide, and even genocide, but these traditions collapse entirely when confronted with biocide, the killing of the life systems of the earth, and geocide, the devastation of the earth itself.

We have a radically new kind of problem. To appreciate this fully, we must understand that the misuse of our scientific-technological powers has not itself come ultimately from the scientific tradition, although this is the general accusation made against the empirical enquiry into the functioning of the natural world. The danger and the misuse have come, ultimately, from the deficiencies of the spiritual and humanist traditions of Western cultural development. These traditions themselves have an alienating emphasis. Both our religious and our humanist traditions are committed to an anthropocentric exaltation of the human.

We have always had difficulty in accepting the human as an integral component of the total earth community. We see ourselves as a transcendent mode of being. Only humans have rights. All other earthly beings are instruments to be used or resources to be exploited. Now, after centuries of plundering the earth for our own advantage, we begin to reflect on who we are and what has happened both to the planet and to ourselves. A sudden reversal has taken place. Our bright, new, antiseptic, mechanical world is collapsing about us or dissolving in its own toxic wastes.

The present urgency is to begin thinking within the context of the whole earth, the integral community of nonliving and living components. When we discuss ethics, we must understand it to mean the principles and values that govern that comprehensive community and the manner in which the community of the entire natural world achieves its integral expression. Human ethics concerns the manner whereby we give expression at the rational level to the ordering principles of that larger community.

The ecological community is not subordinate to the human community. Nor is the ecological imperative derivative from human ethics. Rather, our human ethics is derivative of the ecological imperative. The basic ethical norm is the well-being of the comprehensive community, and the attainment of human well-being within this comprehensive community. The earth is not part of the human story, the human story is part of the earth story.

When we are faced with change of this magnitude, we find that we are dealing with a profound reversal in our perspective on ourselves and on the universe about us. This is not a change simply in some specific aspect of our ethical conduct. Nor is it merely a modification of our existing cultural context. What is demanded of us now is to change attitudes that are so deeply bound into our basic cultural patterns that they seem to us as an imperative of the very nature of our being, a dictate of our genetic coding as a species. In clinical language, we are into a deep cultural pathology. We can no longer trust our cultural guidance in any comprehensive manner. In this situation, we must return to our genetic structure and rethink who we are, where we fit into the community of existence, and what our proper role might be within this community.

Our genetic coding is more comprehensive than our cultural coding. It is integral with the whole complex of species codings whereby the earth system remains coherent within itself and capable of continuing the evolutionary process. For a species to remain viable, it must establish a niche that is beneficial both for itself and for the larger community. The species coding of the human carries within itself all those deeper physical and spiritual spontaneities that are consciously activated by the genius of human intellect, imagination, and emotion. These cultural patterns are handed down as traditions that form the substance of the initiation rituals, educational systems, and lifestyles of the various civilizations.

Our cultural traditions are constantly groping toward their appropriate realization within the context of an emerging universe. As things change, the traditions are forced into new expressions or into an impasse that demands a new beginning. The norm for radically restructuring our cultural codings forces us back to the more fundamental species coding that ties us into the larger complex of Earth codings. In this larger context, we find the imperative to make the basic changes now required of us.

We cannot obliterate the continuities of history, nor can we move into the future without guidance from existing cultural forms. Yet, somehow, we must reach even further, back to where our genetic coding connects with the species codings of the entire Earth community. Only then can we overcome the limitations of the anthropocentrism that binds us.

Perhaps a new revelatory experience is taking place, an experience wherein human consciousness awakens to the grandeur and sacred quality of the earth process. Humanity has not participated in such a vision since shamanic times, but in such a renewal lies our hope for the future for ourselves and for the entire planet.

NOTE

This chapter is based upon a paper delivered to the Harvard Seminar on Environmental Values, Harvard University (April 1996). Copyright © 1996 by Thomas Berry. Used with permission.

REFERENCE

Van der Post, Laurens. 1980. *The Heart of the Hunter: Customs and Myths of the African Bushman.* Harvest Books.

15

Deciding for Life and Our Children's Future

An Interview with David Orr by Mike Seymour

David Orr is a passionate orator barnstorming the country for the environment and a sustainable human future, reflecting his childhood in nature and a family line of preachers. Connectedness is at the hub of his philosophy, and he flows easily between the connections of spirituality and ecology. His is one of the most probing criticisms of education and its contribution to the mess we are in today. Orr chairs the environmental studies program at Oberlin, where he oversaw the development of the Adam Joseph Lewis Center for Environmental Studies, a facility with state-of-the art ecological design that redefines the relationship between humankind and the environment. He is author of numerous books including the must-reads: Earth in Mind *and* Ecological Literacy.

MIKE SEYMOUR: Thomas Berry says that the "great work" of our times involves the reconciliation of the human within the larger ecosphere—humankind finding its place in harmony with the larger community of life. How would you characterize the human mission in this watershed period of human history?

DAVID ORR: In two ways. First, to use a medical analogy, I think we must stop the hemorrhaging of life on Earth, by which I mean stabilize climate, protect endangered species, soils, forests, oceans, and the productive capacity of the biosphere, restore degraded environments, protect the oceans, and improve basic fairness within and between generations.

Those constitute the first order of business. The first stage buys time to answer a much bigger question: Who we are as a species. If successful, the first stage gives us time to mature, to work through what we are to each other and understand our obligations as "plain members and citizens" of the natural world. That conversation must be organized around issues of peace, justice, fairness, and decency. There is another level to that conversation that has to do with what is possible for us in a world governed by the laws of entropy.

We can see the end of the fossil fuel age. When cheap, portable liquid fuels are no longer available, we will have to learn a whole new way of being on the planet that may not be to our liking at first glance. There is a lot of discussion now about the services of nature and natural capitalism and sustainability—as if we can have our cake and eat it too. But we need to reckon with our human limitations and the finiteness of the world itself.

SEYMOUR: Industrial societies live in a very self-oriented and shortsighted way. How do we change the attitudes and values by which we now live?

ORR: We need to ponder: Why is it we should be sustained? What is it that qualifies us as a species for longevity? Why do we deserve the role that we have in the world? This seems pretty esoteric from the standpoint of our current frame of reference in which human value is not questioned, but is absolutely basic.

SEYMOUR: In a sense, we need to stand outside ourselves as a species and look at ourselves from a much larger viewpoint. This is a huge transition.

ORR: This is about growing up spiritually. The current religions, Hinduism, Buddhism, and the roots of Christianity and Islam came out of a period around 700 to 300 years before Christ and represented a significant shift in thinking. We need something like that period now, except condensed from centuries into decades—an enlarged conscious-ness, if you will. We are not dealing with technological issues so much as philosophical and spiritual issues that have technological aspects to them.

SEYMOUR: Please elaborate on your views as to why you think we are in a failure mode to preserve the habitability of Earth.

ORR: There are two different levels of answers, starting with the historical perspec-tive. We began to compromise the habitability of Earth centuries ago. You could trace the origins back to the standard lineup of bad guys: Bacon, Gallileo, Descartes all the way through Ford, Rockefeller, [and] Sloan. What was enshrined was a world, in the Buddhist view, based on illusion, ill will, and greed. This industrial, material-istic world worked at the level of physical science and technology, but was inevitably paradoxical and at great odds with our higher human purposes. From the late twen-tieth century to the present, we have more physical things than ever before, alongside extreme poverty, social injustice and violence. We have more material stuff but less satisfaction; more weapons, yet less security; more control over nature, yet nature is becoming more capricious than ever before. There were flaws in the Western worldview, but these probably didn't matter much in 1750, 1850, or even 1950. However, these flaws have [been] magnified with the passage of time to the point that they are now terribly debilitating, world-breaking kinds of flaws.

The second perspective has to do with why the environmental movement, various justice, peace, and urban renewal movements are failing to make a bigger impact. In part, we are failing because we never learned how to take these issues into the political arena in democratic societies and make winning kinds of arguments out of them. We don't have an environmental crisis; we have a political crisis enabled by a failure of our schools to engage us in a critical pedagogy linked to the real issues of our lives.

SEYMOUR: Talking about politics, people get the leaders they deserve. What is it about Americans that more of us don't see beyond the deception, government minimization of the issues, and the media skimming over the real issues? Why aren't our congressional leaders standing up and loudly speaking out against this?

ORR: I think this suggests something about us at a deep physiological level. I recall a fine book written years ago by Ernst Becker called *Denial of Death* about our capacity to deny our mortality. The environmental crisis is about mortality at the largest possible scale—mortality of living systems on the planet. Faced with this, we humans are not rational near as much as we are creatures who can rationalize—and we rationalize away that which we fear. We spend time at the mall, watch Super Bowls and anything to divert us from serious consideration of who we are and where we are headed—having to reckon with the death that we see all around us. We are now seeing the playing out of deep psychological forces that either we will master or they will master us.

At a political level, democracy grew up in a time of abundance. Walter Prescott Webb wrote that democratic societies began to flourish only as the abundance of the new world opened the great frontier after 1500. Democracy was an artifact of abundance, reflecting a positive ratio between available natural resources and population size. However, we've now gone back to ratios typical of Europe prior to that great boom; we have reason to question whether democracy can survive scarcity.

There is an old critique of democratic society that dates back to thinkers of the last century and earlier that the ideal of the well-informed democratic citizen was a myth. Even if it weren't a myth, can democracy survive scarcity when we have to agree to give up some level of consumer satisfaction, tighten our belts, and pay more attention to equity and decency? If the pie doesn't expand, then the issues of distribution move to the center. As we near the end of abundance fueled by cheap, portable fossil fuels, we have reason to wonder whether democracy can survive that transition.

SEYMOUR: Along with Becker's notion of fear of death and our tendency toward denial, what other thoughts do you have on this?

ORR: Victor Frankl said that humans could survive an incredible amount of deprivation but almost no meaninglessness. We are meaning-making creatures and must have some sense of purpose or larger vision of life or we don't do very well. I think spirituality bubbles out of us like water out of an artesian well. Our choice is not whether we are religious and spiritual creatures but rather whether we are authentically religious and spiritual. You can subvert spirituality any number of ways—into shopping, into nationalism, sports, or war; and when you do that, people lose any sense of true meaning in their lives.

SEYMOUR: You talk about the political economy and the ecology of childhood. Can you expand on that?

ORR: In the sense of the political economist, Adam Smith, the political economy was the total ensemble of the way we organize the conduct of the public business. For Smith and others, the political economy had a moral dimension to it—partly ethics as well as politics and economics. It's how we do our business as a society, but you would not hear talk of political economy in any preindustrial culture. This came as an industrial basis and its economic reasoning began to penetrate the modern Western mind and organize people's lives. From Adam Smith on, the conduct of the public business is dominated by economic thinking.

We have the problem, then, of raising children in a world where economics has become the dominant discourse—economic reasoning, the final arbiter of the allocation of resources, time, attention, and eventually affection. We can't serve two masters. We can either serve the interests of our children and long-term evolution of the human enterprise or we can serve money. The latter will always undermine the former. It does it in a whole variety of ways. We can't afford to take chemicals out of our production process—that would damage some businessman's bottom line. However, those chemicals eventually work their way through the ecosystem. They are spread around by wind, water, and air, and [they] bioaccumulate at a disproportionate rate in our children; their toxic effects being amplified by a young person's growth rate. The current political economy is biased in favor of the bottom line but not in favor of our children's lives, not to speak of other lifeforms. A child-centered world would not be affordable given the way we account for costs now, because the damage to the child both mentally, spiritually, or physically is not accounted for.

SEYMOUR: You speak of the problems "of" education, as opposed to those "in" education. Could you expand on that?

ORR: The national reform effort of education standards and testing to make students productive in the global economy is like equipping students for jobs onboard the *Titanic*. Young people are being educated for an economy that is changing the climate, destroying species, eroding and ruining soils, eliminating whole forests, and poisoning them and everyone else. The education process tends to work against the evolution of life-centered people. It turns out people who are equipped and adapted to the industrial world, but not to [a world] that is decent and ecologically or spiritually sustainable over the long haul.

On the other hand, to honor the child's sense of wonder, in Rachel Carson's words, would be a very different kind of educational process—one in which kids spend a lot more time with grandma and granddad out on the farm or out roaming through the woods than they do in classrooms. Learning would be open to spontaneous things. Kids would read more and watch television less, and they might never be in a classroom at all.

One of the questions haunting us is why our educational system creates such a high percentage of people prone to violence or indifferent to and ignorant of larger spiritual and ecological issues. We turn out people who have difficulty understanding the connections between what they eat, the state of their health, the death of small towns in middle America, the draw-down of the Ogallala aquifer, and a New Jersey–sized toxic dead zone in the Gulf of Mexico . . . in other words: the food system. I am not much interested in the problems in education, but the problems that education has made—the crisis of which education is an integral part.

SEYMOUR: David Abram says we risk losing imagination as we lose biodiversity and the natural context out of which the mind of humanity was born. What are your thoughts on this?

ORR: I think Abram has a lot to say here. I would add that the current metaphors for [the] mind as a machine or a computer are terribly simplified. In an evolutionary sense, the mind evolved over millions of years—through interaction between people, sky, seas, grass, animals, water, rain, seasons, trees, moss, stones—the whole of the natural world. What evolved out of that is this infinitely beautiful calibration of [the] mind and its five senses with the world.

So Descartes' notion, in his statement "I think, therefore I am," that mind was simply a thinking machine is not only wrong, it is a form of evil. This destructive thinking reduces us to a fragment of our human potential. The human mind could not have evolved on the moon, for example. Intelligence of some sort might have—but the human mind and its richness couldn't have. The mind that writes poetry, loves, hates, sees the future, has visions, and affections, is a mind that had to evolve in a diverse, complex and beautiful natural world over eons and eons. That is a mind equipped to be in a particular kind of habitat on a particular planet. So, yes, as the context that gave rise to [the] mind is destroyed, how could our imaginative capacity not be affected?

SEYMOUR: How do you think some of the ideas we're talking about can become more compelling for Americans?

ORR: Well, I am an educator, so it certainly looks like an educational opportunity. One thing that unites us is our children and our desire that they live decent lives. . . . on that we can agree. Aside from the things that are obvious about the education, shelter, clothing, and the necessities of life, we would want them to have a sense of meaning and spirit in their lives. Currently, we are politically divided between Left and Right. There is no Left nor Right. But the real divide is between present and future. People are living in opposition to the future of our kids as we are using up their planet for ourselves; but we can choose to work on behalf of future generations. Our politics need to be reoriented from Left to Right to present/future, allowing us to think about the world in a whole different way.

Let's consider granting children legal standing as the Philippines' Supreme Court did in a recent case. The rights of children now and for future generations should be foremost, and not the rights of corporations. There's no divine right of capital or of the bottom line. Capital needs to be dethroned and children put in its place. In that change of power is our best chance of developing something that is sustainable and sustaining. It says that my interests as a parent are subservient to those of my children. I think people from all walks of life will sacrifice a great deal for their kids, and in that commitment we may find hope. This doesn't mean indulging children. It means daring to give their legitimate interests and rights a priority over everything else.

SEYMOUR: What else besides making our children a priority do you think will help Americans move toward a future that works for all?

ORR: The second is to take back language. For example, words like *conservative* have lost their true meaning when the so-called conservative people who run our country are merely reckless. A true conservative serves future generations. Next, our standards for leadership in this country are pathetically low and need to be reenvisioned. Imagine if the President-elect of the United States has to go to Hiroshima and Nagasaki and pledge to the people of the world that we will never use nuclear weapons again. Imagine the President-elect going to Bhopal, India, and telling those people that we will never again cause something like the industrial disaster that happened there.

Imagine leadership that proposed restoration of the forests in the Harrapan region of India, or the Aral Sea, or even the Chesapeake Bay—environmental restoration that would take perhaps 500 or 1,000 years to [complete], if it could be done at all. Imagine leadership willing and able to define the moral terms of its existence and act within those terms. Imagine leadership that would get the words right—that when the word *conservative* was used it meant something, or when the word *patriotism* was used it was not the cynical manipulation of the public. Imagine leadership committed to the interests of the seventh generation out—the old Iroquois standard. If it is good seven generations out, it is good for us. Seven generations back was Thomas Jefferson's generation—the generation that gave us the [U.S.] Constitution. We need leadership with a vision to span past and future.

And lastly, why not make life the core of education—life in all of its wild, crazy diversity, including the life of the learner.

SEYMOUR: Any last word you would like to leave us with?

ORR: Centuries from now, people will look back and say that the ecological enlightenment began in our time. It began with visions and prophetic voices like that of Tom Berry, who helped us see the "Great Work" before us.

REFERENCES

Becker, Ernst. 1973. *Denial of Death*. New York: Free Press.
Frankl, Victor. 1984. *Man's Search for Meaning*. New York: Pocket Books.

Ecological Education: Extending the Definition of Environmental Education

Gregory A. Smith and Dilafruz R. Williams

Gregory Smith is a professor in the Graduate School of Education at Lewis and Clark College in Portland, Oregon. He is a coauthor of Reducing the Risk: Schools as Communities of Support; *author of* Education and the Environment: Learning to Live with Limits; *editor of* Public Schools That Work: Creating Community; *and coeditor (with Dilafruz Williams) of* Ecological Education in Action: On Weaving Education, Culture, and the Environment. *He is currently exploring the role of place-based education as one means for moving our society in the direction of ecological sustainability.*

I met Dilafruz Williams shortly after her election to the Portland School Board, no small accomplishment and a great win for those who care about sustainability, the environment, and a progressive approach to education. She is professor of educational policies, foundations, and administrative studies for the Graduate School of Education at Portland State University. Among her numerous books and articles, she is coeditor (with Greg Smith) of Ecological Education in Action: On Weaving Education, Culture, and the Environment. *Dilafruz has served on numerous boards and advisory committees that address public education, citizenship participation, and environmental issues and is a founding member of the Environmental Middle School, an alternative school in Portland.*

Except in small measure, environmental education in the United States has not yet challenged the *status quo* of Western notions of progress or monoculturalism, or recognized that moving through the environmental crisis may require significant shifts in generally unquestioned cultural attitudes and beliefs. In the United States, environmental education has instead tended to focus on information regarding environmental problems and to explore topics such as endangered species, global climate change, or the water quality of local streams and rivers. Even this has become a source of controversy in the United States since the mid-1990s as a coalition of right-wing organizations has mounted a well-coordinated political campaign charging environmental educators with bias and a failure to present both sides of controversial issues (Sanera and Shaw 1996, Independent Commission on Environmental Education 1997). Despite this, we believe that if environmental education is to live up to its promise as a vehicle for developing a citizenry capable of making wise decisions about the impact of human activities on the environment, examining and altering fundamental cultural beliefs and practices that are contributing to the degradation of the planet's natural systems will be imperative.

We have chosen to call this extended form of environmental education *ecological education*. For us, ecological education connotes an emphasis on the inescapable embeddedness of human beings in natural settings and the responsibilities that arise from this relationship. Rather than seeing nature as other—a set of phenomena capable of being manipulated like parts of a machine—the practice of ecological education requires viewing human beings as one part of the natural world and human cultures as an outgrowth of interactions between our species and particular places. We believe that the development of sustainable cultures will, in fact, require widespread acceptance of a relationship between humans and the earth grounded in moral sentiments that arise from the willingness to care. As Indian physicist and ecofeminist Vandana Shiva writes, the term "sustainability" implies the ability and willingness "to support, bear weight of, hold up, enable to last out, give strength to, endure without giving way" (1992, 191). Preserving the integrity of natural systems will require human cultures that have accepted this task. Our aim is to help cultivate such cultures.

A small but visible group of educators and writers in the United States has provided inspiration and guidance to us in our efforts to incorporate these cultural and ethical concerns into the teaching of environmental issues and concerns. David Orr (1992), chair of the environmental studies program at Oberlin College in Ohio, is one of the most widely read members of this group. Orr popularized the term *ecological literacy* in the early 1990s. For Orr, ecological literacy calls for the fostering of the mental disposition to seek out connections and to develop broad understandings of the ways people relate to one another, their society, and natural systems—a focus that is fundamentally self-critical in nature.

In the early 1990s, physicist Fritjof Capra sought to achieve similar ends by founding the Elmwood Institute in California. Capra (1993) uses, as the touchstone for this institute, eight principles of ecology: interdependence, sustainability, cycles, energy flow, partnerships, diversity, flexibility, and coevolution. He and his colleagues suggest that these principles be used to guide the creation of all elements of a school, from curriculum and instruction to social relations. Both Orr and Capra urge educators to incorporate an exploration of ways human behaviors and institutions do or do not conform to the functioning of the biosphere.

C. A. Bowers (1993, 1995) has also written extensively about these issues. Primarily from a philosophical and linguistic perspective, Bowers argues that members of industrial growth societies are blinded to their own environmentally destructive practices because of their uncritical acceptance of a number of cultural assumptions. Unexamined metaphors such as linear progress or the individual as social atom propel people to participate in activities that weaken traditional understandings and forms of social reciprocity. These understandings, coupled with the practice of mutuality, once led human communities to construct relations among themselves and with the biotic world that were more socially just and environmentally sustainable than those encountered in industrial societies.

In our own work, we have focused on directing educators to the importance of creating classrooms and schools that induct students into the actual experience of relatedness—to one another and to the world beyond the classroom. We have sought ways to embody a "green pedagogy" that leads teachers and students to construct new ways of being in both the social and natural environments that surround them. We strongly believe that the achievement of sustainable cultures will require attending to all peoples' need for security and economic sufficiency, and that a failure to establish supportive and caring societies will lead to continued environmental degradation (Smith 1992, 1998; Smith and Williams 1996).

In an effort to synthesize this body of work with and for our students, we have developed a set of principles of ecological education aimed at helping all of us develop learning experiences capable of inducing a deeper understanding and experience of relatedness as well as the capacity to critically examine the cultural milieu in which we live. We suggest that teachers who are practicing this more comprehensive form of environmental education strive to accomplish the following:

- Develop among their students a deep personal affinity with the earth through practical experiences out-of-doors and through the practice of an ethic of care;
- Ground learning in a sense of place through the study of knowledge possessed by local elders and the investigation of surrounding natural and human communities;
- Induct students into an experience of community that counters the press toward individualism that is dominant in contemporary social and economic institutions;
- Help students to acquire practical skills needed to regenerate human and natural environments;
- Introduce students to occupational alternatives that contribute to the preservation of local cultures and the natural environment;
- Prepare students for work as activists able to negotiate local, regional, and national governmental structures in an effort to adopt policies that support social justice and ecological sustainability; and

- Engage students in an exploration of cultural assumptions upon which modern industrial civilization has been built, examining in particular how these assumptions have contributed to the exploitation of the natural world and human populations.

With these principles as guideposts, we believe that educators can help cultivate among their students the disposition to care for one another and the earth as well as the knowledge of how to do so. It is still too early to know whether the application of these principles will lead to a more ecologically literate and committed citizenry, but a vision of the possible necessarily precedes evaluation.

In what follows, we will describe these principles in more detail and then discuss how they are evident in three different educational settings: A middle school that has chosen to focus on environmental topics; a set of interrelated courses in a university-level environmental studies program; and an informal adult education process tied to a long-term watershed restoration project. We have chosen to include examples from the fields of higher education and nonformal education because we believe that broad public support for the kind of educational reforms we are proposing cannot wait until today's current students have reached voting age. Adults, as well as children and young people, need to be encouraged to consider these matters. In each of the examples we describe, educators or activists have created learning experiences that are, at least in part, aimed at grappling with the ethical and cultural issues we associate with ecological education. Their practices exemplify ways that teachers, students, and community members are beginning to implement visions articulated by people like Orr, Capra, Bowers, and ourselves. We present them here as examples of what committed educators and environmentalists are creating in the United States. They demonstrate what is possible when a more restricted definition of environmental education is broadened to include cultural as well as scientific and regulatory issues.

PRINCIPLES OF ECOLOGICAL EDUCATION

Development of Personal Affinity with the Earth

Robert Michael Pyle (1993) has written eloquently about the extinction of experience with nature and its implications for environmental protection. Pyle believes that people will not protect what they do not know, and that larger and larger numbers of children have few opportunities to develop a meaningful connection with life outside the context of human society and inventions. One of the hazards of modern life is that the close connection people once shared with the natural world threatens to become "extinct" as an increasing proportion of human activities has been channeled into the built environment. Recent studies (Nabhan and St. Antoine 1993) suggest that over the course of their lives, most people in industrialized societies spend only four to five percent of their time beyond their homes, schools, offices, or shopping malls. Within the context of cities and suburbs, it becomes easy to forget nature and to believe that human beings and our economy are able to exist outside the requirements of natural systems.

In order to rectify this situation, adults need to consciously redirect themselves to the kinds of renewal and reconnection that can occur through outdoor work and recreation. For many children, whose time is absorbed by television or computer games, schools may provide one of the few places where a relationship to nature can be initially engendered. By situating learning beyond the confines of the classroom, teachers can redirect children's attention to the world unmediated by software, video images, or even books. Schoolyards can be turned into laboratories where gardens and small ecological field stations serve, along with textbooks and videotapes, as sources of student learning. Local parks can become the site of nature studies, play, and quiet reflection. All of us need to be encouraged to learn how to look and listen and smell and feel, inhabiting our bodies and our places with full attention. By developing a sense of affinity with land and water, students of all ages may come to recognize their beauty and then take the steps needed to guard their integrity.

Grounding Learning in a Sense of Place

Little exists in modern society to draw youngsters or adults into a sense of membership in their own locales. For many of us, face-to-face interaction has been replaced with relations between "absent" others, fostered through a variety of technologies (Gidden 1990). The mobility of families, the media, and the way automobiles isolate us from nature and our neighbors make it imperative for educators to incorporate learning experiences aimed at connecting students to their own communities and regions. In their development of curriculum, teachers need to seek out local resources, focus on local issues, and help students learn how to ask and answer questions about the phenomena and events that surround them. By locating the curriculum in the local, educators may be able to further the regeneration of the unique responses to particular places that have contributed to the development of diverse cultures. Such a project in no way precludes critical evaluation about the constraining as well as nurturing conditions encountered in most human communities.

Countering the Press toward Individualism

Some social psychologists believe that one of the central contributors to the perpetuation of today's market-driven society is the growing social isolation of individuals and individual families. Paul Wachtel (1989), for example, has argued that Americans' preoccupation with affluence stems from the declining strength and importance of communal institutions. In the past, such institutions were necessary if people were to survive in challenging natural conditions. Now, security rests on our ability to provide for ourselves and our immediate loved ones as individuals rather than as members of interactive and supportive communities. The result is a society-wide drive to compete for the jobs, salaries, and goods that promise to protect us from harm and to neglect forms of cooperation and mutual support that once provided for human welfare.

Transcending the pressure to acquire and consume will not be easy, but formal and nonformal educators can at least introduce students to the potential of community. The creation of smaller schools that incorporate opportunities for informal interaction and joint projects outside the classroom can contribute to the development of a sense of social membership among students (Smith 1998). Bridging the gap between school and community can also help students develop an awareness of their ties to others and the forms of obligation, responsibility, and support associated with those relationships. The experience of these relationships can affirm values other than those encountered in the competitive market and direct learners toward an ethical stance grounded in intersupport.

Acquisition of Skills Needed to Regenerate Human and Natural Environments

People's sense of connection to their community is likely to be further enhanced if they believe that they can contribute to the welfare of others. One way to engender the experience of connection is to invite children and adults to participate in projects aimed at restoring damaged ecosystems or improving the lives of others in their community. Current efforts in schools to include community service reflect an understanding of the importance of this kind of labor. These efforts are likely to be most powerful if they are coupled with the teaching of practical skills. Young people who learn how to renovate deteriorated homes, replant damaged riparian zones with appropriate species, grow food, create parks, or set up businesses that meet previously unfulfilled community needs are able to discover their own capacity to contribute to beneficial projects. Adults who participate in such projects can encounter a similar form of affirmation.

INTRODUCTION TO OCCUPATIONS THAT FOSTER ENVIRONMENTAL HEALTH AND SOCIAL JUSTICE

Few adults or children in our society are able to conceive of economic activities that will provide for their support but not contribute to growing social and environmental degradation. Given the primacy of economic relations in our lives, finding ways to imagine other vocational paths seems critical. Youngsters, for example, could be introduced to what it means to practice sustainable forestry, run a community-supported farm, maintain a credit union that makes low-interest loans available to local residents, design and/or construct energy-efficient and low-polluting buildings, or assist low-income people to organize and improve the quality of their lives. From such experiences, a generation of adults could emerge who are willing to use their energy, intelligence, and good will to craft institutions and technologies aimed at fostering the long-term health of human and natural communities.

PREPARATION FOR WORK AS SOCIAL JUSTICE AND ENVIRONMENTAL ACTIVISTS

The creation of viable community and regional governments that are responsive to the needs and viewpoints of all citizens will necessitate inducting the young, and reeducating their elders, into the give and take of public life. The building of such skills can begin in the classroom, where students can be asked to shape classroom rules and expectations and to participate in the development of curriculum and learning activities. This process can be extended into the community of adults through the creation of organizations, such as watershed councils, that bring citizens together to grapple with serious local issues often overlooked by other governmental entities. Schools, too, can draw much more heavily on student participation in important institutional decisions. This does not mean that teachers and administrators should abrogate their responsibilities, but that the voices of children and young adults be given significant weight in decisions that affect their lives (Purpel 1987; Gregory and Sweeney 1993). Young people can also be given the opportunity, through their coursework, to participate in research that has bearing on local problems or controversies. There are instances in which such activity has prodded adults to rectify problems identified by the children of their communities (Lewis 1991).

Exploration of Cultural Assumptions Underlying Modern Industrial Civilization

The enactment of all of the preceding principles must be founded on a recognition of the failure of industrial growth societies to acknowledge their embeddedness in natural systems. It is imperative, for example, that people understand that the human economy is a subset of the ecology of particular places and the planet as a whole (Daly 1996). If human economic activities threaten the well-being of these ecosystems, our own well-being will eventually be threatened. We must come to understand that a way of life based on the celebration of human inclinations of greed and avarice will eventually come to injure ourselves and the communities in which we live. From this perspective, the pursuit of self-interest without an awareness of our broader relationships will be seen for what it is—a tear in the fabric of the world. Ecological education must call into question the assumptions that underlie industrial and postindustrial societies, and encourage teachers and their students to thoughtfully consider aspects of our lives that either contribute to or detract from the creation of a culture that is at once environmentally sound and socially just.

PRACTICES OF ECOLOGICAL EDUCATION IN THE UNITED STATES

We know of only a few schools or programs where all of these principles are being put into practice. There are, however, a number of formal and nonformal educational institutions, in the United States and elsewhere, where elements of this agenda can be observed. While we recognize that other countries have similar programs, we will focus on experiences in the United States about which we have a grounded understanding. Our book, *Ecological Education in Action: On Weaving Education, Culture, and the Environment* (1999), offers a collection of accounts by practitioners and researchers about thirteen programs that can serve as models of the possible. In this section, we will describe three of the thirteen, relating their activities and educational approaches to the principles discussed above.

The Environmental Middle School

We begin with Portland's Environmental Middle School (EMS), an institution we both know well since we participated in its founding and continue to serve on its site council. EMS, as the school is known to its participants, was started in the fall of 1995. Educators there have placed the environment at the heart of the curriculum. From this focus, school-wide projects on rivers, mountains, and forests that orient students to an exploration of local watersheds and geologic phenomena have emerged. One of the most striking elements of EMS is its schedule which reserves Mondays, Wednesdays, and Fridays for inside classwork, and Tuesdays and Thursdays for fieldwork or service activities that take students into the community. Learning at EMS is not walled off from surrounding social and natural environments; teachers use those environments as the basis for students' education. Because EMS is located in an older school building close to public transportation, teachers have been able to engage in projects located throughout the Portland metropolitan region without incurring the added expense of school bus rentals. EMS students pull English ivy that has invaded Forest Park in the northwest sector of the city, study the Willamette River closer by, and travel to the Johnson Creek watershed southeast of the school to remove invasive Himalayan blackberries and plant native species. Students also help in downtown soup kitchens and homeless shelters. Much learning at the school, itself, has also been situated out-of-doors. A sizable vegetable and flower garden has been created with the help of parents and community members, and a section of the school grounds has been "naturescaped" with plantings of indigenous species and the construction of a small wetland.

Beyond its curricular focus and hands-on teaching approaches, the social environment in the school encourages the formation of close interpersonal ties. Students can stay with the same teacher for three years in classrooms that blend grades six through eight. Each morning begins with a community meeting that features announcements, group singing, and occasional presentations by outside speakers. Because the school is small—180 students—the anonymity encountered in larger middle schools is absent. Students are drawn into a sense of community membership and participation on a number of levels: the immediate school, the broader social environment, and the "community of all beings" in which humans play only one part.

To one extent or another, EMS enacts all of the principles of ecological education enumerated earlier. Students are provided with multiple opportunities to develop a personal affinity with the earth. During field studies, it is not uncommon for them to be given time to observe quietly what is going on around them and to be encouraged to write poems or journal entries about what they have perceived. In addition to work during regular school days, students, teachers, and parents participate in weekend camp-outs at the Oregon Coast, in old growth forests, or in the high country of the Cascade Mountain Range.

These experiences, as well, provide an opportunity for young people to be outside in ways that deepen their sense of connection to nature. Teachers, furthermore, expose students to a curriculum that focuses on local phenomena. Field studies, obviously, contribute to this end. EMS students, in fact, are surprised when they learn that their counterparts in other schools do not know the names of indigenous flora and fauna. Students also explore local history, investigating the relationship between human beings and our region over time. During a year devoted to a study of the forests, for example, students researched the history of logging in the Pacific Northwest and constructed a model of a traditional logging operation.

Perhaps one of the most powerful elements of EMS involves the degree to which students are drawn into an experience of community membership. More than anything, EMS is an emotionally safe place to be. Teachers care about students, and students care about their teachers and one another. At EMS, young adolescents can be kids and not be embarrassed about it. Despite peer pressure elsewhere, eighth-grade boys, for example, sing along with everyone else during morning meetings. EMS has also consciously reached out to the Native American community in Portland, striving to provide educational experiences and support for children more likely to drop out than any other population group in the United States. Parents of Native American students describe their teachers as being like "aunties and uncles." A disciplinary approach that emphasizes kindness, honesty, and flexibility underscores much of what makes EMS friendly and supportive. Students learn what it means to be part of a caring and cooperative community.

Through fieldwork and community service, students are given the chance to learn many practical skills. They become knowledgeable about the use of native species in home gardens, and share what they know with residents of the neighborhood surrounding the school during plant sales. They acquire genuine gardening skills, as well as skills associated with restoration ecology. And they learn how to organize major events—such as school celebrations held at the completion of major thematic units—or other events such as the monthly community luncheon prepared by different classes. In this process, they are exposed to a variety of socially responsible occupations as they work shoulder to shoulder with local farmers at subscription farms, participate in the delivery of food at local soup kitchens, or interact with Americorps volunteers at the school. Students at EMS have an ongoing chance to see and try out vocations premised on service to the community.

Although EMS avoids organizing events that might be politically controversial, students have had a number of opportunities over the preceding years to make their voices heard with regard to welfare of their school. At the end of the Environmental Middle School's first year, three of the school's six teachers were told they would not be rehired for the coming school year because they were not yet tenured in the Portland district. Students and their parents were outraged that people who had become like family members could be supplanted by displaced teachers from other schools with little interest in EMS or environmental education. They organized a march and rally to Portland's Pioneer Square, where their speeches and songs were reported by local news media.

Finally, although the school does not explicitly attempt to critique the cultural values of postindustrial civilization, something that is the explicit aim of the program described immediately below, students are encouraged to question our society's casual attitudes toward resource use and disposal. Students reflect on their experiences in school and out-of-doors, and are encouraged to think critically about their place within the broader culture of consumption.

Radical Ecology at the University of Vermont

Stephanie Kaza is an associate professor in the Environmental Studies Department at the University of Vermont. Trained as an ecologist as well as an ethicist, she combines the perspectives of the scientist and the humanist in a set of courses aimed at transforming the understanding and social practices of her students. She strives to help undergraduates confront the facts of the environmental crisis, but does so in a way that enables them to move beyond despair to an understanding of their own capacity to effect change. Her courses on ecofeminism, radical environmentalism, religion and ecology, and international environmental studies push her students to acknowledge the link between central cultural assumptions and practices of our own society and the environmental crisis. Through a variety of highly personalized experiences that combine community building, "conscientization," and activism, Kaza asks students in her classes to shine the light of new knowledge and understanding on their own lives and decisions, and then to embody the implications of what they are learning in new behaviors. This process violates some of the norms of liberal education because of its obvious partisanship—many sides of an issue may be explored, but Kaza does not hesitate to distinguish the life-affirming from the life-denying. In doing so, she models an educational practice with deep ethical and spiritual roots that reclaims the moral ground upon which an ecologically sustainable and socially just culture must be built.

Kaza says that her intent in her classes is to "generate both awakening and empowerment, freeing students to act responsibility in a relational world" (1999, 149). It would be fair to say that Kaza's teaching approach is primarily aimed at examining the central values and assumptions of industrial growth societies and equipping her students to become activists capable of stimulating the cultural and institutional changes required to reverse environmental degradation and social injustice. She achieves this end through combining the activities and liberatory analysis of Joanna Macy (1983) and Gerard Fourez (1982). Macy's work is aimed at releasing energy contained by unexpressed despair about modern developments such as nuclear armaments and environmental degradation through workshops built on the assumption that people are better able to confront their own grief in the context of community. Out of that community emerges the ability to take action to address conditions that threaten the well-being of humans and the earth. Fourez's approach is more analytical, tied as it is to liberation theology and liberation ethics. Kaza uses his methodology to critically examine power and institutional relationships and to unravel our society's legitimating myths. These approaches provide a means for helping students grasp the nature of their own relationship to one another and the world.

From that experience of relationship and community, Kaza goes on to assign projects that involve researching local and global environmental issues and taking local action. One group of students from her ecofeminism class developed a campus awareness program to alert their peers to the relationship between breast cancer and environmental hazards. Another group focused on the toxic chemicals in tampons and placed stickers in all women's restrooms on the University of Vermont campus to warn their classmates and instructors about these products. Students in the radical environmentalism course have become closely involved with a campus effort to "green" the university by reducing the use of pesticides and paper, purchasing food from local producers, and examining campus investments with an eye to their social and environmental implications. In addition to immersing students in social action, this research also directs them to an exploration of local issues.

The Mattole Restoration Council

The Mattole Restoration Council is a nonprofit organization that, for the past decade, has been helping adults and young people in northern California begin to understand the complex relationships that link human activities to the health of the local environment. It works primarily with adults in nonformal educational settings to develop, among the general populace, a deeper grasp of ecological principles and their cultural and economic implications. Located in Petrolia, California, the council grew out of the concern of a group of local residents about the declining health of indigenous king salmon stocks. During the years of its existence, its members have stimulated the development of what might be called a watershed consciousness among people who live on California's "lost coast," through their work to restore stream habitat, replant clear-cut slopes, erase unused logging roads, install hatchboxes (to ensure higher rates of salmon propagation), and document and publish the consequences of their efforts. Although the council offers no degrees or licenses, its activities are educating a corps of activists and leaders in the practical skills and intellectual understandings associated with the emerging field of restoration ecology. Musical comedies written, produced, and staged by some of the council's members take that learning to members of their own community and interested audiences along the Pacific Coast and elsewhere.

In subtle yet powerful ways, the Mattole Restoration Council, like the Environmental Middle School, practices all of the principles of ecological education. Most obviously, people involved in this work acquire a variety of practical skills associated with restoration ecology. They learn how to enhance the productive capacity and survival rate of spawning salmon; they learn how to assist in the reforestation of damaged forestlands and riparian zones; they learn how to map and analyze the consequences of human activities that both injure and help their region. Such skills, in some instances, can be translated into new occupations; a former heavy equipment operator, for example, now repairs or eliminates poorly constructed roads. Much of the learning that occurs in the field also contributes to a deepening of the affinity council members feel toward their own region and other species. Restoration ecologist Freeman House, one of the founders of the council, has written about the impact that catching live salmon and not harming them has had on his own thinking.

"To enter the river and attempt to bring this strong creature out of its own medium, alive and uninjured, is an opportunity to experience a momentary parity between human and salmon. Vivid experiences between species can put a crack in the resilient veneer of the perception of human dominance over other creatures. Information then begins to flow in both directions, and we gain the ability to learn from salmon, from landscape itself" (House 1990, 112).

Such learning is also predicated upon a deepening understanding of local phenomena. House tells a story of an effort early on in the council's work, when a group of people had decided to replant alders along sections of the Mattole River that in aerial photographs showed virtually no vegetation. When individuals had scouted out this area, they were unable to locate the sites, discovering instead stands of alder that were four to twelve feet in height. They later deduced that during a dry period in the 1980s, ripe alder cones had been deposited on the scoured channels. While stream flows remained low, the young trees were able to reestablish themselves. From such experiences, council members have learned the importance of paying attention, as House has observed, "not only systematically, but systemically, over time and space" to the land and rivers that surround them (1995, 2).

The Mattole Restoration Council also exemplifies what it means to regenerate the human community. The council's success has, from the beginning, been contingent on the ability of diverse groups from the region to work together. Environmentalists, loggers, fishermen, ranchers, and representatives from state agencies needed to learn how to discover what they shared in common and then act from that base of agreement. In the process, people came to believe that they could reverse the dramatic decline in the salmon population that followed heavy logging and siltation of the Mattole River in the 1950s and 1960s. Although these groups have found it difficult to cooperate on other issues beyond salmon restoration, their ability to cooperate on this problem suggests that, in time, they may be able to extend their energies and activism to other domains.

THE PROMISE OF ECOLOGICAL EDUCATION

The human capacity to connect to the earth and to other people is at the heart of sustainable cultures that must emerge in coming decades. Among the indigenous residents of North America and elsewhere, the formation and sustenance of such relationships was the bedrock upon which their cultures and moral systems were created. Modernity has allowed human beings to achieve an apparent liberation from many of these relationships and the obligations and responsibilities they entail. Geographic and social mobility, freedom from the limitations of particular communities and places, and the ability to define our own identities have been some of the benefits associated with this liberation. The consequences, however, are uprootedness and detachment, qualities that further the goals of an extractive economy and curtail the possibilities of care.

For us, ecological education provides one means for reestablishing connections and reaffirming relationships. The promise of ecological education lies in its potential to move teaching and learning away from the detached objectivity encountered in most conventional classrooms to experiences that involve students as engaged participants. Instead of being spectators to the knowledge of others, they can become the producers of knowledge and active citizens embedded in meaningful cultures. Ecological education opens the door by providing more space for feelings, values, and commitments, extending these to include relationships with other people. Strengthening the experience of mutual identification and relatedness, it holds out the possibility of regenerating patterns of interconnection and reciprocity that must become widespread if human beings are to learn to live in partnership with the natural world and with one another in new ways.

NOTE

This chapter was originally published in the *Australian Journal of Environmental Education* and is reproduced with permission of the Australian Association for Environmental Education.

REFERENCES

Bowers, C. A. 1993. *Education, Cultural Myths, and the Ecological Crisis: Toward Deep Changes.* Albany: State University of New York Press.
———. 1995. *Educating for an Ecologically Sustainable Culture: Rethinking Moral Education, Creativity, Intelligence, and Other Modern Orthodoxies.* Albany: State University of New York Press.
Capra, F. 1993. *Guide to Ecoliteracy: A New Context for School Restructuring.* Berkeley, Calif.: Elmwood Institute.
Daly, H. 1996. "Sustainable Growth? No Thank You." Pp. 192–96. In J. Mander and E. Goldsmith, eds. *The Case Against the Global Economy and Toward the Local.* San Francisco: Sierra Club Books.
Fourez, G. 1982. *Liberation Ethics.* Philadelphia, Penn.: Temple University Press.
Gidden, A. 1990. *The Consequences of Modernity.* Stanford, Calif.: Stanford University Press.
Gregory, T., and M. E. Sweeney. 1993. "Building a Community by Involving Students in the Governance of the School." Pp. 101–28. In G. A. Smith, ed. *Public Schools That Work: Creating Community.* New York: Routledge.
House, F. 1990. "To Learn the Things We Need to Know: Engaging in the Particulars of the Planet's Recovery." Pp. 111–20. In V. Andruss, C. Plant, J. Plant, and E. Wright, eds. *Home! A Bioregional Reader.* Philadelphia, Penn.: New Society Publishers.

————. 1995. "Reinhabitation and Ecological Restoration. A Marriage Proposal." Talk delivered at the Society for Ecological Restoration's International Conference, Seattle, Washington, September 14–16.

Independent Commission on Environmental Education. 1997. *Are We Building Environmental Literacy?* Washington, D.C.: George C. Marshall Institute.

Kaza, S. 1999. "Liberation and Compassion in Environmental Studies." Pp. 143–60. In G. A. Smith and D. R. Williams, eds. *Ecological Education in Action: On Weaving Education, Culture, and the Environment.* Albany: State University of New York Press.

Lewis, B. 1991. *A Kid's Guide to Social Action: How to Solve Problems You Choose and Turn Creative Thinking into Positive Action.* Minneapolis: Free Spirit Publishing.

Macy, J. R. 1983. *Despair and Personal Power in the Nuclear Age.* Philadelphia, Penn.: New Society Publishers.

Nabhan, G. P., and S. St. Antoine. 1993. "The Loss of Floral and Faunal Story: The Extinction of Experience." Pp. 229–50. In S. R. Kellett and E. O. Wilson, eds. *The Biophilia Hypothesis.* Washington, D.C.: Island Press.

Orr, D. 1992. *Ecological Literacy.* Albany: State University of New York Press.

Purpel, D. 1987. *The Moral and Spiritual Crisis in Education: A Curriculum for Justice and Compassion in Education.* Granby, Massachusetts: Bergin and Garvey.

Pyle, R. M. 1993. *The Thunder Tree: Lessons from an Urban Wildland.* Boston: Houghton Mifflin.

Sanera, M., and J. Shaw. 1996. *Facts, not Fear: A Parents' Guide to Teaching Children about the Environment.* Washington, D.C.: Regnery.

Shiva, V. 1992. "Recovering the Real Meaning of Sustainability." Pp. 187–93. In D. Cooper and J. Palmer, eds. *The Environment Question: Ethics and Global Issues.* London: Routledge.

Smith, G. A. 1992. *Education and the Environment: Learning to Live with Limits.* Albany: State University of New York Press.

————. 1998. "Rooting Children in Place." *Encounter* (Winter).

Smith, G. A., and D. R. Williams. 1996. "The Greening of Pedagogy: Reflections on Balancing Hope and Despair." *Holistic Education Review* 9, 1: 43–51.

————. 1999. *Ecological Education in Action: On Weaving Education, Culture, and the Environment.* Albany: State University of New York Press.

Wachtel, P. 1989. *The Poverty of Affluence: A Psychological Portrait of the American Way of Life.* Philadelphia, Penn.: New Society Publishers.

17

Returning Home with Empty Hands

David Jardine

David W. Jardine is professor of education in the faculty of education at the University of Calgary. He is the author of Speaking with a Boneless Tongue *(1992),* To Dwell with a Boundless Heart *(1998), and* Under the Tough Old Stars *(2000) as well as being the coauthor (with Patricia Clifford and Sharon Friesen) of the book* Back to the Basics of Teaching and Learning: Thinking the World Together. *His main work is with student teachers in elementary education and in the area of hermeneutic inquiry. He lives with his family in Bragg Creek, a small community in the foothills of the Rocky Mountains, west of Calgary, Alberta.*

> It is impossible to divorce the question of what we do from the question of where we are—or, rather, where we think we are. That no sane creature befouls its own nest is accepted as generally true. What we conceive to be our nest, where we think it is, are therefore questions of the greatest importance.
> —Berry, 1986, p. 51

I

During the recent twentieth-anniversary celebrations of the first moon landing, one of the former Apollo astronauts was asked how he would sum up what the Apollo program was all about. He replied, "It's about leaving." It is interesting to speculate as to whether there is any connection between the lack of success in generating any great excitement about "further, deeper penetration into the solar system" or "getting

175

it [the space program] up again" (and a great deal of other unintentional, but rather blatant phallocentric talk) and the recent flourish of ecological awareness.

Ecological awareness is not about leaving, but about responsibly staying put here on Earth. It has to do with the logos of our home, our dwelling, and with how we can come to be at home here in a way that does not overstep the real possibilities of dwelling responsibly, sanely, in a way that does not befoul the very "nest" that houses us. Ecology is about returning our attention to home. It is about tending anew to where we dwell, to our nest, to the delicate and difficult reliances and debts that intertwine our fleshy lives with the fleshy life of the earth; it is this moist texture that bestows our lives and makes them possible.

Becoming attentive to this original bestowal, this "original blessing" (Fox 1983) requires more than "understanding" and "knowing" as they have come to be. Our issuing up out of the earth is not a set of objective relations that we can place in front of us for our perusal. Understanding such issuance requires cultivating "the continuity of attention and devotion without which the human life of the earth is impossible. The care of the earth is our most ancient and most worthy and, after all, our most pleasing responsibility. To cherish what remains of it, and to foster its renewal, is our only legitimate hope" (Berry 1986, 14). Attention, devotion, care, worthiness, cherishing, fostering, renewal, and hope: These are not just words. They echo a deep sense of place, remaining, dwelling, and settling. These words bring with them a sense of memory, continuity, and regeneration; a mindfulness of what is needed for life to go on and a passing of such mindfulness to the young.

Children are already present in these words. "Leaving" once described our fanciful hopes for the future. It is now becoming one of the traumatic and painful features of ecological insight—we cannot just leave, for the exhaust(ion) left in the wake of such leaving inevitably returns and, just as inevitably, it always returns precisely here. Even if the ecological consequences of our actions do not return to this specific place, we return here slightly more insane, slightly more "out of place" and "out of touch" with where we really are. We carry this consequence in our hearts along with the both displaced and displacing belief that we live somewhere other than on the whole of the earth, needing to believe, to protect our sanity, that we have left those consequences "someplace else."

If home is abandoned altogether—if we all get caught up in "leaving"—our care for and devotion to the conditions, sources, and intimate dependencies of renewal and generativity are also abandoned; and with these is abandoned our only legitimate hope (van Manen 1983). If we abandon our care for and devotion to the conditions of renewal and generativity, we abandon our care for and devotion to our children.

Ecopedagogical reflection thus involves drawing together our concern, as educators, for the presence of new life in our midst (Smith 1988) (and for bringing forth this new life into the world, our world—*educare*) and "our most pleasing responsibility," caring for the earth. Such reflection simply asks: In what ways do questions of pedagogy interweave with questions of the continued existence of an earth in the embrace of which pedagogy is possible? Ecology and pedagogy interweave to the extent that separating them or separating our responsibilities for them can be accomplished only at a tragic cost. "No matter the distinctions we draw, the connections, the dependencies, remain. To damage the earth is to damage our children" (Berry 1986, 57). Perhaps we will see that pedagogy, too, is "our most pleasing responsibility." It, too, requires the very same love, care, and generosity of spirit that ecological awareness does. Ecology is silently and inevitably interwoven with pedagogy. In the face of this interweaving, we cannot just "leave."

II

Loving and savoring the articulate beauty of mathematics is interlaced with the ability to love and savor the actual conditions under which mathematics is possible. The indigenous articulations and beautiful inner workings and intimate interrelationships of mathematics must be re-thought as "human formations" (Husserl 1970, 170) in the full, embodied, "fleshed-out" sense—full of humus, earthly. This re-thinking has two moments: the first rather long and convoluted, the second frighteningly straightforward.

First, articulation of "that anciently perceived likeness between all creatures and the earth of which they are made" is needed (Berry 1983, 76). For example, "symmetry," as detailed in the grade two curriculum guide, is not some abstract and cerebral concept, but is right before us as we stretch out our arms and clap our hands in time, right there in the pinwheel patterning of an orange we divide with a child, again in the turns we take dividing the pieces (there also, implicit in the unfairness of "unsymmetrical" turns), again in the radiating needles of a pine tree outside the window, again in the rhythm and rhyme of language, in the change of days, of seasons, and in the cycled repetition of inhaling and exhaling. Loving and savoring the articulate beauty of mathematics entails being mindful of how mathematics rests in the embrace of the earth and the resonances and relationships that issue up out of the earth. It entails realizing that mathematical "forms" are not identical with our operations (Piaget 1952): We do not make these connections. They are findings, anciently perceived. We "come upon them," abstract from them in the name of clarity and distinctness, and then all too easily forget their earthly origin. In spite of this, however, and even for the professional mathematician, the cycled rhythms of breath persist as a deeper and moister "knowing" of mathematics than its professional articulations might allow, a knowing that someone (to use Jean Piaget's formulation) "at the logico-mathematical stage of cognitive development" shares with the very young child, more deeply, with all of life: a common knowing, a "kinship" that the idealizations of the "discipline" of mathematics often appear to disavow (Piaget 1952).

More pointedly, it can appear that it is precisely this disavowal of kinship that mathematics must profess in order to attain its discipline. Many of my student teachers deeply believe that clapping your hands in time to a song is not really mathematics. "Real" mathematics requires occult symbols, chalk and dust, and the mechanical repetition of the meaningless, done as some sort of terrible, inevitable penance for being only human in the face of this divine science. Here is the grand reversal that Edmund Husserl enacted with his phenomenology: It is not either necessary or possible to draw all of life up into the idealizations of mathematics and logic. Rather, our earthly life already resonates with ambiguous, living mathematical forms of which the well-bound "discipline" of mathematics is the idealization (Jardine 1990).

Realizing the mathematical character of breath is not making the sacred discipline of mathematics profane. It is tying its idealizations back (*religare*) to their generative analogical sources. It is a remembrance of its deeply earthly character. Mathematics lives and is at home here. Even its idealizations are earthly dreams, dreamt by humans. Mathematics is not only deeply about the life of the earth. It is a feature of that earthly life, laced to the logos of that home. It is the resting of mathematics in the embrace of this generative source that makes it a living discipline, one that can always be re-thought, one that can always seduce us anew with its "eloquent gestures" (Merleau-Ponty 1972, 42).

Ludwig Wittgenstein named this analogical interlacing "family resemblances" or "kinships" (1968, 32). The idealizations of mathematics are not identical to its sensorimotor, kinaesthetic, embodied analogues, but these analogues are the "kin" of mathematical idealizations. The young child, stretching out her arms and saying in an ever louder voice, "I have a milllllllion stickers at home!" is dwelling in kinships to the mathematical notion of numerical quantity—the stretch of arms, the increasing volume of voice and the stretching out of the word *million* displays a rich and ambiguous understanding of such a big (so to speak) number. The idealized mathematical notion of numerical quantity belongs here in the midst of this diversity of instantiations. That is to say, the idealized mathematical notion is not of an aloof paradigm that sits above these instances; neither does it sit at the end of a developmental sequence of these instances. It is one of the instances, belonging here, on Earth, with these other instances which are its kin, its kind.

Ecopedagogical reflection thus concerns the belonging-together-in-diversity of the full range of human understanding. It is these anciently perceived likenesses or "family resemblances" that make children our kind, them, with us, the kind of the earth. And it is this anciently perceived kinship that makes the most fundamental pedagogical (and ecological) response one of "kindness." It is these anciently perceived likenesses or family resemblances that make the earth our home, and therefore make the most fundamental ecological (and pedagogical) response also one of kindness. If these analogical links are not recovered, mathematics begins to appear to be capable of drawing up into itself and becoming identical with its idealized articulations (precisely the sort of hard, fossilized notion of science that Husserl critiqued).

We can imagine ourselves breaking the threads of kinship and likeness that bind our lives to the life of the earth (such idealization is possible, as is the forgetfulness that goes along with it). Mathematics can appear to be no longer at home here (just like our sad inheritance of the Cartesian "I think" that orients the "subjection" we bring upon the earth). Once we can imagine the threads of kinship being severed, we find that the pristine and articulate beauty of mathematics can henceforth take it upon itself to make demands upon the earth out of which it has arisen.

The clarity and distinctness of Descartes' "I think" became the criterion of any reconnection to the earth that could make a claim to knowledge—that is, we are only connected to things again insofar as that connection is forged with the clarity and distinctness of self-presence. Once the original kinship and "at-homeness" on Earth has been lost, the achieved clarity of mathematics is turned back upon Earth as a weapon of domination. The earth becomes an inert thing to which mathematics owes nothing and which it can henceforth inseminate with its own forms. Mathematics, looking upon itself in its own image, imagines that it has not issued up out of the earth, that it has no kinship to this place, that it is not at home here. For it to feel at home here, it must violate what is here by giving order(s) of its own meticulous making.

Consequently, to dwell here is not to be mindful of this place and its delicate contours, but to make this place "mind." Mathematics owes only to itself, needing nothing but itself in order to exist. (This is a paraphrase of Descartes' notion of substance, taken from the Scholastic, and earlier, Aristotelian traditions.) Mathematics is at home only with itself and with that which it produces after its own image. It cannot tolerate infestations with anything other than that which it has formed itself. Mathematics and its brethren (formal logic and the meticulous methods of the sciences) thus become the home (office) from which order(s) is (are) issued. The moist and ambiguous contours of the earth and our delicate kinships with our home become violated, colonized with demands for unequivocal clarity and distinctness. Logico-mathematical operations become the right of passage (colon—home office is where the colonized must get a "pass") for the earth. The whole earth must pass through the sphincter of Reason because (it is believed) without the organizing activity of (adult, white, male, European) human intervention, the earth possesses no indigenous "order" of its own. In the face of this colonizing impulse, the earth becomes what the colonizer has always understood any Other (women, children, foreigners, different races, creeds, colors, smells) to be: dark, disorderly, unorganized, unruly, unmethodical, unreasonable, unreliable, untrustworthy, possessing no indigenous integrity at all, in desperate need of imposed order, needing to be "whipped into shape." (Consider the potential violence in naming children "our greatest natural resource.")

Being enamored with ourselves, it becomes less and less possible to understand why the colonized refuse our gracious bestowals of law and order. Here is the final(izing) pedagogical twist: The rejection of our gracious bestowals of order become incomprehensible betrayals, pointing to the fact that we have simply not been diligent enough. How could they do this to me after all I have done? I'll have to show them. (I can't help but hear the voice of Marc Lepine.) Violence. And, sadly, violence with a pedagogic voice: We must teach these unruly Others a lesson they'll never forget.

III

The second moment of ecopedagogical reflection is blunt and obvious. For pedagogy to be possible, there must be an earth that can sustain our lives. We cannot befoul the earth that grants us breath and then, with that very befouled breath, speak of the beauty of mathematics and of our eloquent pedagogical aspirations. And, bluntly put, we do this all the time, for we bear within our hearts a long and sad inheritance (sketched in the barest of detail above) of belief in the ascendancy of Reason, of humanity, of Europe, of being male, of the potency, irresistibility, and inherent morality of our own actions, our own dominion, of the immorality of not doing anything we can conceive of doing.

And yet, the sting of ecological awareness faces this inheritance with the inevitability that it is not accumulated curricular knowledge that we deeply offer our children in educating them. It is not their epistemic excellence or their mastery of requisite skills or their grade-point average, but literally their ability to live, their ability to be on an earth that will sustain their lives. A thorough grounding in mathematics is of little use if that knowledge is understood in such a way that there is no longer any real ground that is safe to walk (Jardine 1990, 112).

There is required, in ecopedagogical reflection, a sense of breaking through the scholastic notion of substance. It is difficult to comprehend, standing as we do in the shadow of Western and Christian philosophical traditions. A substance, in this tradition, is that which needs nothing but itself in order to exist. (Consider how much of a stake we have in this notion and how it underwrites images of American democracy and individuality.) The disorienting character of ecopedagogical insight lies precisely here: anything requires everything else in order to exist. Thereby, in attempting to understand, to know, to experience any one thing, all things are ushered forth in a nest of interdependencies with this one thing—interdependencies that cannot be severed without this thing's losing its integrity, its wholeness. This makes fully naming, fully understanding, fully experiencing, fully knowing this thing impossible. And this impossibility is not a matter of the nest of interdependencies being very large and complex. Rather, understanding, knowing, experiencing, and naming are features of this nest of interdependencies.

IV

Ecological awareness begins and remains within a paradox regarding human life. We can do the impossible. The unnoticeable law of the earth preserves the earth in the sufficiency of the emerging and perishing of all things in the allotted sphere of the possible, which everything follows and yet nothing knows. The birch tree never oversteps its possibility. It is [human] will that drives the earth beyond the sphere of its possibility into such things that are no longer a possibility (and are thus the impossible). It is one thing to just use the earth, another to receive the blessing of the earth and to become at home in the law of this reception in order to shepherd the mystery and watch over the inviolability of the possible (Heidegger 1987, 109).

"The inviolability of the possible" here is not commensurate with what we can do, assuming "that the human prerogative is unlimited, that we must do whatever we have the power to do. What is lacking (in such an assumption) is the idea that humans have a place and that this place is limited by responsibility on the one hand and by humility on the other" (Berry 1983, 54–55). Human action, human will, can, so to speak, spiral out of order, out of proportion, breaking the analogical threads of kinship that might delimit our prerogative. Our truly sane, human prerogative finds itself interwoven with the earth and the fundamental dependencies and reliances that "limit" our actions, not to what is conceivable, but to what is sustainable. The problem is, of course, that we can act without having a strong sense of where we are, of what reliances and harmonies "house" us (we can leave), and we often believe that this "can" is our freedom.

Ecology (and pedagogy) remind us that if what we do despoils the conditions under which our doing can continue (if what we do befouls the earth which houses the possibility of doing anything), then such doings are not freedom, but insanity. Such supposed "freedom" is insanity if it undercuts its own continuance, its own possibility. Thus, ecology concerns not what we can do (in some Utopian sense, which is literally no place), but what is proper, what is properly responsive to the place in which we find ourselves, those actions that have propriety, those that are "fitting," and that issue up out of a place as a considerate response to that place (i.e., a response that somehow acts in accordance with the sustainability of that response). Again, this language contains the notions of family resemblance and kinship—being at home in a place. It requires action and thought that preserve the integrity of the place that houses us.

Some people are beginning to try to understand where they are and what it would mean to live carefully and wisely, delicately in place, in such a way that one can live adequately and comfortably. Also, children, grandchildren, and generations one thousand years in the future would still be able to live there. That's living in terms of the whole fabric of living and life (Snyder 1980, 86). The ecopedagogical response thus involves not just the possibility, but the necessity of returning, of renewal, and regenerativity. Reproduction is nurturing, patient, resigned to the pace of seasons and lives, respectful of the nature of things. Production's tendency is to go "all out"; it always aims to set a new record. Reproduction is more conservative and more modest; its aim is not to happen once, but to happen again and again and again, and so it seeks a balance between saving and spending (Berry 1986, 217).

Loving and savoring mathematics is preserving the ability to return to mathematics again and again. It involves preserving its generative, living character, shepherding its mystery. This means, put in the simplest fashion, that an understanding of mathematics involves attention to its integrities, dependencies, and possibilities that draw us in repeatedly. It means that an understanding of mathematics that fails to open up the possibility of being drawn in continually is, albeit unwittingly, self-degenerative. Its boundaries are unresonant, closed, fixed, allowing only the specialist to enter. An understanding of mathematics that has no opening for or toward "the new ones" unwittingly cuts itself off from its own living sources; it breaks the kinships that house its own regeneration.

It no longer knows where it is. It can thus believe that the mathematization of all things is not an act of befouling its own nest, but simply a consummation of its own indigenous destiny that needs nothing but itself in order to exist. Living somewhere as if you, your children, and their children will live there for one thousand years is, therefore, not a matter of building impermeable edifices that will remain unchanged for one thousand years. It is a matter of building things that can be returned to, that are not "finished once and for all" but that are sustainable, repairable, modifiable, changeable, adaptable, reinterpretable, renewable, and regenerable. To live carefully, wisely, and delicately is to live such that this care, wisdom, and delicacy can continue, and this sort of living-as-continuance already has room for children. Put more strongly, such living is impossible without children, for without them a continuity of attention and devotion is impossible.

V

There is a peculiar etymological twist involved in the ability to do mathematics. It is the ability to "be at home with it." *Habilité:* inhabitation, being at home with something, being able. And being at home with something is being familiar, having familialness, finding family resemblances and kinships. The parallel Sanskrit root of *kin* is *gen*: genesis, genealogy, generativity, generousness. Kin/kindness, generativity/generosity. Kindness and generosity. Affection, freely given.

VI

Where is our comfort but in the free, uninvolved, and finally, mysterious beauty and grace of this world that we did not make, that has no price, that is not our work? Where is our sanity but here? Where is our pleasure but in working and resting kindly in the presence of this world? (Berry 1988, 21). In the end, our comfort is our strength. Resting kindly in the presence of the world is resting "in kind" or "with kindness." It is resting in those kinships, reliances, and dependencies. It is in cultivating the attention and devotion required not to sever these reliances, but to sustain them, nurture them. The peculiarity of ecopedagogical reflection is that it equates interdependency, reliance, and indebtedness with comfort, strength, and freedom. The resistance to such reflection is found in our inherited belief that we gain our strength in the severing of reliances, debts, and dependencies.

Descartes' *cogito ergo sum* is a perfect example of the impulse toward severance and the equation of truth with such severance and what follows from it. Thinking we can live without "dependents" is precisely a closing out of children from our lives, and therefore, a closing off of ourselves from the conditions of generativity and re-newal. The interweaving of ecology and pedagogy requires recovering a sense of faith-fulness to these conditions, a sense of being true to the "finally mysterious beauty and grace of this world which we did not make" (Berry 1989).

But this recovery must always be chosen anew and chosen repeatedly: Mind-fulness of our place on Earth is neither simple nor inevitable, nor achieved once and for all. Fidelity to human order, if it is fully responsible, implies fidelity also to natu-ral order. Fidelity to human order makes devotion possible. Fidelity to natural order preserves the possibility of choice, the possibility of renewal of devotion. Where there is no possibility of choice, there is no possibility of faith.

One who returns home, desiring anew what was previously chosen, is neither the world's stranger nor its prisoner, but is at once in place and free (Berry 1986, 130–131). This passage makes these matters a little too grand. Our love and atten-tion and devotion to Earth is always worked out in small and meticulous ways. The full weight of our ecological and pedagogical responsibility comes to bear here and here and here, in this next gesture, this next world. The kindliness and generosity it speaks of is not a theory. It is borne out in how we live our lives on this precious Earth.

Ecopedagogical reflection thus has two vital inseparable moments. It involves the deeply spiritual attention required to be mindful of each gesture, each breath, and the cherishing of the interdependencies and inevitabilities that house us. It re-quires, in this sense, a phenomenology. Also, it requires an ability to read and be-come mindful of the violations and compromises of such attention, of the violence and severance out of which so much of our lives and the lives of our children are built. It requires being able to read these violations back into the linguistic, cultural, social, political, economic, and philosophical soil out of which they have emerged. This, too, is our "everyday life." This task, too, is a phenomenology. Without these two moments, ecopedagogical reflection becomes a romanticism that refuses to face where it actually is and the threads of culpability that bind it here and here and here.

VII

My son took his mother out into our forest and asked, in a matter-of-fact way, "Mom, this is my life tree. As long as I live, it lives. When I die, it dies, and when it dies, I die. Which one do you have, Mom?" Coupling this with thoughts of the schooling he has in store brings the horrible thought that he is bearing, for all of us: The weight of a long-standing orientation to our earthly lives that makes nonsense out of much of the life he actually lives.

This whole, longstanding edifice is brought down upon his innocent doing of this little, meaningless, mathematics worksheet. He is bearing a schooled laughter on our behalf, cut off so sharply and so easily from the deep belly laughs of springtime when he runs, unnamed and unnumbered, into the forest. His unnamed bearing is ours and he will one day ask me what I've done. But my hands are so full.

NOTE

This chapter is copyright © 2004 by David Jardine. Used with permission.

REFERENCES

Berry, Wendell. 1983. *Standing by Words.* San Francisco: North Point Press.
———. 1986. *The Unsettling of America.* San Francisco: Sierra Club Books.
———. 1988. "The Profit in Work's Pleasure." *Harper's Magazine* (March 1989): 19–24.
Fox, M. 1983. *Original Blessing.* Santa Fe, New Mexico: Bear and Company.
Heidegger, M. 1987. *Overcoming Metaphysics: The End of Philosophy.* New York: Harper & Row.
Husserl, E. 1970. *The Crisis of European Science and Transcendental Phenomenology.* Evanston: Northwestern University Press.
Jardine, D. 1990. "To Dwell with a Boundless Heart: On the Integrated Curriculum and the Recovery of the Earth." Pp. 107–19. In *Journal of Curriculum and Supervision* 5, no. 2. Reprinted in Jardine, 1998.
Merleau-Ponty, Maurice. 1970. *Signs.* Evanston: Northwestern University Press.
Piaget, J. 1952. *Origins of Intelligence in Children.* New York: International Universities Press.
Smith, D. G. 1988. "Children and the Gods of War." *Journal of Educational Thought* 22A, no. 2.
Snyder, G. 1980. *The Real Work.* New York: New Directions Books.
Wittgenstein, L. 1968. *Philosophical Investigations.* Cambridge: Basil Blackwell.

PART V

Educating for Spirit: The Quest for Heart, Character, and Meaning

Mike Seymour

SCHOOL'S OUT FOR RELIGION—BUT THEN WHAT?

The First Amendment of the Constitution guarantees religious freedom safe from governmental interference. We all breathe a sigh of relief that our dearly treasured religious or spiritual practices are not subject to state influence—especially today— in a society of far greater cultural and religious diversity than the founding fathers could have imagined. I'm glad that, when my sons were in school, they were not made to feel odd because they did not subscribe to one particular religion or another and were not proselytized by their teachers or by the system.

Removing religion from schools, however, does not mean we are free from spiritual influence on our lives. By dividing church from state, are we not leaving a vacuum to be filled by new gods—the materialistic gods of success, achievement, getting ahead, and partaking of the "American way of life?" Most pernicious is that we are blind to the fact that these lesser "gods" are eroding the spirit and moral character that traditional religions serve to develop. We don't see, or don't care enough, that our very reticence about matters of faith, heart, and spirit—in itself—greatly

185

diminishes every child's inner life and tends to undermine each child's religious and spiritual fiber.

To avoid something is to minimize it—to cloak it in shadows, fear, and controversy. The unspoken communication in avoidance implies that faith and spirituality are something that *can* (or *should*) be avoided or are best relegated simply to a "personal matter." In fact, matters of faith and spirit *can never be avoided*. The gods are ever with us; Their names change according to what we place faith in and give significance to. That might be science, our own ingenuity, money, or a charismatic person. Moreover, our individual paths are inseparable from our relationship to others, whether we are Christian, Jew, Buddhist, Hindu, or none of these.

This section joins the growing chorus of voices on all sides of the aisle—some calling for more godly schools, others for character education in school, and some for spirituality in education. All voices in the choir realize that we have a crisis of character and morals in our society and in our schools. Additionally, some recognize that this moral and spiritual crisis lies at the center of our problems in learning. The motivation to learn has as much to do with spirit and meaning as anything else we could talk about. So, as spirit and meaning leave the classroom, so goes the fire that ignites young minds.

SPIRIT IS THE WATER IN WHICH WE LIVE

In each individual, the presence of spirit reveals itself as a natural part of human life from a young age. We all have childhood stories of spirit making itself known in ordinary or extraordinary ways. As a child, you may have gazed in wonder at the sunset and marveled as its magnificent beauty, stirred by something within you that could not easily be put into words.

Spirit infuses our curiosity. I recall the time when my then three-year-old son David seized on several small sticks, promptly tied them together with some string, and wove them through the air, happily making whirring sounds and saying, "Look Dad! An airplane." A child surprises us with a question about where the cat goes when it dies or does God mind if we sneak a spoon of peanut butter before dinner, and we pause to wonder where those thoughts come from. Perhaps we observe our child's rapt attention for story-time—and, afterwards, they say, "That felt good." One of the most obvious signs of spirit is in our child's joy and effervescence.

Spirit is the water in which we all live. It is as natural to us as the fingers on our hands. But since we cannot see spirit with the naked eye, the thought of consciously experiencing ourselves as spiritual beings does not necessarily occur without guidance. We need a conscious spiritual literacy and the benefit of traditional wisdom to help us live more fulfilled and meaningful lives.

Religions, wisdom traditions, and indigenous knowledge all provide a spiritual roadmap to guide people in their quest for personal truth, authenticity, and moral growth. What happens if we are not guided by a conscious spiritual literacy? What happens if our spirituality is limited or colored by religious sectarian bias? What if our spiritual natures are compromised by the materialistic world in which we live? What if the people we live with and learn from have no language of the heart?

We suffer a spiritual and moral crisis.

This is where we find ourselves today, both in society and in our schools—which too often fail our children and their teachers by not meeting them in the most important spaces in their lives.

SPIRITUALITY VERSUS RELIGION

Spirit is a universal energy that gives life a sense of aliveness. All religions recognize a universal spirit or life force within and around all beings. Spirit, however, is not confined to religious life and practice. It is the energetic river connecting all life and matter.

Spirituality is not bounded by religion. Nurturing the spirit is something we could integrate into our notions and practices in education. But, for a number of reasons, we have avoided the issue of spirituality in school—the main "reason" being our concern about trespassing on students' rights or raising parents' concerns. Another reason is the widely held belief that spirituality lives primarily within religious experience, which teachers feel guarded about discussing. However, as Rachael Kessler notes in her book, *The Soul of Education*, it is legal to have students discuss their beliefs—providing teachers do not impose their belief on students. In walling off spirituality from the classroom, we have widened the rift between the sacred and the secular, between the inner and outer lives of our young people and ourselves.

A COMMON SACRED GROUND

Writers in this section give us hope that there is not only an emerging realization of the need to address spirit and meaning in education, but that there are also practices that help mature the spiritual lives of children and teens without violating religious principles and the separation of church and state.

All the subjects we teach resonate with their own mystery when we comprehend them in their rightful and larger context. As Rachael Kessler and Parker Palmer make clear, the teaching day is full of wondrous, teachable moments in which we can stir young hearts and help children see the beauty and connectedness in life.

We have a way to go in understanding how to fashion the language and practices that would provide a common, sacred ground that is acceptable to parents and children of diverse religious and secular perspectives. As we move forward cautiously, we must remember the urgent dangers in how the strict privatization of moral and spiritual discourse in our society is contributing to social division, loss of public good will, and moral illiteracy. We must see our way through to making a language of the heart and spirit a core purpose in education.

SPIRITUAL INTELLIGENCE AND MAKING MEANING

Following his ground-breaking work in multiple intelligences, Howard Gardner (in *Intelligence Reframed*) considered spirituality as a possible intelligence, understanding it as the desire to know about and experience a cosmic domain beyond our five senses. While spirituality, defined this way, fell short of his tight criteria for an intelligence, Gardner did feel comfortable considering our existential yearning and questioning as signs of an additional intelligence which he calls "existential intelligence." The writers in this section make a strong case for education that helps young people to encounter the enduring and significant questions of life. Children's intellectual formation cannot be divorced from their spiritual formation. We cannot authentically engage children's minds when their deepest questions are neither sought nor received.

An aspect of spirituality, existential intelligence deals with issues of ultimacy, or our most significant and often transcendent questions. From earliest times, humans have pondered the stars, built burial mounds to house the dead, and wondered about death, life, and the ultimate fate of themselves and the world. Such reflections are not purely intellectual. They stem from a deeply emotional predisposition in our nature to wonder, question, and make meaning about who we are in relation to the vast, magnificent, and highly complex universe in which we live. Holocaust survivor and psychoanalyst Victor Frankl said we can endure much physical deprivation but not a loss of meaning and purpose in our lives.

In *SQ: Spiritual Intelligence: The Ultimate Intelligence* (2000), Danah Zohar and Ian Marshall make a strong case for spiritual intelligence, or SQ, and explain its importance in healthy reasoning (IQ) and emotional ability (EQ): "By SQ, I mean the intelligence by which we address and solve problems of meaning and value, the intelligence with which we place our actions and our lives in a wider, richer meaning—giving context, the intelligence with which we can assess that one course of action or one life-path is more meaningful than another. SQ is the necessary foundation for effective functioning of both IQ and EQ. It is the ultimate intelligence" (4).

To Zohar and Marshall, SQ is the ultimate intelligence because it integrates thought and feeling, enabling a coherent experience of the world. SQ also plays a central role in the brain's neurological development and our potential for value formation, growth, transformation, and the evolution of human potential.

EXPERIENCE OF MYSTERY AND BEAUTY

A group of young people sits in a circle, becomes quiet, and then listens deeply and respectfully as each one shares a story about herself or himself. Something this simple evokes a presence, a sense in the heart, that can be felt. Creating a space for the heart in school calls on teachers to lead by being emotionally open, vulnerable, and hospitable to the inner life in themselves and in their students. When we rest in the stillness of our being together, we make space for spirit to emerge. When we hurry, are anxious, or are trying to "do something" or "get somewhere," the sensitive, feeling part of us is closed down.

Similarly, the spirit in our subjects can be liberated as we uncover the mystery in them. Do we have minds to understand and hearts to feel the mystery of a tree, the sacred origins of mathematics, the exquisite beauty of a Beethoven symphony? The very fact of our being deeply moved by anything is, in itself, a wonder of this human life and the very core of our humanity. The experience of mystery and of the beauty in life is the common ground and a foundation for spirit in education.

CHARACTER AND THE MORAL LIFE

No parents want their children moralized according to someone else's values. Yet, most parents want a school culture and curriculum that enhances positive character attributes and moral literacy. Who would argue against the need to nurture our young with a prosocial awareness, an inclination to think about the ramifications of their actions, and the need to weigh the complexities involved?

We know from experience that children have an innate capacity for moral judgment, which is part of their spiritual predisposition to make their experience coherent. Children's moral formulations cannot be avoided.

Robert Coles's early work with Ruby Bridges was significant in opening his eyes to the moral nature of children. Ruby was one of the black children who, in the face of abusive, even violent, resistance, initiated school desegregation in New Orleans. Her mother told Coles that Ruby prayed every night for those in the mob who threatened and harassed her.

> I think of the many black children my wife and I came to know, in Arkansas and Louisiana and Georgia and Alabama and Mississippi—and of the white children too, who braved awful criticism to befriend them. . . . Whence that moral capacity, that moral spirit, that moral leadership? How are we to make sense of such moral behavior in psychodynamic terms? (Coles 1986, 8)

Coles speaks of children having a different "moral notice" than adults; the issues and circumstances they find morally compelling are linked directly to their lives. Abstract moral issues, values that don't emerge from lived experience, simply find no place in the concrete logic of a young person's thinking. So, concerns about who pushed who and why, or why did so-and-so get more time on the slide, or how come we are bombing that country—these and a host of other issues are the food for a child's moral diet.

For these reasons, educators in this chapter (and others) argue for moral and character development in the context of young people's lived experience. The classroom, playground, or sports field becomes the mirror to life in which moral reflection can be deepened in children. Moral lessons must not be separated from the spirit of the moment. The most opportune time to talk about kindness—or what it feels like to another when you say something hurtful—is in the immediacy of life.

REFERENCES

Coles, Robert. 1986. *The Moral Life of Children.* New York: Atlantic Monthly Press.

Kessler, Rachael. 2000. *The Soul of Education: Helping Students Find Connection, Compassion, and Character at School.* Alexandria: Association of Supervision and Curriculum Development.

Gardner, Howard. 1999. *Intelligence Reframed: Multiple Intelligences for the Twenty-first Century.* New York: Basic Books.

Zohar, Danah, and Ian Marshall. 2000. *SQ: Spiritual Intellgence: The Ultimate Intelligence.* New York. Bloomsbury Publishing.

18

A Vision of Schools with Spirit

Linda Lantieri

As did many reading these pages, I read Schools with Spirit, *the book Linda Lantieri edited in 2001. I did so with great enthusiasm, not only for the articles, but also for the fact that such an important subject was being addressed by someone held with such a high regard in the education community. Linda Lantieri has over thirty years of experience in education as a teacher, administrator, university professor, and an internationally known expert in social and emotional learning and conflict resolution. She serves as the founding director of the Resolving Conflict Creatively Program (RCCP) of Educators for Social Responsibility, which supports the program in 400 schools in the United States. She is also the director of the New York satellite office of the Collaborative for Academic, Social, and Emotional Learning (CASEL), whose central offices are at the University of Illinois at Chicago. Linda is coauthor of* Waging Peace in Our Schools *(1996) and editor of* Schools with Spirit: Nurturing the Inner Lives of Children and Teachers *(2001).*

> Education should be a source of nurturance for the spirit as well as a means of reaching understanding.
> —Linda Darling-Hammond

This essay is dedicated to all children who would benefit from having their inner lives more present in our classrooms, and to the adults who have the courage to help evoke that change. A bold new vision for our schools is needed—one that reclaims them as soulful places of learning where the spiritual dimension is welcomed. My intention here is to explore some of the possibilities and practicalities of creating such a movement and the role you and I can play in it.

I would like to make it clear at the outset that I am not talking about the teaching of religion or religious doctrine, but about ways to attend to what I would call the spiritual life of young people while respecting both the wide range of religious convictions held by many in our diverse and pluralistic society and the more secular worldviews shared by others. The kind of spiritual development I am advocating is not about allowing schools to display the Ten Commandments in their classrooms. I am concerned with fostering and inventing educational approaches that encourage a commitment to those matters of the heart and spirit that are among the positive building blocks of healthy development.

Because this is a complex topic, perhaps the best place to begin is with a bit of personal history.

I've always considered it a great blessing that my occupation and my vocation have coincided—that my professional life has also been my calling. For more than three decades now, I have worked in the field of public education. I have worn many hats: classroom teacher, school administrator, education activist, college faculty member. For the past sixteen years, I've served as the director of one of our country's largest and most successful efforts to teach social and emotional skills in the classroom—the Resolving Conflict Creatively Program (RCCP) of Educators for Social Responsibility. Throughout my career, I have always felt that the education of young people involved not only their intellectual, emotional, and social development but also their spiritual growth. However, the challenge of connecting the inner life of mind and spirit and the outer world of secular education is not an easy one to meet, because, for several reasons, our society seems to have built an almost impenetrable wall between the two.

When I began teaching in a fifth-grade classroom in East Harlem in 1968, I was only twenty years old. I couldn't even vote in the presidential election and yet I was entrusted with nurturing the hearts and minds of thirty-seven children. My training for this task was barely adequate in many ways, but one thing I did know for certain: I was to remember the First Amendment's separation of church and state. I don't recall a time when any education professor or school official actually went over the specifics of what this meant, but it had seemed to me that I was forbidden to discuss with my students those vital questions about life's purpose and meaning that all of us must confront. I had been raised in a faith-based home, and my spiritual experience was and is a central and defining aspect of my life. But this part of me, I concluded, was not welcome in any form in my classroom or my teaching. And so my very rewarding life as a teacher was also a divided one. I realize in hindsight that as long as I was fully present with those thirty-seven children, which happened often, my inner life was being expressed. But it didn't feel that way at the time, and I suspect my experience is not unique.

I was asking myself the most basic of questions: How can I teach my students well? What am I doing here at this school, in this world? I soon noticed that the children at P.S. 171 were often confronting deep questions as well. Depending on how old they were, they were even asking the questions out loud. Among the youngest, what I would call the spiritual dimension was still integrated enough into their lives that they hadn't yet learned to repress it. During the first week of school, a six-year-old came up to me in the lunchroom, told me his name was Jason, and asked, "Where did my grandmother go when she died?" I remember saying something like, "Maybe you should ask your mother. We can talk about it sometime, but not now." I now regret that I didn't answer, "That's an interesting question, Jason. I also wonder about that. What do *you* think?" (Then, and now, perfectly permissible, by the way, under the Constitution.)[1]

As a fifth-grade teacher, though, I didn't often hear this kind of question from my own students. By the time they were nine or ten, it seemed that young people's thoughts about such matters had gone underground. Excluding the promulgation of religion from publicly funded schools, it appeared, had somehow come to mean that nurturing the inner life was not the business of public education. So both children and teachers have had to leave their deeper questions about the mysteries of life at home. I have spent the last several years in the field of public education, struggling with what it would mean to allow those questions back into the classroom—to live, as Parker Palmer puts it in *The Courage to Teach* (1998), "divided no more"[2] Is it possible for schools to nurture the hearts and spirits of students in ways that do not violate the beliefs of families or the constitutional principle of the separation of church and state that safeguards our religious freedom? Although this is a difficult question to answer, many educators are beginning to acknowledge that teaching the whole child can include welcoming the wisdom of a child's soul into our classrooms. The original intent of the First Amendment was to protect our nation from the establishment of any specific religion or dogma while giving all citizens the right to freely express their own beliefs. Certainly it was never meant to suffocate such an important part of life as our spiritual experience—rather the opposite.

But how this aspect of human existence can be addressed in public schools is still a thorny matter, and I am well aware of how far I am deviating from the status quo in suggesting such a thing. Indeed, numerous well-meaning colleagues have tried to warn me against doing so, and I've thought long and hard about rocking the boat. Luckily, I've had a little practice. In the 1980s and 1990s, we wouldn't have imagined that public schools would embrace the teaching of conflict resolution or emotional intelligence as a normal, natural part of the curriculum, yet I've spent the last decade playing my part in making that happen. So I'm no stranger to mustering up the courage to say and do what I know in my heart will be better for children and teachers.

I take this risk because I strongly feel that the dilemmas of our times are deeply spiritual ones that our children need to be prepared to meet. Most of our young people growing up today, from the poorest to the most affluent, are imprisoned by our obsession as a culture with material things. They get the message early on that to feel good about themselves or to feel the love of their family, they need to own the latest *Star Wars* toy, designer sneakers, or fancy car. We are teaching children, by our example, that we should look to the outside for meaning, not the inside. We are, in Dr. King's words, "judging success by the index of our salaries or the size of our automobiles rather than by the quality of our service and our relationship to humanity" (Children's Defense Fund 2000).

By not welcoming the sacred, by not considering "that which is worthy of respect," as Palmer puts it, our schools run the risk of raising a whole generation of young people who will be bereft of the wisdom and connectedness they need to live a fully human life.

Having been in the field of violence prevention in schools for so many years, I'm concerned that we don't make the same mistake twice. Amidst the social crises of the 1980s and 1990s, we waited for young people to really get in trouble, even kill each other, before we responded with programs to create safe schools in our inner cities. More recently, we have seen a number of high-profile killings, including multiple murders linked to suicide by the perpetrators, among young people in the more affluent suburbs. These environments differ, as do the particulars of each individual case of "senseless" violence, but the common threads include fatalism, despair, and a lack of human connectedness. I hope we have learned from that past not to wait for more and more young people to lose their sense of positive meaning and purpose before we invite spirit into education.

Webster's defines *spirit* as the "animating or vital principle held to give life." It is the spiritual dimension of our lives that helps us to place our actions in a wider, richer context. I am only one of a number of educators, social scientists, and concerned citizens who are beginning to explore the role of public schools in nurturing a broader, deeper vision that takes us beyond ourselves and gives us and our actions a sense of worth in the context of community.

For me, this vision has deep roots in a very specific experience and history. The Resolving Conflict Creatively Program, which I cofounded in 1985, started as a joint initiative of Educators for Social Responsibility/Metropolitan Area and the New York City Board of Education. Today, under the auspices of Educators for Social Responsibility's national office, I serve as the director of a very successful research-based K–12 curriculum and training program that is now reaching more than 400 schools in eight states, with beginnings in Brazil, England, and Puerto Rico.

From the very start, our aim was to create safe, caring school communities. Over the years, as we worked with teachers, administrators, young people, and parents, I started to notice that sometimes our efforts reached beyond our aim of equipping children and adolescents with practical skills in conflict resolution. The insight and courage that some of our young people exhibited in the most difficult of circumstances seemed to be more than the byproduct of a good prevention program. I began to think about how to intentionally foster the inner strength and resilience that made this possible.

SPIRITUALITY AS BELONGING, CONNECTEDNESS, MEANING, AND PURPOSE

When we open a discussion of nurturing children's and teachers' spiritual lives, it's important to say exactly what we are talking about. Although connected to moral development and ethical principles, nurturing the spiritual is neither. Morality is about right and wrong, and although certain basic moral principles seem to be universal, their interpretation is often heavily influenced by custom and culture, and may lead to judgmental attitudes and/or separation between people and groups of people with different cultural values. The word "spiritual" often conjures up religious dogma, a set of beliefs and practices one might have, and although religion can indeed be an expression of one's spiritual nature, it too can be divisive, and many people nurture the spiritual dimension of their lives without adhering to a specific religion.

The definition of *spiritual* that we are exploring here encompasses a realm of human life that is nonjudgmental and integrated. It is about belonging and connectedness, meaning and purpose. Spiritual experience cannot be taught. But it can be uncovered, evoked, found, and recovered.

Humans have the capacity for creativity, for love, for meaning and purpose, for wisdom, beauty, and justice. All these are aspects of our spiritual lives. When they are evoked, the experience is often subjective and intense. Apollo 14 astronaut, Captain Edgar Mitchell, describes it this way:

> On February 9, 1971, when I went to the moon, I was as pragmatic a test pilot, engineer, and scientist as any of my colleagues. But when I saw the planet Earth floating in the vastness of space . . . the presence of divinity became almost palpable and I knew that life in the universe was not just an accident based on random processes. It was a knowledge gained through subjective awareness, but it was— and still is—every bit as real as the objective data upon which the navigational program was based. (The Institute of Noetic Sciences 1998, 1)

Spiritual experience can be described as the conscious recognition of a connection that goes beyond our own minds or emotions. It's the kind of experience that sometimes leaves us without words to describe it.

Most of us have experienced this essence of our human spirit in powerful encounters with nature—from witnessing a glorious sunrise to being captivated by the sound of ocean waves as they meet the shore, from watching ants toil in the dirt to contemplating the moon and the stars. Or we may have been deeply moved by a piece of music, by a painting or a story, or by a certain soul-to-soul flow between ourselves and someone else that lifts us beyond the mundane. Swiss psychologist Carl Jung used the term "synchronicity" to describe meaningful coincidences that are so timely that they seem beyond chance. If we have engaged with intensity in a sport or in physical labor, we may have experienced the "high" of a sensory experience that brings a natural spiritual release. And social issues or work within a community can arouse our passions and connect us to a consciousness that touches what I would call the divine within us.

What would it mean to nurture these experiences in schools in more intentional ways so that our classrooms could be places that facilitate spiritual growth? In the "schools of spirit" that I envision, the following would be true:

- The uniqueness and inherent value of every individual would be honored and education would be seen as a lifelong process;
- Students and teachers alike would be engaged in inquiry, exploring and learning about what has heart and meaning for themselves. Different ways of knowing would be respected—those we could test for and others too subjective to be measured—and we would pay as much attention to whether a student has a sense of his or her purpose in life as we do to his or her SAT scores;
- School leaders would shift from a centralized concept of power to approaches that help individuals and groups to self-organize;
- We would be less concerned with the kind of school spirit that comes from winning a football game and more concerned with the spirit of collaboration and partnership, and with an appreciation of diversity within the school community;
- We would acknowledge our interconnectedness with one another and with all of life, by a commitment to ecological principles, environmental limits, and social responsibility;
- We would enlarge our ability to put to use our gifts of intuition, imagination, and creativity, and we would value personal change as a vehicle for systemic change and social justice; and
- There would be places and time for silence and stillness, to help us face the chaos and complexity of life yet stay in touch with inner truth and the web of interconnectedness.

In short, I believe we need to see schools as active and alive organisms that place a high value on self-knowledge, healthy interpersonal relationships, the building of community, and care for our planet. These goals are not incompatible with the pursuit of academic excellence—indeed, they foster it—and without care, respect, and kindness, what purpose does intellectual competence serve?

Recently, the RCCP released one of the largest scientific evaluations of a school-based social and emotional learning program ever completed. The results supported the conclusion that two years of teaching five thousand young people concrete skills in managing their emotions and resolving conflict actually interrupted developmental pathways that could otherwise lead to violence and aggression. When I had the privilege of being on a panel with Archbishop Desmond Tutu, soon after the presentation of this report at an Appeal for Peace international conference at The Hague, he twinkled when he heard of the study's results. "By the looks of things," he joked, "we could be in deep trouble. Imagine these peace-making skills being incorporated throughout a child's entire education. I'm not sure we would have enough people in the world who would be willing to kill or be killed in wars or who would want a job that has the power to press the button that could cause a nuclear holocaust."[3]

As we step into the new millennium, we are holding in our individual and collective hands the opportunity to use our civilization's new knowledge and advances for unbearable evil, devastation, and moral breakdown—or for goodness, trans-formation, and hope. The choices we make today regarding how we nurture our children's development will have critical implications for generations to come. Even as we make huge advances in the world of technology and our understanding of the brain, in this country, we are struggling to rescue generations of young people who are growing up without the supports they need to feel valued and to participate in community. Although Yale psychiatrist James Comer tells us: "We are doing the least harm to the most privileged," according to the Annie E. Casey Foundation's *Kids Count* report for 1999, 21 percent of American children still live in poverty and "are growing up with a collection of risk factors that are profoundly unsettling." Many young people today are cut off from an understanding of their lives as having a "higher purpose"—or any purpose at all. Many have trouble even imagining what their future will look like. Psychiatrist James Garbarino, author of *Lost Boys,* calls this terminal thinking, which he warns can undermine young people's motivation to contribute to their community and invest in their present life circumstances. He also discusses what he calls juvenile vigilantism, speaking of violent boys who have lost confidence in the ability of adults to protect and care for them and so join gangs in order to feel a little safer.

Too many young people experience mental health and adjustment difficulties, and our schools don't have the resources to provide appropriate help and attention. It is estimated that one out of five nine- to seventeen-year-olds has a diagnosable men-tal disorder (Shafer et al. 1996, 865–77). The fact is that an increasing number of children are entering schools in crisis—unprepared cognitively and emotionally to learn—while educators confront the challenge of higher public expectations and di-minishing internal resources to do their jobs well.

This complex set of social conditions tries the best of us who work in public education. Instead of fostering meaningful discourse, tolerance of divergent think-ing, and the opportunity to get to know ourselves and each other, most public schools today look more like what social psychologist Alfie Kohn calls "giant test prep cen-ters." In most, the deeper questions of life have been put on the back burner. As educators, we are somewhat aware of this void, yet we are not sure what to do about it. Many of us recognize that a one-size-fits-all standardized system of education may have been useful during the industrial age but will not be adequate to prepare our children for living together in the new millennium.

In my work with teachers, principals, and parents, I've asked hundreds of groups in the United States and other countries: If you could go to bed tonight and wake up in the morning with the power to ensure that you could teach one thing to all the children of the world, what would it be? The responses are similar no matter where I am or whom I ask: That children feel loved, that they know they have a purpose, that they learn tolerance and compassion, that they have a sense of their interconnectedness with other people and with the natural world. As educators, how can we not con-sciously and systematically attend to that which we dearly feel matters most?

In a recent survey of 272 "global thinkers" from around the world, five shared values emerged: compassion, honesty, fairness, responsibility, and respect (Loges and

Kidder 1997). These values seem to be so universal that it appears that they are agreed upon regardless of one's religious or spiritual perspective. And when the American Association of School Administrators asked fifty education leaders a similar question—(What would students need to know and be able to do to thrive during the next century?)—civility and ethical behavior were on the list along with math and science (Uchida et al. 1996, v). So we seem to agree on some of the fundamental tasks of education, and that these tasks extend beyond helping young people stay out of trouble and achieve academic competence. However, we have not yet outlined the steps needed to strengthen these shared values.

When we look carefully at the literature on resilience—those capacities that foster healthy development—we find an attempt to coordinate the social, emotional, moral, physical, and cognitive development of young people. Researchers and practitioners who focus on resiliency go beyond the identification of risk factors such as poverty and social dislocation to the study of how young people's strengths and capabilities can be developed in order to protect them from the potential harm that these circumstances represent. This body of research has direct relevance for our concerns about the nurturing of the inner lives of young people. For example, the Search Institute studied over 100,000 sixth through twelfth-graders in 213 towns and cities throughout the United States in order to identify the "building blocks of healthy development" that assist young people in choosing positive paths, making wise decisions, and growing up to be caring and responsible adults. The Institute's research identified forty positive experiences or qualities, called developmental assets, which have a significant, positive influence on young people's lives (1997, 1–4).

According to the Search Institute, the presence of these assets serves to protect young people from engaging in problem behaviors and harmful and unhealthy choices ranging from alcohol and drug abuse to gang violence and attempted suicide. Several of them pertain to what I would describe as their inner lives:

- *Service to others*—serves in the community one hour or more per week;
- *Religious community*—spends one or more hours per week in activities in a religious institution;
- *Creative activities*—spends three to four hours per week in lessons or practice in music, theater, or the arts;
- *Caring*—places high value on helping others;
- *Integrity*—acts on convictions and stands up for his or her beliefs;
- *Honesty*—tells the truth even when it's not easy;
- *Personal power*—has a sense of control over "things that happen to me;"
- *Sense of purpose*—reports that "my life has a purpose;" and
- *Positive view of personal future*—is optimistic about his or her personal future.

This kind of research points to some of the ways in which our educational institutions can contribute to positive outcomes for youth. The facilitation of these protective factors is important for both adults and young people, and clearly, it involves developing inner strengths that can serve to prevent or repair harm.

Another trend in educational theory that has paved the way for nurturing children's spirits in schools is the social and emotional learning movement. Howard Gardner, with his "multiple intelligences" model, was instrumental in this expansion of our concept of intelligence. The "personal intelligences" Gardner first outlined in the early 1980s included intrapersonal intelligence, which involves knowing and managing one's own feelings, and interpersonal intelligence, which is the ability to understand and get along with others. (He has since considered the addition of three new intelligences to the list. They include a naturalist, a spiritual, and an existential intelligence. While the evidence to support the inclusion of each is varied, Gardner's ideas have a lot to do with the kind of abilities or capacities that schools with spirit would promote) (1999).

Social psychologist Daniel Goleman, author of the best-selling book *Emotional Intelligence* (1995), has contributed much to our thinking about the need to nurture the social and emotional lives of children. He summarizes research from the fields of neuroscience and cognitive psychology that identifies emotional intelligence (EQ) as being as important as IQ in terms of children's healthy development and future life success. He writes:

> One of psychology's open secrets is the relative inability of grades, IQ, or SAT scores, despite their popular mystiques, to predict unerringly who will succeed in life. . . . There are widespread exceptions to the rule that IQ predicts success—many (or more) exceptions than cases that fit the rule. At best, IQ contributes about 20 percent to the factors that determine life success, which leaves 80 percent to other forces. (1995, 34)

Goleman's work helped educators understand the importance of emotional intelligence as a basic requirement for the effective use of one's IQ—that is, one's cognitive skills and knowledge. He made the connection between our feelings and our thinking more explicit by pointing out how the brain's emotional and executive areas are interconnected physiologically, especially as these areas relate to teaching and learning. The prefrontal lobes of the brain, which control emotional impulses, are also where working memory resides and all learning takes place. Goleman's summary of recent neuroscientific research has made us aware that when chronic anxiety, anger, or upset feelings are intruding on children's thoughts, less capacity is available in working memory to process what they are trying to learn. This implies that, at least in part, academic success depends on a student's ability to maintain positive social interactions. As a result of Goleman's work, schools across the country have begun helping children strengthen their EQs by equipping them with concrete skills for identifying and managing their emotions, communicating effectively, and resolving conflicts nonviolently. These skills help children to make good decisions, to be more empathetic, and to be optimistic in the face of setbacks.

Many school systems across the country have used the frameworks developed by social scientists to bring together under one umbrella various different efforts for preventing "risky" and/or antisocial behavior among young people. This approach acknowledges that the development of social and emotional skills is a critical factor in school-based prevention efforts, and it calls for an integration of the cognitive and affective domains for all students as a means of enhancing their chances for academic and personal success.

In the late 1990s, Danah Zohar, a visiting fellow at Oxford University, and Ian Marshall, a practicing psychiatrist, did for spiritual intelligence what Daniel Goleman did for emotional intelligence. Zohar and Marshall brought together an array of recent research that showed evidence that there is an "ultimate intelligence based on a third neural system in the brain"—a spiritual intelligence (2000).

Spiritual intelligence, or SQ, as Zohar and Marshall call it, is "the intelligence with which we address and solve problems of meaning and value, the intelligence with which we can place our actions and our lives in a wider . . . context." They point out that neither IQ or EQ can fully explain the complexity of human intelligence or richness of the human soul. Computers have high IQs; animals can be highly sensitive to their owner's moods. The "why" questions—asking how things could be better or different—and the ability to envision unrealized possibilities or to wrestle with questions of good and evil are all in the realm of SQ. Zohar and Marshall call spiritual intelligence the ultimate intelligence because it is the necessary foundation for the effective functioning of the other intelligences and because it has a transformative power:

> My emotional intelligence allows me to judge what situation I am in and then behave appropriately within it. This is working within the boundaries of the situation, allowing the situation to guide me. But my spiritual intelligence allows me to ask if I want to be in this particular situation in the first place. Would I rather change the situation, creating a better one? This is working with the boundaries of the situation, allowing me to guide the situation. (2000)

Zohar and Marshall's work attempts to distill what scientific evidence we do have concerning this realm of experience, even though they are the first to admit that existing science is not well-equipped to study something like meaning and its role in our lives. They also outline some of the competencies, skills, or qualities of a "spiritually intelligent" person:

- *A high degree of self-awareness*—knowing who we are, what our strengths and limits are, what we live for;
- *The capacity to be inspired by vision and values*—a caring that transcends self-interest, a sense of service;
- *The ability* to *face and use suffering and transcend pain*—learning from mistakes, our own and those of others; acknowledging our weaknesses and cultivating our strengths;
- *A holistic worldview*—an ability to see connections between diverse things and take "the bigger picture" into account;

- *An appreciation of diversity*—being grateful for differences that challenge our assumptions and values and help us grow;
- Being *"field independent"*—possessing the capacity to stand against the crowd or work against convention;
- *Spontaneity*—the ability to be flexible and actively adaptive;
- *A marked tendency to ask "why" or "what" questions and seek "fundamental" answers;* and
- *Compassion*—a reluctance to cause unnecessary harm.

British researchers David Hay and Rebecca Nye, coauthors of the book *The Spirit of the Child,* have done research on the lives of young children that suggests that spiritual awareness and expression may be a natural predisposition, a biological reality that is a given of the human condition and a byproduct of evolution. Among the areas of childhood experience they link to the spiritual dimension are an intense awareness of being "here and now" as opposed to living in the past or the future, an awareness of the mystery of life, and an intensity of feeling about what we most value.

To investigate such elusive concepts, Hay and Nye asked children to respond to a series of photographs depicting subjects such as a girl gazing into a fire, a boy looking out at the stars, a girl mourning the death of a pet. Their first and most important finding was that, although they scrupulously avoided prompting for religious concepts, they did not come across a single child without a sense of spirituality. Indeed, the majority of the children in their sample did not come from faith-based homes and had very limited religious vocabularies but used the language of fairy tales or science fiction to express what Hay and Nye call "relational consciousness," that is, an intense awareness of relatedness—to god, to nature, to other people, or to self.

Clearly, such a predisposition connects closely to ethical and moral behavior. It helps us begin to make the link between damage to oneself and damage to others, care for oneself and care for others. Acknowledging these connections between social and moral development and the implications of research on spiritual awareness in young children can help us begin the dialogue about what the content of a spiritual curriculum might include.

How successful will we be in welcoming spirit into our secular schools? It will depend on how honestly those of us who are struggling to live an integrated life are willing to talk about and share our struggle with our more skeptical colleagues. And we've got a few challenges ahead of us in terms of giving this movement some momentum.

First, we have to continue to redefine what it means to be an educated person. This is a worldwide challenge to widen the vision of education beyond mastering a body of knowledge as measured on standardized tests. Even teachers who use our well-established RCCP are telling us that they are hanging on by a thread to make room for teaching our curriculum.

It will help to meet the educational field where it is by acknowledging that academics are, and always will be, central. The new vision of "soulful" education that

I am writing about has the potential of producing students who not only have direction and purpose in life but are also emotionally and socially skillful, *and* more academically competent as well. It is not an either/or situation and we have to communicate that.

The second challenge is for adults to let young people show us how we can help them cultivate their inner lives, including openness and creativity. J. Robert Oppenheimer, one of the pioneers of nuclear energy, once said, "There are children playing in the streets who could solve some of the top problems in physics because they have modes of sensory perception that I lost long ago." Exploration, innovation, and creativity often come more easily to children and young people, and children are interested in life's most basic questions. Our task is to remember how integrated young children's spirituality is and to find ways to protect it from being trampled. This is part of what Nancy Carlsson-Paige of Lesley University calls teaching the whole child.[4]

Sadly, as children move through our schools, they often receive spoken and unspoken messages that extraordinary experiences related to their inner lives are not honored as part of their reality. The older they become, the more repressed, forgotten, and locked within themselves this awareness and these experiences become. Adolescence offers an opportunity to reopen this line of inquiry, yet young people at this stage are usually met with the adult tendency to ignore or trivialize transcendental experiences. What complicates matters is that few of us have experienced as learners the kind of holistic education we want to put into practice as teachers. If we hope to be a part of bringing this work into schools, we will each need to find positive models and experiences that can show us how to live and teach in a more integrated way. In my own case, as a senior scholar at the Fetzer Institute (a foundation that investigates the implications of mind-body-spirit unity), being a part of this community over a three-year period was one such experience.

The third challenge we face in welcoming children's inner lives into our public schools is developing a common vocabulary for how we talk about these things. How can we create a common ground for discussing the ultimate questions of meaning and purpose? For some of us, various words that I've used in this essay may have been an obstacle. Perceptions of terms like *sacred, inner life,* and *spiritual* are different for different people. We haven't yet developed an inclusive way to describe this realm of experience. We also need to find practices and approaches in the classroom that celebrate and respect the diversity of our individual religious and spiritual beliefs. We need to find ways to talk about these concerns that are as palatable to an evangelical Christian as to someone whose inner life is not defined by a specific religion. It will be important for schools and districts to reach a consensus through a democratic process in which decision making includes all of those affected. It is only through building trust and truly listening to one another that fair guidelines can be developed for discussing matters of belief and values.

The fourth challenge is to root this work in scientific research, as well as in sound pedagogy and child development theory. Most child development theory has focused on personality development and on the emotional and intellectual realms;

only rarely does it consider the spiritual or intuitive dimensions of experience. However, recently we are seeing more and more studies that point to the benefits of nurturing children's spiritual development. Current research in social/emotional learning and positive youth development has already begun to make this connection; it is important that we encourage further work in this direction.

The fifth challenge is how to go about integrating the inner lives of students into the curriculum of a school district. I believe that this calls for a process very different from what we see happening in the prevention field or in the field of social and emotional learning, in which we institutionalize innovation by standardizing promising practices. To nurture children's spiritual development, I don't think we will need to implement programs or create teachers' guides with prescriptive directions. Instead, this movement will rely on people—teachers, parents, principals—who are committed to the idea of reaching the whole child and to sustainable systemic change that will make that possible. I hope we won't write scripts that tell us the right things to say; we will have to improvise and evaluate our effectiveness by means other than test scores. Practitioners will have to be the "change masters" Angeles Arrien talks about—designing, developing, and sharing flexible approaches to this domain. [5]

Finally, we can't think about doing this work in classrooms without supporting teachers in the nurturing of their own inner lives. Many of us want to help young people find deeper purpose and meaning, but we can't give what we don't have. In *The Courage to Teach*, Parker Palmer writes, "We teach who we are."

> Teaching, like any truly human activity, emerges from one's inwardness. . . . As I teach, I project the condition of my soul onto my students, my subject, and our way of being together. . . . Knowing myself is as crucial to good teaching as knowing my students and my subject. When I do not know myself, I cannot know who my students are. . . . When I do not know myself, I cannot know my subject—not at the deepest levels of embodied personal meaning. (1998, 2)

Soul work isn't about giving our students a road map. This teaching must flow from the quality of each teacher's own inner life.

Box 18.1 is a self-assessment tool for organizing our thoughts about how we might begin to welcome what I have called the spiritual domain into our classrooms—how we can more intentionally create a larger space in our schools for children's inner lives.

Nel Noddings, educator and author of *The Challenge to Care in Schools*, beautifully sums up the kind of education we are advocating:

> I have argued that education should be organized around themes of care rather than traditional disciplines. All students should emerge in a general education that guides them in caring for self, intimate others, global others, plants, animals, and the environment, the human-made world and ideas. Such an aim doesn't work against intellectual development or academic achievement. On the contrary, it supplies a firm foundation for both. (1995, 679)

Box 18.1 A Self-Assessment Quiz

1. Is there a sense of community in your classroom?
2. Do both you and your students feel comfortable sharing thoughts and questions about values, meaning, and purpose?
3. Do you encourage respect for diversity of opinions, beliefs, and cultural backgrounds among your students?
4. Are there opportunities in the school day or week to appreciate the beauty of a work of art or to allow students to make art—poems, pictures, sculptures, music, drama—themselves?
5. Do you provide regular activities to explore and spend time in nature? Are elements from nature present in the classroom?
6. Do you and your students have ample opportunity through studying history or through storytelling to honor the power of ancestors and the past?
7. Is there some free time in the school day, including time for silence and reflection?
8. Do you have the flexibility to allow for moments of spontaneity in which intuition redirects a discussion or an activity?
9. Are there opportunities for students to become involved in volunteering, or to participate in community or social action projects?
10. Do you and your students feel that most of what is being taught and learned is authentic, meaningful, and useful?

And Daniel Goleman writes:

> This new focus moves some of the key elements of emotional intelligence into a deeper dimension. Self-awareness takes on a new depth of inner exploration; managing emotions becomes self-discipline; empathy becomes a basis for altruism, caring, and compassion. And all of these basic skills for life can now be seen as building blocks of character. (2001, ix)

A window of opportunity exists right now in the field of education for soul to enter. The advocates of character education have provided a framework that respects the vital constitutional principle of the separation of church and state. We must use this opening to broaden our work even further, and we need to support one another and engage people of all persuasions in this unfolding process.

Our mission is to insist that we develop policies and approaches that enable all of our children to have their human spirits uplifted and their inner lives nourished as a normal, natural part of their schooling. It will take enormous courage and energy to work across the existing boundaries. Far from being marginal or irrelevant, attention to our inner life of mind and spirit will help us achieve the equilibrium we need in this chaotic world; we must foster the compassion, insight, and commitment to community that will be necessary to tackle the deep emotional, social, political, and spiritual dilemmas of our time.

As I look at the huge problems our young people will inherit—racism, poverty, violence, the degradation of nature—I can't imagine how we will make it if we neglect soul. My hope is that each of us finds a way to act to make sure that no child is left behind and that every aspect of the human spirit is welcomed in our homes, communities, and especially our schools.

NOTES

This chapter was first published in *Schools with Spirit* by Linda Lantieri. Copyright © 2001 by Linda Lantieri. Reprinted by permission of Beacon Press, Boston.

1. The clause of the First Amendment regarding religion reads, in its entirety, "Congress shall make no law respecting an establishment of religion." At the very least, this means the U.S. Constitution recognizes religious faith as a fundamental right of the individual, superseding government intervention. In interpreting this amendment with reference to public education, the U.S. Supreme Court has clearly supported the study of religion, as well as the inclusion of religion in the curriculum in historical and cultural contexts. Public school teachers are not to advocate a particular point of view, but they may accept the expression of young people's religious views as germane to an open discussion, a homework assignment, or any other academic project. Freedom of religious expression in schools does not include the right to force a "captive audience [to] listen or to compel other students to participate" in religious activities or discussions, but it does allow individual students to pray, read scripture, discuss their faith, and even to invite others to join their own particular religious groups, as long as this is not coercive or disruptive to others.

Although school officials may not organize religious activities, including prayer, they may lead a group in a moment of silence. The use of music, art, drama, and literature with religious themes is also permissible if it serves an educational curriculum goal, as long as this does not become a vehicle to promote a particular religious belief. See U.S. Department of Education, "Religious Expression in Public Schools: A Statement of Principles," June 1998.

2. Parker J. Palmer writes and teaches on issues of education, community, spirituality, and social change. *The Leadership Project* has named him as one of the thirty "most influential senior leaders" in the field of higher education today.

3. Archbishop Desmond Tutu, remarks during the Appeal for Peace International Conference, The Hague, Netherlands, May 12, 1999.

4. Nancy Carlsson-Paige teaches social development and early childhood education, and is cofounder, with Linda Lantieri, of the masters degree program in Conflict Resolution and Peaceable Schools at Lesley University.

5. Angeles Arrien is an anthropologist, educator, and author who is also president of the Foundation for Cross-Cultural Education and Research.

REFERENCES

Annie E. Casey Foundation. 2000. *Kids Count Databook: State Profiles of Well-Being 1999.* Baltimore, Md.: AECF.

Children's Defense Fund. 2000. *The State of America's Children.*

Gardner, Howard. 1999. *Intelligence Reframed: Multiple Intelligences for the Twenty-first Century.* New York: Basic Books.

Goleman, Daniel. 1995. *Emotional Intelligence.* New York: Bantam Books.

———. 2001. *Schools with Spirit: Nurturing the Inner Lives of Children and Teachers.* Edited by Linda Lantieri. Boston: Beacon Press.

Hay, David, and Rebecca Nye. 1998. *The Spirit of the Child.* London: HarperCollins.

The Institute of Noetic Sciences. 1998. Program Brochure. Sausalito, Calif.: 1.

Loges, W. E., and R. M. Kidder. 1997. *Global Values, Moral Boundaries: A Pilot Survey.* Camden, Maine: Institute for Global Ethics.

McLuhan, Marshall, and Quentin Fiore. 1984. *The Medium Is the Message.* New York: Bantam.

Noddings, Nel. 1995. *The Challenge to Care in Schools: An Alternative Approach to Education,* 3rd ed. New York: Teachers College Press.

Palmer, Parker J. 1998. *The Courage to Teach.* San Francisco: Jossey-Bass.

Shafer, D., P. Fischer, et al. 1996. "The NIMH Diagnostic Interview Schedule for Children," *Journal of the American Academy of Child and Adolescent Psychiatry* 35.

Search Institute. 1997. *The Asset Approach: Giving Kids What They Need to Succeed.* Minneapolis, Mn.:1–4.

Uchida, Donna, Marvin Cetron, and Floretta McKenzie. 1996. *Preparing Students for the Twenty-first Century.* Arlington, Va.: American Association of School Administrators.

Zohar, Danah, and Ian Marshall. 2000. *Spiritual Intelligence: The Ultimate Intelligence.* London: Bloomsbury.

Making Meaningful Connections in School

Nancy Carlsson-Paige

Nancy Carlsson-Paige is professor of education at Lesley University and a co-founder of Lesley's masters degree program in conflict resolution and peaceable schools. For more than twenty years, Nancy has been studying both the effects of violence—especially media violence—on children's social development and how children learn the ideas and skills for caring relationships and positive conflict resolution. She has coauthored four books and many articles on media violence and its effects on children and how children learn the skills of conflict resolution. She is the author of Best Day of the Week, *a children's book about conflict resolution. I was delighted to finally meet Nancy on a trip back to Boston. I found her to be a kindred spirit and a compassionate advocate for all the values expressed in this book.*

From their first days of life, children are trying to make sense of things. They actively engage with the world around them, exploring, manipulating, and interacting with everything and everyone within reach. Just watching a baby lay a piece of string on top of a shoe as if it were a shoelace or a toddler cover up a stuffed animal before bed reminds us that children's actions have purpose and meaning for them. This striving to make meaning involves a child's thoughts and feelings as one inseparable whole.

The mounting body of literature known to many educators today as constructivist education is united by the central idea that children actively construct meaning for themselves. These meanings, unique to each child, are embedded in family and culture. They are built over time and shaped by the developmental changes that occur throughout childhood and adolescence. New learning builds on what is already known, in an active, hand-over-hand process. Because of this, a basic aim of education should be to begin with children's personal meanings as the basis on which to build new learning.

LOSING ONESELF IN SCHOOL

When children enter school, they bring with them their natural capacity for making meaning. But for many children, arriving at school means leaving some of themselves behind. Much of school curriculum requires children to meet the demands of tasks that do not build on their understanding; the emphasis on right answers begins early to separate children from themselves.

A student teacher in my seminar wrote this in her journal:

A First Grade Classroom
Jasper sat with the worksheet page on two-place addition in front of him. He was supposed to add 35 and 23 in the first problem. I came over and saw that he was trying to add the numbers horizontally instead of vertically! He didn't understand at all what he was doing. I've done Piagetian number tasks with Jasper and I know he doesn't even conserve numbers yet! This assignment can't make any sense to him. He needs to be working on pre-number concepts with manipulatives. He was getting so frustrated and upset. He said to me, "I think I'm gonna cry. Do I go down? Go down, right? I don't know what to do." I tried to help him even though I knew this was all wrong. He got more and more upset so I finally suggested he stop. The head teacher came over and said, "If he was made to do it through recess, you'd see how quickly he'd learn it."

Unfortunately, in school, experiences like Jasper's are not uncommon. When children are expected to complete tasks that are not geared to their understanding, they become confused, begin to feel inadequate, to doubt their own ability to make sense. More and more children are experiencing this separation from self as schools try to meet the requirements of standards-based reform and high-stakes tests.

As schools become increasingly driven by standards, tests, and accountability, teachers spend more and more time teaching to tests: The curriculum narrows and students have less and less of a role to play in their own learning. Their capacities for making meaning through drawing, drama, music, social exchange, and inner exploration are increasingly left out of school curriculum. Schools today look more like what social psychologist Alfie Kohn calls "giant test prep centers" (Lesley University's Peaceable School Conference 2001). In this climate, the aspects of the school curriculum that young people most need for the world they are living in and will inherit are disappearing: the social curriculum, multiple ways of knowing and being, multicultural curriculum, and civic engagement—aspects that engage their minds, hearts, and spirits in authentic, whole experiences that have meaning and purpose for them. This is a time when young people are in profound need of this kind of education both for their lives today and for their lives as citizens inheriting the global, multicultural world of the future.

A CULTURE THAT SEPARATES

In the United States, one percent of the population holds forty-eight percent of the wealth and twenty percent of children still live below the poverty line. A host of risk factors such as violence, poverty, racism, and poor health add up to what James Garbarino (1995) calls a "socially toxic environment" for many children. These risk factors are compounded by the negative effects of the media-driven commercial culture, with its aggressive marketing campaigns aimed at children and youth. In the last decade, children have become a major target of corporate marketing. Corporations spend more than $12 billion a year marketing to children—well over twenty times the amount spent a decade ago. Many young people growing up today, from the poorest to the most affluent, are imprisoned by our culture's obsession with material things. From an early age, they get the message that to feel good about themselves or to be accepted, they need to look a certain way, to own the latest *Star Wars* toy or designer jeans.

Children spend more than thirty-five hours per week consuming media outside of school, much of it violent (Kaiser Family Foundation Report 1999). The hours spent alone in front of a screen rob children of vital social lessons they need to be learning from spontaneous play and interactions with peers. The lost hours of positive learning with peers are replaced by interactions with antisocial media messages. By the end of elementary school, the average child will have witnessed 8,000 murders and 100,000 other acts of violence on television (Diamant 1994).

In addition to the pervasive influence of media and the commercial culture, children and youth today are struggling to make sense of a world where war and the threat of terrorism create a climate of fear, violence, and uncertainty. Many students in the United States have had difficulty understanding the events of September 11, 2001, in a broader context and wonder whether they are still living in a meaningful universe. A third-grade boy said recently about the war on Iraq: "They want to kill Saddam Hussein but they are killing a lot of other kids in the process." Children need help making sense of what they hear about the world. They need to be able to bring their feelings, thoughts, and questions to school where they can work through them in a climate of safety and support.

The need for schools to become communities that embrace the wholeness of the human experience is greater now than ever before. But the current standards-driven educational climate has edged out the social curriculum and driven even a bigger wedge between curriculum expectations and children's needs and views of the world. This is a time when the need for attending to the inner lives, deeper selves, and spiritual longings of students is crying out for educators' attention.

Even in this climate, when schools are weighed down by the demands of curriculum standards and testing, many educators continue to implement a kind of education that is meaningful and relevant to young people of all ages. They are finding ways to provide students with authentic experiences that actively engage their heads and their hearts. They are learning that schools can be places where young people practice constructive ways of being with others and learning about the world at the same time that high academic standards are met (Aber, Brown, and Henrich 1999). Schools can be places that not only promote in the young a unity of one's sense of self but also an interconnectedness to others and a sense of meaning. What do classrooms that nurture this kind of wholeness look like?

CONNECTING TO SELF AND TO OTHERS

Classrooms that nurture every aspect of a child's being are places where activity thrives, where different points of view are embraced and respected, where curriculum is based in the real concerns and interests of students. Classrooms such as these employ structures that foster connection among students. One such structure is the class meeting. Although class meetings look different at different grade levels, they are always rooted in the interests, feelings, and needs of students.

Kirsten's kindergarten classroom is in an urban public school. Kirsten holds daily class meetings where children are free to talk about their schoolwork and their lives. She listens a lot, for the meanings behind what children say.

At one class meeting, Carlos asked if he could share something with the class. He began to talk about the fighting that had happened at his house over the weekend. Here's how Kirsten tells what happened:

> Carlos asked if he could share something with our class at sharing time. He said that his parents were fighting over the weekend and it made him feel scared. Then he said, "I'm ready for questions and comments." One of the students told him they were sorry that had happened. Another student wanted to know if they were fighting with words or with their bodies. Carlos told him that it was a fight with words, but it was really loud and lasted for a long time. He felt really scared because he wasn't sure what to do. The same student wondered if they fought a lot, and Carlos told him that they didn't which was why he was so scared. When all of the questions were finished, we asked Carlos what we could do to make him feel a little bit better. He thought we could send him lots of love and hugs (something that our class sends to each other when we are feeling sad or vulnerable).
>
> During lunch and nap time, my student teacher and I talked a lot about this because Carlos had obviously been very upset and the children had a lot to say. We talked about our own feelings when we heard arguments between family members as children. We decided to focus afternoon work time on this idea: What happens when you hear or see other people fight? How do you feel? We centered this in four areas of the classroom:

Writing: In the middle of the table we wrote: "When I see people fight, I feel
_____."

Art: We taped the words *angry* and *sad* on the four sections of the easel and
children painted pictures of how those emotions looked, times that they had felt
that way, and what they did when they felt angry or sad.

Dramatic Play: Children built houses out of blocks and used our play people to
act out fights and arguments and what happened afterward.

Table Top: We put out small wooden cubes and teddy bear counters for the
children to act out arguments and what might happen when arguments occur.

Before work time, I talked with Carlos to find out if there was an area where he
would like to be in charge to re-create what happened with his friends around to
help him work through it. He really liked that idea. "You mean I get to show what
really happened?" he asked. He chose to be in charge in the dramatic play area. The
other children rallied around the idea of Carlos being in charge. They wanted him
to feel better about the whole thing.

Our work time was spectacular. Everyone had their own experiences to draw
upon to enrich what was going on in each area. Magical conversations occurred
between children at the easel as they were painting. At the table top, the "fight"
pulled in more and more teddy bears until there were so many that the children
decided to have the police come to stop it. Children were writing down their feelings at the writing table, as well as specific incidents where they had seen people
fighting. In the dramatic play area, Carlos directed the construction of his house
and how the fight occurred. The children with him had ideas about what the Carlos
doll could do when he saw the fight; they were actually giving him strategies for
how to cope with a situation like this in the future!

I am lucky to own a digital camera, so I took pictures of each of these areas
during work time. At our afternoon circle, we talked about what happened in the
areas and I took notes. I told the children that I was going to try to write on the
computer what we had done so we could post it in our class. The next day a few
children illustrated a few key pieces of our book and I assembled it that night: the
writing, digital pictures, and student illustrations. We laminated it and posted it on
the back of our easel so we could all see each page.

Several times throughout the year Carlos would talk about "that time that I was
in charge in the blocks when my parents were fighting." He later told me that the
students in our community are his friends and he knew they could make him feel
better; that is why he shared that day. What a testament to the amazing children in
our class and the safety they create for each other.

Kirsten understood right away that Carlos had said something very significant to the
class. He had described a potent family scene and his feelings of fear. I have heard
many teachers quickly dismiss similarly potent statements made by children in school,
but Kirsten wants a classroom climate where children feel safe expressing what is of
true meaning to them.

Kirsten gave Carlos her full attention. She acknowledged his feelings of fear. She understood that the children listening might have stories similar to Carlos's or that they might feel worried this could happen to them. She wanted to help all of the children explore and work through the powerful feelings that arise around a topic such as this and to come to some sense of closure; even to feel that they have some ideas about what to do in emotionally charged situations.

Kirsten and her student teacher spent time talking together about their own childhood experiences with family fighting, making space in their planning time for their own feelings. They planned curriculum activities that helped children construct their own understanding of conflict. They used open-ended materials, which allowed for children's experience to come forth in a dynamic mix with the materials and the ideas of others. The open-ended nature of these tasks invited children to bring their full personal and cultural identities into the process. There was room for the children to invent their own story and invent a safe ending for it. Children were engaging in the active process of making meaning through play that can transform and heal. This opened up an avenue to feelings of empowerment and generosity as children gave their ideas and strategies to Carlos.

In these activities, academic skills such as literacy and math were connected to the meaningful content of children's lives, instead of being taught as isolated skills to be learned apart from experience. The book Kirsten made captured children's first-hand experience in writing and with pictures. Deep personal meaning fueled the children's interest in literacy; the pages spoke of their reality in their own words.

Meetings such as this can be a part of school throughout a student's school life. They provide a way for students to talk about what matters to them—to discuss problems, share feelings, and make decisions as a group. Because the content for class meetings is rooted in the experience of the students in the class, there is always an opportunity for building community—for connecting to oneself and to others. At the same time, class meetings give students first-hand experience with the tools of dialogue, perspective-taking, and democratic decision making—tools that students will carry with them into other parts of their lives and into the future.

The Child Development Project, a comprehensive school-change effort to help elementary schools become inclusive communities and supportive places to learn, has made class meetings a central focus of their approach. Their materials show how meetings are the glue of the classroom community; they provide many developmentally based suggestions for how to hold meetings with both younger and older elementary students. For example, teachers can build on the experiences children have had in earlier grades with older elementary students but use techniques that fit their changing needs and interests. For example, teachers can make decision-making processes more explicit: "What we just did was called 'reaching consensus.'" And teachers can present problems for discussion that are relevant to this older age group: "I would like to have a discussion about ways we form friendships or 'small groups' that benefit our community and ways we form groups that detract from our community" (Development Studies Center 1996). Presenting a problem in this way can be cognitively interesting to older elementary school children who like to categorize, reflect on their behavior, and compare things. As students engage in a meeting such as this, they are connecting meaningfully to themselves and each other, in addition to building values and social skills: how to see their own needs in relation to the needs of a larger group; how to listen effectively and respect different points of view; and how to reach a shared understanding with others through dialogue.

In her curriculum guide entitled *Partners in Learning,* Carol Miller Lieber emphasizes how important class meetings are to the optimal functioning of a learning community in secondary school. High-school students are able to take more responsibility for generating the agenda and facilitating class meetings. As they become comfortable, students can take on the roles of facilitator, summarizer, note taker, time keeper, and person who gives feedback. In so doing, they are practicing the many skills that have been used in class meetings throughout their school experience, but integrating them at a level suited to their development. High-school students can hold meetings on many topics, some of which are unique to their age group such as discussions on hypothetical topics (e.g., What would a world without wars be like?) and discussions about schoolwide issues such as policies, events, and ways to change the overall school climate (Lieber 2002).

MAKING CONNECTIONS TO SOCIAL JUSTICE AND THE WIDER WORLD

Schools can be places where children of all ages connect to themselves and others in their community in meaningful ways. They can also be places where caring connections to the wider world are fostered. Teachers can engage even young students in activities that build meaningful connections to issues of social justice; within these they can integrate academic skills as tools for learning about issues of importance rather than as ends in themselves.

Even young children can begin to care about the wider world when it arises from an issue in their immediate experience. A good example occurred at Pacific Oaks Children's School in Pasadena, California. There, a parent who was wheelchair-bound was driving one of the children to school every day. The children in the class began realizing that the parent had nowhere in the school lot to park because there was no handicapped parking space. Teachers helped the children think about this problem: What do we know about where handicapped people park their cars? What could we do at the school to help this situation? Eventually, the children decided to make a handicapped parking space at their school. With help from their teachers, they went outside, figured out where and what size to make the new parking space, drew it, mixed paint, and then painted it. They "wrote" their own tickets with the teacher's help and put them on cars that parked in the spot "illegally." When an issue of social justice such as this one is rooted in the direct experience of young children, and when they have a chance to invent a solution to a problem and carry it out themselves with concrete steps, it is a meaningful and empowering experience for them. Academic skills such as math and literacy can be integrated into authentic experiences such as this one that empower children, connect them to the wider world, and to their own growing sense of social justice.

Teachers can work with children of all ages in this way; as children grow and change, so will the approaches and techniques teachers use. *Rethinking Globalization* (Bigelow and Peterson 2002) is a book packed with examples of teaching about world justice issues to children as young as nine and ten years of age. In his fifth-grade class, Bob Peterson uses simple stories and a problem-posing approach to help students connect their own lives to the lives of children they don't know. He tells his class that 30,000 children die daily from malnutrition and preventable illness. He asks, "How many schools with the same student population as ours would it take to equal the number of children who die each day?" In this way he creates a math lesson just right for his students' developmental level that helps raise their awareness of a social justice issue.

To begin to introduce issues of globalization, a complex topic that many would say is too abstract for fifth-graders, Bob Peterson places a shopping bag in front of the class and asks the students to guess what's inside. He pulls out a T-shirt, a McDonald's Happy Meal toy, and a Nike shoe. He asks how far these items have traveled. At first students answer, "from McDonald's" or "from the store." Then, he has students come up and read where each item is from. As a class, they locate the country on the world map. For homework, students do a "Where Are My Things From?" activity in which they list ten household items, the brand names, and where they are made. In school, they share their lists and label and color maps that show the origins of their things. These activities integrate math, reading, social studies, and science skills. Later, he shows the video, *When Children Do the Work*, which portrays the harsh conditions child workers endure. He uses photos of child laborers to spark poetry writing. These concrete experiences connect these fifth-graders to other children in the world and to a larger social justice issue. Invariably the students ask: "What can we do?" and he helps them figure out how they can write letters, buy things made in places that don't use sweatshops, educate young children about the issue, and set up their own organizations. One year, his students set up a No Child Labor Club that included third-, fourth-, and fifth-graders. Among other things, they marched at a rally sponsored by labor organizations against NAFTA and two of the children spoke there. A curriculum experience such as this one connects to the students' deep sense of what matters most; they are inspired and activated as their minds and hearts connect to other children through an issue of social justice.

Bill Bigelow, author of *Rethinking Schools*, has designed many different activities on globalization for his high-school students that are presented in his book. Through these activities, secondary students begin to discover some of the abstract economic and political concepts underlying globalization. They participate in a simulation that Bill invented, called Transnational Capital Auction: A Game of Survival, and learn how governments lure transnational corporations with attractive investment climates that maintain low wages, use child labor, and harm the environment. Through acting out roles as Third-World elites trying to attract corporate investors, students come to understand abstract concepts such as capital and the complex social, economic, and ecological consequences of globalization. They look at global sweatshops and, through poems and videos, students see the lives behind the products they buy. Students are encouraged to write in the voices of those who make these products for pennies an hour—clothes, soccer balls, and Barbie dolls—and to feel what their lives are like. Students look at the "Nike Code of Conduct" and do a "loophole search" that makes full use of their critical thinking skills. Toward the end of the unit, Bill steers his students to their final project—to do something positive with the knowledge they have gained. He gives them a "Making a Difference" assignment sheet full of possible ways to take action within or outside of school.

Some of the projects students have developed include giving presentations on global issues to other classes, writing articles for local papers, and writing letters to Phil Knight (CEO of Nike) and to the Disney Company. One student discovered that, at the five nearby Portland schools, the soccer balls were made in Pakistan, where children as young as six who work in factories making these balls are sold and resold as virtual slaves and treated with extreme cruelty. This student wrote to the school district's athletic director, describing the conditions under which the soccer balls are made, and asked school officials to rethink their purchasing policies.

This entire unit from beginning to end captures the developmental energies of adolescents: their sense of justice and their ability to imagine a better world; their ability to think abstractly and critically and to relate complex ideas; their ability to empathize with how someone else feels and to imagine their life through role playing, drama, and writing. This unit accomplishes academic goals at the same time that it captures the momentum unleashed by the developmental changes of adolescence and gives it meaning and purpose through new knowledge, awakened compassion, and social action. This is the kind of education that inspires young people to care about the world by building connections that grow from authentic experiences rooted in issues that have meaning for them.

CONCLUSION: A CHANGING VISION OF EDUCATION

These are difficult times in education. Outside forces such as state standards and high-stakes testing, the influence of a violence-saturated commercial culture, and life in a country preoccupied with the threat of war and terrorism put conflicting pressures on teachers: a more holistic, student-centered curriculum is needed at a time when it is harder for teachers to provide it. At a time when students need a curriculum to help them cope with the world in which they are living, and to learn the concepts, values, and skills they will need for the world they are inheriting, many classrooms are stepping backward into a pedagogy driven by predetermined content that leaves little room for the needs and passions of students.

Even under the weight of conflicting political and cultural forces, many teachers are finding ways to draw in and nurture every dimension of humanity that children bring to school. Inspiring educators are showing us how to put the principles of a new kind of education into practice with real curriculum content for students of various grade levels. They are showing us how schools can teach academics in a broader context of social values through a kind of teaching that will outlast any rise in test scores. But, we need to work for these exceptions to become the norm in education today. We need to insist that schools develop policies and approaches that enable all young people to have their ethical, political, social, and emotional selves welcomed, their spirits uplifted, and their capacity for active, meaningful learning fully engaged as a normal, natural part of their education. We need nothing less than compassionate, insightful, and committed young people and adults who will learn how to do the extraordinary things necessary as we tackle the profound political, emotional, social, and spiritual issues of our time.

NOTE

This chapter is copyright © 2003 by Nancy Carlsson-Paige. Used with permission.

REFERENCES

Aber, J., J. Brown, and C. Henrich. 1999. *Teaching Conflict Resolution: An Effective School-Based Approach to Violence Prevention*. New York: National Center for Children in Poverty.

Bigelow, B., and Bob Peterson. 2002. *Rethinking Globalization*. Milwaukee, Wisconsin: Rethinking Schools, Ltd.

Developmental Studies Center. 1996. *Ways We Want Our Class To Be*. Oakland, Calif.: Developmental Studies Center.

Diamant, A. 1994. "Special Report: Media Violence," *Parents Magazine* 69, 40–41: 45.

Garbarino, James. 1995. *Raising Children in a Socially Toxic Environment*. San Francisco, Calif.: Jossey-Bass, Inc.

Kaiser Family Foundation. 1999. *Kids and the Media at the New Millennium: A Comprehensive National Analysis of Children's Media Use*.

Kohn, Alfie. 2001. Presentation at Lesley University's Peaceable Schools Summer Institute at Lesley University, Cambridge, Mass.

Lieber, Carol Miller. 2002. *Partners in Learning*. Cambridge, Mass.: Educators for Social Responsibility.

Quart, Alissa. 2003. *Branded: The Buying and Selling of Teenagers*. Perseus Publishing.

Making Space for the Mystery: Reawakening Life and Spirit in Teaching and Learning

An Interview with Parker J. Palmer by Mike Seymour

After the first interview on authentic living and learning, I devoted the rest of my time with Parker to discussing the role of spirit in education. This lively dialogue between us generated its own momentum and creativity well beyond what I had planned. I now have a deeper appreciation for the role of mystery in awakening our wonder and love of the world.

MIKE SEYMOUR: We learn most from teachers who couple a true passion for their subject with a respect and caring for those they teach. So let's talk about the spirit in teaching and what it is that animates learning.

PARKER J. PALMER: My thoughts about teaching are rooted in some reflections on what it means to know. We've had this outmoded, objectivist idea of knowing which assumes that to know anything well you must stand at a distance from it, holding the object of knowing at arm's length. Supposedly, this keeps our subjectivity from messing up the truth of the thing itself. But in the past sixty years, there has been a revolution in our understanding of how we know. Truth is known not by building a wall of separation between the knower and the known but through engagement and relationship. The biographies of many great scientists—like Barbara McClintock, for example—are stories of love, passion, and a deep relationship to a subject. If relationship is the heart of knowing, then it has to be the core of teaching as well,

217

because teaching is about inducing knowing, creating the conditions under which knowing can happen.

Then we start thinking about all of the things that make relationships possible—not only between a teacher and his or her subject, but between a teacher and his or her students. Intuitively, we know a lot about what makes relationships possible. We know, for example, that if someone tries to present themselves as perfect, it is really hard to relate to that person. Most of our relationships happen in the broken or open or needy places in our lives where our humanity shines through. So, vulnerability is integral to making teaching and learning come alive. When teachers understand and operate from their own need to be related to students because of what teachers don't know, wonderful things start to happen in a classroom.

For example, teachers can employ question asking as a technique, hoping to get students involved in learning. But if you already know the answer to the questions, you are really testing the student's knowledge, which means you are not asking out of your own need to know. Students catch on quickly and sit back, figuring the teacher will get frustrated with the silence and eventually give them the answer—so why should we, as students, have to invest ourselves? On the other hand, when you ask out of your own need to know, your vulnerability creates a space that invites students in.

So, vulnerability is certainly a condition for a spiritual quality of aliveness in learning. Hospitality is another. Hospitality is about making space inside oneself to receive, to be interested in and learn from the stranger, which brings something new into the learning experience.

SEYMOUR: Strangers or guests in the Hebrew and other traditions were always received in the belief that they just might be "angels of God." In teaching and learning, I take this to mean that revelation, like the teachable moment, emerges from our unknowing, from surprise, and from how we welcome unexpected guests.

PALMER: Exactly. The stranger always brings insights that are alien and stunning—and that we ourselves could never have thought up because we are caught in our own mindset. So the act of hospitality, as Henri Nouwen notes, is always more of a gift to the host than to the guest because it brings knowledge that enlivens you.

I am convinced that when a classroom is not hospitable, real rigor is not going to happen. A classroom becomes rigorous, for example, when students are willing to raise their hands to disagree with the teacher or with another student—or to admit that they don't understand anything the teacher has said! Those behaviors invite rigor because they force us to explain ourselves, to interpret, to look at things from different angles or to go over the ground again. But those vulnerable acts of asking honest questions, admitting ignorance, or disagreeing will not happen if the classroom is a place of combat or fear rather than hospitality.

SEYMOUR: I want to connect what you're saying about hospitality and making an opening for spirit with your suggestion that spirituality is about the heart's longing or burning for the largeness of life. This brings to mind a great example of hospitality—when the two disciples on the road to Emmaus meet the risen Christ whom they don't recognize. This seems to me a great story about how the stranger or guest in our midst enlarges our lives.

PALMER: Yes. The disciples were walking home defeated and discouraged by the crucifixion which seemed to have destroyed everything they believed in. They meet this stranger on the road who asks why they are downcast, and they say "You must be the only person in town who doesn't know what just happened,"—which turns out to be one of these comically ironic points in scripture! Then the disciples ask this stranger to come with them and have dinner. They finally understand during the breaking of bread—as "their hearts burned within them"—that the person they have been talking to is the risen Christ. Revelation, the story tells us, comes from the act of hospitality.

There are two movements in this tale about the gift of mystery that the stranger or "otherness" brings to us. One is that burning in the heart, the sense that something important is happening here that defies explanation. That's a movement of intuition, of empathy or inner self-awareness. The other movement is a simple, explicit, outer act of hospitality, of setting out the food. Translated to the classroom, this is when teachers keep asking those questions, setting out problems to be solved, inviting life stories to be shared so that a journey can be taken together. Do that often enough, with purity of heart, and you will find yourself with a sense of amazement that something remarkable is happening.

SEYMOUR: The teacher here is the lead questioner, authentically musing about life and this questioning is part of the food, so to speak, that is set out on the table.

PALMER: Yes, and at the same time, we want to honor the fact that the teacher has knowledge that students don't have that can also feed them. We're talking about a rhythm where the teacher as lead questioner, with authentic questions, invites students into the mysteries that help engage students with the world, and helps them past the walls of ignorance that keep them from stepping into the mystery.

SEYMOUR: Teachers both orchestrate and are orchestrated by the larger context of learning and its mystery, and their knowledge arises at the moment it is called for. When well given, the piece they bring feeds everyone, including themselves.

PALMER: The parallel that comes to mind is a good Outward Bound instructor who shows you how to jam the piton into the rock, or how to hold your body when rappelling down the cliff. This knowledge is essential—but the true teacher is the rock and gravity and your bodily experience of them.

SEYMOUR: So, if the spirit in teaching and learning is about relationship and experiencing the world, like the rock, as teacher, it seems crucial that teachers retain the wonder about their subject. This is another way of saying they need to stay at the borders of their unknowing. But when we tell teachers what to do, or when expertise is emphasized (being good means knowing a lot), teachers quickly lose the mystery and spirit, and get trapped within the finite borders of [both] their own and the institution's thinking. We only get to a place of unknowing when we realize that whatever subject we teach has no borders. For instance, geology is connected to cosmology and is the context for all the subsequent processes of animate life. Maria Montessori suggested that we can't understand anything without also understanding the whole cosmos. We have to recontextualize our discipline within the much larger sphere which maintains the mystery, and therefore sustains our own childlike wondering, which fires the same in those we teach.

PALMER: I can't imagine not being on the borders of my own unknowing. As a writer, people sometimes treat me as if I were the master of whatever subject I write about. The only reason I write a book is that it is about something I haven't figured out, something that baffles me—and writing is simply my next stage of exploration into that bafflement. If I had mastered something, I would never write a book about it—because it would be too boring! But if I write to probe the frontier of my own sense of mystery, then the book has meaning for me. So the book or the teaching takes me the next step into this *terra incognita*, this unmapped territory.

SEYMOUR: What happens when teachers run out of the mystery and the aliveness goes away? How do they keep the spirit alive?

PALMER: This is a complicated question. Sometimes things simply die for us. We need discernment to know when we truly need to move out of a field or profession—or go deeper into it and find a new wellspring of inspiration. Part of the sadness of the life of an educator is that people are required to stay in the same discipline year after year, and so they often dry up by being locked into something that no longer engages them. Knowing when you need to find the next great thing that is alive for you—or when you need to probe more deeply into what you haven't yet fathomed—takes patience and courage.

In the Courage to Teach program, we see a lot of teachers who renew their sense of vocation in part by renewing their relationship to their subject. They revisit those early moments of excitement and insight and realize that those moments are still available to them if they just twist the prism a little and look at their subject in a slightly different way. But other teachers come to understand that they are no longer called to this field, that math or literature has died for them, or maybe that they are no longer called to teaching itself. Some in this situation wonder if they should continue in the Courage to Teach program—and we always say we are not here simply to advocate for teaching, since the person of the teacher is far bigger than their work. We try to help them make good judgments about what is true and alive for them and how that translates into the next step of their journey—where that deeper calling of their life now is.

In this society we have a very hard time acknowledging that something has simply died! We want to pretend that it hasn't. So, part of honoring aliveness is acknowledging the death of interests and passions. When something is not engaging you, maybe the issue is not that it's no longer alive for you, but that you are no longer alive to yourself or to the world. In that case, I think we go back to an earlier moment in our conversation when we were talking about all the ways we have of anesthetizing ourselves because we don't want to take risks or face the fears that being alive involves.

I am very taken with a Guatemalan writer named Julia Esquivel whose collection of poems has the stunning title *Threatened with Resurrection.* This is a striking set of words because we usually take death as the great threat and resurrection as the great hope. But the truth is that we often cling to living deaths because we fear the vitalities of real life. Embracing new life takes us into fearful places within ourselves. You might have to change your line of work, you might have to change your way of thinking. I love this insight that resurrection can be even more threatening than death.

SEYMOUR: Let's talk about hearing the voice of what we study. You've said—about a poem—that the most objective voice in the room belongs to the poem itself. Some more literal-minded people might argue that believing that a poem or a tree can speak to us is fanciful, just a matter of our imagination, that we are making it up and that the subject has no life or inwardness of its own. How do you answer that kind of objection when people say it's just imagination or just an unreal fiction that poems or trees have their own inner life that communicates to us?

PALMER: Well, I guess my first response would be, "What's your point?" Because imagination *is* a mode of hearing. I would challenge the misuse of that word *fiction,* because one of the things we know about great fiction—like all great art—is that it illuminates what we fondly call our "real life" in a way that facts never can. Recently I reread a 1969 article by Robert Coles called "The Words and Music of Social Change." [It was] about several black and white civil-rights workers who had been murdered by the KKK in Mississippi. Their colleagues in the movement were trying to find the courage to go back down there, into the mouth of the beast, after their idealism had been challenged by the sheer brutality of the situation. Coles wrote a brilliant article about how these people drew courage to return to Mississippi from reading Greek mythology and biblical stories, and from singing folk songs, as opposed to studying social scientific data or strategies. Myth, story, and the arts have always empowered courageous movements in a way that shows how much more powerful fiction can be than facts.

SEYMOUR: This is the power of art, the pen being mightier than the sword. So the complaint of it's not being real then, is really a statement of disbelief of the fact that there is such a thing as truth that is independent of the human project.

PALMER: I would also say that denying the belief in the "voice" of a tree or a poem is related to an instrumental view of the world as a body of raw material which has no nature and identity of its own, but exists simply to be shaped by our plans and manipulated for our purposes. Let me give you another example. I have been down the river through the Grand Canyon three times and have such awe for that piece of geology and geography. But I have read about people who really believe that the Grand Canyon has little value apart from its use for hydroelectric power. I can't begin to understand the mentality that says that the Grand Canyon has no identity and integrity of its own.

To me, it is self-evident that a poem has a voice of its own apart from the poet. Too many English departments want to do no more that deconstruct that poem and reduce it to a piece of sociology, linguistics, or psychology. At best, that's a disrespect-ful thing to do to a work of art. I can see how, for some, the "voice" of a tree may be a bigger leap—but then I recall Annie Dillard and the image she gave us of the mystery of a tree [in *Pilgrim at Tinker Creek*].

Dillard was arguing with the view that a tree is merely the outcome of a mecha-nistic process, evolved to perform certain biological functions, rather than having a dimension of mystery. So she asks us to consider two things. First, if all that was needed was to have a function performed—the function of photosynthesis—then why not cover Earth with great lakes of green glop and achieve the same goal? Why the majesty, the complexity, the intricacy of a tree as contrasted with the essential simplicity of masses of green glop? Second, Dillard says, if you doubt the complexity and the intricacy of a tree, just pick one and try to build a scale model of it! If I ever doubted that there was a mystery of selfhood at the heart of a tree, Annie Dillard removed my doubt!

In this society, we devalue the life of the world because we want to run big corporations that cut down all those trees and mine the land for profit. There is a huge drive to master the world of objects by defining it as inert and valuable only for human needs. We need to look at the underpinnings of why we are thinking that way—and we're paying the price for it.

SEYMOUR: Ernest Becker, in *Denial of Death*, addresses those underpinnings when he talks about fear of death being the driver in the human psyche. Fearing surrender as ego death, we get cut off from the living spirit in all things and project our inner deadness onto the outer world which, seen as dead, is now something we neither feel nor respect.

PALMER: I concur. I think fear is huge in our culture—and in education—so huge we can't even see it. It's so all-pervasive, like the air we breathe, that people have a hard time recognizing how fear dominates our lives. We can feel fear when airplanes are crashed into the twin towers of the World Trade Center, but it is rare to find people who truly realize that fear has long been endemic in our culture and, in fact, drives our international relations, with the United States and our global partners exploiting fear and violence around the world.

SEYMOUR: We can't, then, address the issue of spirit in education without also dealing with fear, asking people to become conscious of the ways in which fear colors their work and personal lives.

PALMER: In that regard, John MacMurray, a Scottish theologian, said years ago that, every time in the New Testament that Jesus uses the word *faith*, the word he contrasts it with is never *doubt* but always *fear*. The dynamic in our lives is between faith and fear, and the response to fear is faith. I'm talking about the faith that makes possible a kind of open-hearted, open-minded receptivity to myself and others—not faith in certain doctrinal propositions, but faith which helps me look past my fear to life on the other side.

SEYMOUR: You're talking about the kind of openness which is not afraid. One of the refrains in Christianity and other religions is about not being afraid. Perhaps we can conclude with more thoughts on having faith as it relates to the spirit alive in ourselves and our work as teachers.

PALMER: If you had to boil the great wisdom traditions down to a few words, those words might be, "Be not afraid." The spiritual traditions all point to this underlying problem of fear, and the various forms of faith that they invite us into are all responses to fear. What I find interesting is that these words don't say you shouldn't *have* fear. They say you don't need to *be* fear, or allow fear to run you. This is a crucial distinction which, as I began to understand it, has made my own journey through fear more doable. Most people *have* fear; I certainly do. But I can have fear without *being* fear, or fear controlling [me]. I can choose the place within myself that I come from. I have a place of fear in me, but I also have a place of hope and resilience. I can make choices about being and doing from one of *those* places rather than from the place of fear—which I will always have, but don't need to be.

SEYMOUR: It's about finding what has heart and meaning and, therefore, hope to sustain us along our journey.

PALMER: Absolutely—and that is what we want to help each other do as teachers so we can help children and young adults do it as well.

Way of the Brave: An Indigenous Perspective on "Character Education"

Don Trent Jacobs

I had the pleasure of meeting Don Trent Jacobs at the National Coalition of Alternative and Community Schools at Antioch College in Yellow Springs, Ohio. Don's Native American roots in the Creek and Cherokee people show in his easy, natural pace, his groundedness, and humor. Don, whose native name is Four Arrows, has a thoroughly holistic perspective on education, reflecting the ways of indigenous peoples who see themselves, their community, Earth, and spirit as one whole. Don is associate professor in the Department of Teaching and Learning in the College of Education at Northern Arizona University and is a faculty member at the Fielding Graduate Institute. He is the author of eleven books, including Teaching Virtues: Building Character across the Curriculum; Primal Awareness: A True Story of Survival, Awakening and Transformation; *and* The Bum's Rush: The Selling of Environmental Backlash. *He can be reached at www.teachingvirtues.net.*

Character education will be another failed effort at school reform unless we replace ideas associated with authority and conformity with a more spiritual awareness about the authentic goals of a virtuous life. A successful model for this alternative exists within indigenous ways of knowing.

The Lakota scholar Vine Deloria, Jr. describes modern American education as "indoctrination" that may produce "professionals" but not "people" prepared to be responsible, "contributing members of a society" (Deloria and Wildcat 2001, 42–44). If this is true for education in general, it is especially so for "character education" that, by and large, relies upon similar indoctrination strategies or upon disconnected references to heroic dispositions.

An alternative approach is recommended by a number of educators. For example, Patrick Slattery, in *Curriculum Development for the Postmodern Era,* writes: "Curriculum development in the postmodern era also includes attention to the wisdom embedded in Native American spirituality, for it is in the very sacred land of the native people that American education now finds its home" (1995, 79). Similarly, the authors of a widely used text for troubled youth state: "Native American philosophies of child management represent what is perhaps the most effective system of positive discipline ever developed. These approaches emerged from cultures where the central purpose of life was the education and empowerment of children" (Brendtro, Brokenleg, and Van Bockern 1990, 35). Parker Palmer and Noam Chomsky both write that the deep knowing of the American Indian people brings to education one of the most neglected resources of our continent (Jacobs and Jacobs-Spencer 2001, back cover). This recognition of the value of traditional Indian philosophies emphasizes a "spiritual" approach to character in that the goal of one with good character is about living life as if everything in life was related in a sacred way. For example, courage is regarded as one of the highest virtues by most American Indian and Alaskan Native peoples, but the greatest manifestation of courage is generosity. Initiation rights designed to build character generally teach children to turn their fears into virtues rather than escaping from them.

Thus in a modern classroom, a way to teach character with this understanding would be to help students identify their many fears and then show them how to use core universal virtues to replace them. As an extreme example, consider the options of a young brave encountering a grizzly bear to better understand this concept:

> *Humility:* Ah, bear, you are so magnificent! I am so pitiful in comparison. Do with me what you will.
> *Patience:* I will turn slowly and, inch by inch, move away, ever so patient.
> *Generosity:* If you are more in need of food than I am of a few more breaths of life, I offer myself to you."
> *Honesty:* In truth, had I been aware, I would not have stumbled into your area. I will accept whatever consequences are to be.
> *Fortitude:* He uses all of his strength and endurance to climb a tree without letting up.
> *Bravery:* He draws his knife and challenges the bear to come at him.

Of course, in all of the above scenarios, the bear turns away. For when we see our fears as a catalyst for living a virtue, they *do* go away.

The American Indian/Alaskan Native (AI/AN) traditional reason for developing good character in children is to enhance harmony in all relationships. It is not about just following rules and obeying external authority. Teaching virtues is not relegated to a one-day-a-week, "virtue of the month" status. "Bonus Bucks" are not offered as motivation and standardized tests are not used to measure outcomes.

According to the AI/AN view, we can only build character if we weave a critical awareness of its value into every teachable moment, in every subject throughout the day. To do this, teachers themselves must explore their own assumptions about the following concepts, because if a more Western view dominates thinking, it will be difficult, if not impossible, to truly integrate authentic spiritual awareness with virtues, and teachers will fall into the authority/compliance trap.

- Authority
- Equity
- A View of Children
- A Focus on Values versus Virtues
- Transmission Models of Teaching
- The Absence of Nature in Character Education

AUTHORITY

American Indian views of authority have little to do with relinquishing power to others. As the old ways are understood, authority is about using life's experiences to put oneself into harmony with all things and not about creating cultures of fear and dominance. American Indians typically, regardless of which unique tribal perspective they possess, view personal experience as the ultimate authority—social mores and ceremonies cultivate this understanding. Because they believe that the central purpose of teaching is to nurture this empowered way of being in the world that resides naturally in children, the idea of having authority over them is not considered. Character education that uses extrinsic motivators or "carrots and sticks" runs counter to this understanding of inner authority. When extrinsic motivation dominates character education programs, children emerge less generous than those who grow up in more intrinsically motivated environments. What does this say about "bonus bucks" in character education programs?

EQUITY

Many Western views about courage, fortitude, patience, and so on, relate to the "pick yourself up by the bootstraps" theme of rugged individualism. They assume that merely being virtuous will solve life problems without the need to address issues of equity and injustice. Typical indigenous economic and social systems do not condone such great discrepancies between people as those that exist in Western societies. Neither socialistic nor communistic in nature, American Indian customs and the cultivation of intrinsically motivated generosity help assure that excessive material wealth is shared and that no one suffers economic misfortune when that person's neighbors are rich. How can we teach about relatedness, responsibility, generosity, and humility when we have a society that tolerates the huge discrepancy between five-dollar-an-hour workers versus CEOs who make one hundred million dollars a year?

A VIEW OF CHILDREN

People of all cultures love their children. However, I believe Western consciousness typically views children somewhat differently than do American Indians. Charles Dickens comes to mind regarding European perspectives that call for children to be "seen and not heard" until they gain economic value. Children are automatically of infinite value in American Indian value systems, as are elders. Early Christian missionaries were confused by American Indian attitudes toward children. In 1634, Jesuit Father le Jeune wrote: "These Barbarians cannot bear to have their children punished, nor even scolded, not being able to refuse anything to a crying child" (Thwaites 1896, 153–154).

In Lakota and a number of other American Indian languages, words that represent or relate to children incorporate a syllable that means "sacred." In traditional native worldviews, babies enter the world as spiritual beings and they are born into a sacred relationship with the universe and its creatures. This view is not a romantic notion or a new-age vision, but a practical way of seeing the world. With it, a character education that attempts to "control" inherently "bad" children, take away their willfulness, or "fix" their problems would not lead to good character.

A FOCUS ON VALUES VERSUS VIRTUES

It is useful to distinguish between values or individual/cultural preferences and core universal virtues like courage, generosity, honesty, humility, fortitude, and patience that all cultures tend to honor. Western schools, in spite of rhetoric about character education, tend to focus on certain values like respecting authority or consumerism, even when attached to a virtue like honesty. In *I'm Only Bleeding: Education as the Practice of Social Violence against Children* (Block, Kincheloe, and Steinberg 2002), fields of neuroscience and psychology reveal the negative impact of typical public education. Is it possible that such violations occur because the priority of education is hegemonic? (I refer here to both political and religious hegemony.) Could it be that certain values relating to compliance to authority are more important than virtues that might challenge authority?

TRANSMISSION MODELS OF TEACHING

American Indian children tend to have assumptions about learning that are different than those of Western children. They expect more opportunities for personal reflection, critical thinking, observation, experience, and autonomy. They are more comfortable with a constructivist model that involves continual awareness of complex interconnections between individuals, communities, Mother Earth, and all of her creations. A study by Swisher reflects this idea:

> The values which produced significant differences between American Indians and non-Indians provide an interesting point of discussion. When considering which values affect socialization practice and subsequently one's approach to learning, the American Indian respondents selected discipline, group harmony, and holistic approaches to health and spirituality to a greater extent than non-Indians. These values all speak to the integral aspects of one's life, which communicate balance and respect and apparently affect the way in which one approaches a new learning situation. (Swisher 1994, 9)

When character education is an exhortation and virtues are "ordered or else," it is unlikely that a deep understanding can emerge sufficiently for children to realize that they truly possess virtues. Such realization is crucial, for as Coopersmith says, "The self-realization that one possesses virtues is a requirement for a spiritually fulfilling existence (1967).

THE ABSENCE OF NATURE IN CHARACTER EDUCATION

Even a constructivist approach to education has a missing link—nature. Focusing too much on the student's need to construct knowledge can still play into the hazards of anthropocentrism if we do not also teach about human connections with nature and ecological sustainability.

Foremost in the character education of American Indians is a sense of survival (Reyhner and Eder 1989, 9). Survival, however, is not separate from the realization of life's beauty, even amidst the struggles for survival. In essence, this idea of "surviving with beauty" is an ultimate spiritual priority because it recognizes that human beings, like all the other living creatures on this wonderful planet, share the mandate for survival. This view honors the wonderful connectedness and symbiosis in nature. It honors life. Moreover, it has lead to the famous priority often assigned to American Indian thinking about the survival of the seventh generation; perhaps the most spiritual, virtuous concern any of us could have in our lives.

This concern is reflected in the spiritual message to America from more than 1700 elders from 108 tribes that resulted from the National Indian Council on Aging Year 2000 Conference in Duluth, Minnesota, referring also to survival of the Seventh Generation:

> To the Seventh Generation: Survive, keep hopes and dreams alive. Take care of yourself and remember your spirit. Be there for one another. Respect courage. Be generous. Share knowledge for the benefit of all. Always keep learning. Treat the Earth and all that dwell thereon with respect. Be truthful and take responsibility for your actions. Remember the true values.

NOTE

REFERENCES

Brendtro, Larry K., Martin Brokenleg, and Steve Van Bockern. 1990. *Reclaiming Youth at Risk, 2d edition.* Bloomington, Indiana: National Educational Service.

Coopersmith, S. 1967. *The Antecedents of Self-Esteem.* San Francisco: W. H. Freeman.

Deloria, Vine, Jr., and Daniel R. Wildcat. 2001. *Power and Place: Indian Education in America.* Golden, Colo.: Fulcrum.

Jacobs, Don Trent. 1998. *Primal Awareness: A True Story of Survival and Transformation.* Rochester, Vt.: Inner Traditions International.

Jacobs, Don Trent, and Jessica Jacobs-Spencer. 2001. *Teaching Virtues, Building Character across the Curriculum.* Lanham, Md.: Scarecrow Education.

Keely, Lawrence. 2001. *War before Civilization: The Myth of the Peaceful Savage.* N.Y.: Oxford University Press.

Reyhner, Jon, and Jeanne Eder. 1989. *A History of Indian Education.* Billings: Eastern Montana College.

Shepard, Krech. 2000. *The Ecological Indian: Myth, and History.* New York: W.W. Norton and Co..

Slattery, Patrick. 1995. *Curriculum Development in the Postmodern Era.* New York: Garland Publishing.

Swisher, K. 1994. "American Indian Learning Styles Survey: An Assessment of Teacher's Knowledge." In *The Journal of Educational Issues of Language Minority Students* (Spring).

Thwaites, Reuben Gold. 1896. *The Jesuit Relations and Allied Documents.* Translated by J. C. Covert. Cleveland: The Burrows Brothers Co.

Trevor-Roper, Hugh. 1965. *The Rise of Christian Europe.* London: Thames and Hudson.

Nourishing Soul in Secular Schools

Rachael Kessler

I met Rachael Kessler in 1997 at a conference in Boulder, Colorado, on Spirituality in Education and again in 2000. I knew education had come to a new and exciting crossroads when The Association of Supervision and Curriculum Development (ASCD) devoted the January 1999 issue to spirituality in education and then published Kessler's The Soul of Education: Helping Students Find Connection, Compassion, and Character at School *(2000). I find Rachael thoughtful, aware, and dedicated. She is a highly engaging presenter whose workshops we have sponsored for several years in Seattle through The Heritage Institute. The PassageWays Institute, which Rachael founded, is accessible online at: http://www.mediatorsfoundation.org/isel/institute.html.*

It is our first senior honoring ceremony, designed to celebrate each graduating senior—not just the few who have shown outstanding achievement in academics or athletics. A small cross-section of the community is gathered in the softly lit room. In the center of the circle is a large vase filled with a variety of long-stemmed flowers. The first circle of chairs holds twenty-five students and the teachers who will address them. In the chairs behind them are parents and other faculty.

After a welcoming address by the school principal, a teacher goes to the center, selects a flower from the vase, and stands before a surprised and curious student. The teacher begins:

> I have watched you grow this last year and become strong like the sturdy stalk of this giant Iris. When you came into my class, I could tell that you were used to

230

being one of the clowns. Yet when it came time to share our stories, you took the first risk. You inspired all of us with the courage of your vulnerability. I want to honor you for the warmth you brought to each one of us, and the initiative and courage you've shown. I respect you as a leader and value you as a friend.

The young man beams. His father behind him looks stunned. This is his younger son, the cut-up—the disappointment after the academic achiever who went before him. The one who has brought the father too many times to the disciplinary dean's office. Now, after listening to one of the most respected teachers in the school describe the outstanding gifts of character his boy has demonstrated in his final year of high school, the father's face begins to soften. Tears glisten. He places his hands on the broad shoulders of his son. One squeeze tells this boy that his father has heard, is willing to see him in a new light.

In the father's eyes looms perhaps the largest question of all: What went right? And the answer, though elusive, is quite simple: At the heart of every adolescent experience is an exquisite opening to spirit. An awakening of energy when larger questions of meaning and purpose, of ultimate beginnings and endings, begin to press with both an urgency and a loneliness much too powerful to be dismissed as "hormones." What went right is that this year, this young man found experiences that nourished his spiritual development. This secular school created a place for his soul, and he flourished. Your school can do it too.

For fifteen years, I have worked with teams of educators around the country in both private and public school settings to create curriculum, methodology, and teacher development that can feed the awakening spirit of young people as part of school life. I call this approach "The Passages Program"—a set of principles and practices for working with adolescents that integrates heart, spirit, and community with strong academics. This curriculum of the heart is a response to the "mysteries" of teenagers: their usually unspoken questions and concerns are at its center.

I first discovered this approach at the Crossroads School in Santa Monica, California, where I worked for seven years as chair of their department of human development, building the team that created the Mysteries Program. In the 1990s, I began to take the gifts of Mysteries into schools around the country—adapting, refining, and expanding the curriculum to include what I learned from colleagues in the new and growing field of social and emotional learning. In those first years, I could not explain how our classes invited soul into the room. We were not—and are not—practicing religion or even talking about religion. Yet the students reported that there was something "spiritual" about our classes. We had to figure out what they meant.

CLASSROOMS THAT WELCOME SOUL

Most high school students grapple with the profound questions of loss, love, and letting go, of meaning, purpose, and service—of self-reliance and community, and of choice and surrender. How they respond to these questions—whether with love, denial, or even violence—can be profoundly influenced by the community of the classroom. When students work together to create an authentic community, they learn that they can meet any challenge with grace, with love, and with power—even wrenching conflict, prejudice, profound gratitude, or death. Creating an authentic community is the first step in soul of education.

When soul is present in education, attention shifts. We listen with great care not only to what is spoken but also to the messages between the words—tones, gestures, the flicker of feeling across the face. We concentrate on what has heart and meaning. The yearning, wonder, wisdom, fear, and confusion of students become central to the curriculum. Questions become as important as answers.

When soul enters the classroom, masks drop away. Students dare to share the joy and talents they have feared would provoke jealousy in even their best friends. They risk exposing the pain or shame that might be judged as weakness. Seeing deeply into the perspective of others, accepting what has felt unworthy in themselves, students discover compassion and begin to learn about forgiveness.

How can classroom teachers invite soul? To achieve the safety and openness required for meaningful exploration of spiritual development, students and teachers work together carefully for weeks and months. We create ground rules—conditions that students name as essential for speaking about what matters most to them. Games help students fully focus, relax, and become a team through laughter and cooperation. Symbols that students create or bring into class allow teenagers to speak indirectly about feelings and thoughts that are awkward to address head on. And we work with a highly structured form of discourse called Council.[1] With everyone sitting in a circle where all can see and be seen, the council process allows each person to speak without interruption or immediate response. Students learn to listen deeply and discover what it feels like to be truly heard. Silence becomes a comfortable ally as we pause to digest one story and wait for another to form, when teachers call for moments of reflection or when the room fills with feeling at the end of a class.

Since "we teach who we are," teachers who invite heart and soul into the classroom also find it essential to nurture their own spiritual development. This may mean personal practices to cultivate awareness, serenity, and compassion, as well as collaborative efforts with other teachers to give and receive support for the challenges and joys of entering this terrain with their students. When this climate of honor and respect is co-created with our students, stories emerge about what matters most to young people. I have listened to these stories for years now, and a pattern has emerged.

GATEWAYS TO THE SOUL OF STUDENTS

Based on students' stories and questions, I have mapped spiritual development in adolescents who may or may not have a religious tradition or other beliefs about the nature of spirituality. This mapping comprises seven interrelated yearnings, needs, or hungers. Meeting these spiritual yearnings supports, strengthens, and fosters the development of a young person's spirit.

1. *The search for meaning and purpose* concerns the exploration of existential questions that burst forth in adolescence: Why am I here? Does my life have a purpose? How do I find out what it is? What does my future hold? Is there life after death? Is there a god? I've read these questions time and again when students write anonymously about their personal "mysteries"—their wonder, worries, curiosity, fear, and excitement.

This domain of meaning and purpose is not only crucial to motivation and learning for students but also paradoxically simple and uncomfortable for teachers to deal with. Teachers who predicate their authority on the ability to know, or to have the right answer, are profoundly uncomfortable with questions that appear to have no answers. In most schools, purpose is primarily taught through goal setting and decision making—often with strictly rational techniques. But when the spiritual dimension is omitted, or if the inner life of the adolescent is not cultivated as part of the search for goals or careers, they will most likely base their decisions on external pressures—from peers, parents, teachers. One student writes:

> So many of my friends are so clueless. They don't know what they want to do, they know what they're supposed to do. They don't know how they feel—they know how they're supposed to feel. And here I find myself in a group of people going through all my same stuff, and although I don't have the answers to all the questions, I find myself feeling like everything is perfect and right. . . . I have this "community" that gives me a home base and a sense of security.

Educators can provide experiences that honor the big questions. They can also allow students to give their gifts to the world through school and community service, through creative expression, or academic or athletic achievement. In the way we teach, we can help students see and create patterns that connect learning to their personal lives. A student helps explain:

> When I go over to the local elementary school to tutor two Spanish-speaking children, they are so excited to see me. I guess they don't get too much attention from a teacher and a classroom that is strictly English-speaking. When I am with them, I feel special. I am an average student at my school. I don't hold any elected positions. I am not on any varsity team. I do not stand out in any way, and that is okay with me. It is okay with me because for 3 hours each week, Maria and Miguel make me feel like I am the most important person in the world.

2. *The longing for silence and solitude* can lead to identity formation and goal setting, to learning readiness and inner peace. For adolescents, this domain is often ambivalent—fraught with both fear and urgent need. As a respite from the tyranny of busy-ness and noise that afflicts even our young children, silence may be a realm of

reflection, calm, or fertile chaos—an avenue of stillness and rest for some, prayer or contemplation for others. Another student writes:

"I like to take time to go within myself sometimes. And when I do that, I try to take an emptiness inside there. I think that everyone struggles to find their own way with their spirit and it's in the struggle that our spirit comes forth."

3. *The urge for transcendence* describes the desire of young people to go beyond their perceived limits. "How far can I be stretched, how much adversity can I stand?" writes one student. "Is there a greater force at work? Can humans tap into that force, and bring it into their daily lives?" writes another. Transcendence includes not only the mystical realm but also secular experiences of the extraordinary in the arts, athletics, academics, or human relations. By naming this human need that spans all cultures, educators can help students constructively channel this urge and challenge themselves in ways that reach for this peak experience.

4. *The hunger for joy and delight* can be satisfied through experiences of great simplicity, such as play, celebration, or gratitude. "I want to move many and take joy in every person, every little thing," writes one student. Another asks: "Do all people have the same capacity to feel joy and sorrow?" Educators can also help students express the exaltation they feel when encountering beauty, power, grace, brilliance, love, or the sheer joy of being alive.

5. *The creative drive* is perhaps the most familiar domain for nourishing the spirit of students in secular schools. In opportunities for acts of creation, people often encounter their participation in a process infused with depth, meaning, and mystery. Writes one student: "There is something that happens to me in pottery class—I lose myself in the feeling of wet clay rolling smoothly under my hands as the wheel spins. I have it last period, so no matter how difficult the day was, pottery makes every day a good day. It's almost magical—to feel so good, so serene."

6. *The call for initiation* refers to a hunger the ancients met through rites of passage for their young. As educators, we can create programs that guide adolescents to become conscious about the irrevocable transition from childhood to adulthood, give them tools for making transitions and separations, challenge them to discover the capacities for their next step, and create ceremonies with parents and other faculty that acknowledge and welcome them into the community of adults.

7. *The common thread is deep connection.* As my students tell stories about each of these domains, I hear a common thread: the experience of deep connection. This seventh domain describes a quality of relationship that is profoundly caring, resonant with meaning, and involves feelings of belonging, of being truly seen or known.

Through deep connection to the self, students encounter a strength and a richness within that is the basis for developing the autonomy central to the adolescent journey, to discovering purpose and unlocking creativity. Teachers can nourish this form of deep connection by giving students time for solitary reflection. Classroom exercises that encourage reflection and expression through writing or art can also allow a student access to the inner self while in the midst of other people. Totally engrossed in such creative activities, students are encouraged to discover and express their own feelings, values, and beliefs.

Connecting deeply to another person or to a meaningful group, they discover the balm of belonging that soothes the profound alienation that fractures the identity of our youth and prevents them from contributing to our communities. To feel a sense of belonging at school, students must be part of an authentic community in the classroom—a community in which students feel seen and heard for who they really are. Many teachers create this opportunity through "morning meetings," weekly councils or sharing circles offered in a context of ground rules that make it safe to be vulnerable. The teacher must continue to support the autonomy and uniqueness of the individual while fostering a sense of belonging and union with the group. The more that young people are encouraged to strengthen their own boundaries and develop their own identity, the more capable they are of bonding to a group in a healthy, enduring way.

Some students connect deeply to nature: "When I get depressed," revealed Keisha to her "family group" members in a Manhattan school, "I go to this park near my house where there is an absolutely enormous tree. I go and sit down with it because it feels so strong to me."

"It was my science teacher who awakened my spirit," said a teacher about his high-school days in Massachusetts. "He conveyed a sense of awe about the natural world that would change me forever."

Some students discover solace in their relationship to God or to a religious practice, as well as a place to explore urgent questions. One student writes: "I try to practice being present—that's what Buddhism has given to me that I really cherish. It's really the most important thing to me now." Another writes: "I became a Christian a few years back. It's been the most wonderful thing in my life. I can't tell you what it feels like to know that I'm loved like that. Always loved and guided. By Jesus. And it's brought our family much closer."

When students know there is a time in school life where they may give voice to the great comfort and joy they find in their relationship to God or to nature, this freedom of expression itself nourishes their spirits. The First Amendment actually protects students' freedom of expression of religious beliefs. (However, we teachers must be careful not to share our religious beliefs because, given the power and public nature of our role, students may experience a teacher's sharing as proselytizing.) But in our fear and confusion about violating the law, we have actually suppressed student freedom and the rich exchange that comes when such an important part of their lives has been acknowledged and respected.

Students who feel deeply connected don't need danger to feel fully alive. They don't need guns to feel powerful. They don't want to hurt others or themselves. Out of connection grows compassion and passion—passion for people, for students' goals and dreams, for life itself.

In a pluralistic society, educators can provide a forum that honors the ways individual students nourish their spirits. We can offer activities that allow them to experience deep connection. In the search itself, in loving the questions, in the deep yearning they let themselves feel, young people will discover what is sacred in life, what is sacred in their own lives, and what allows them to bring their most sacred gifts to nourish the world.

NOTE

This chapter is copyright © 2004 by Rachael Kessler. Used with permission.

1. See Jack Zimmerman and Virginia Coyle's *The Way of Council*. Bramble Books, 1996.

Appendix: Resources

PROGRESSIVE SCHOOLS

Codman Academy Charter School
637 Washington Street
Dorchester, Mass. 02124
Phone: (617) 287-0700, ext. 103
Principal: Meg Campbell
www.codmanacademy.org

This public high school serves a mostly minority student population in Dorchester, Massachusetts, and is guided by the principles of expeditionary learning. An equal emphasis is placed on intellectual and character development, with emphasis on an ethic of service and a healthy lifestyle. There is a strong emphasis on post-secondary education.

El Puente Academy for Peace and Justice
211 South 4th Street
Brooklyn, N.Y. 11211
Phone: (718) 599-2895
Fax: (718) 599-3087
Principal: Alfa Anderson
http://www.nycboe.net/OurSchools/Region8/K685/default.htm

El Puente Academy is a four-year comprehensive high school and its mission is to inspire and nurture leadership for peace and justice. El Puente strives in all activities to create community, develop love and caring, achieve mastery, and promote peace and justice. These goals are based on a view of human beings as holistic, thriving in collective self-help, seeking safety and requiring respect.

Environmental and Adventure School
Finn Hill Jr. High
8040 N.E. 132nd Street
Kirkland, Wash. 98034
Phone: (425) 825-1411

Lead Teacher: Eileen McMackin
http://www.eas.lkwash.wednet.edu/

This middle school is one of a growing number of "choice," thematically focused schools where students achieve academic, personal, and social goals in a challenging educational program with an environmental focus.

The Environmental Middle School
2421 S.E. Orange Street
Portland, Ore. 97214
Phone: (503) 916-6490
Principal: Sarah Taylor
http://www.pps.k12.or.us/schools-c/pages/environmental/

EMS is a small, multicultural, urban, public middle school that draws students from all of Portland's diverse neighborhoods. The teachers teach a holistic, integrated curriculum. Exploring themes of their many overlapping environments, students develop academic knowledge and skills while demonstrating personal and social responsibility for all living things.

Greenfield Center School
71 Montague City Road
Greenfield, Mass. 01301
Phone: (413) 773-1700
Principal: Laura Baker
http://www.centerschool.net

This independent K–8 school started as a laboratory school of the Northeast Foundation for Children, where their highly acclaimed program, *The Responsive Classroom,* was developed. Their program is an excellent example of integrating social and academic learning and building a strong learning community.

Hudson Public Schools
155 Apsley Street
Hudson, Mass. 01749
Phone: (978) 567-6100
Superintendent: Sheldon Berman
http://www.hudson.k12.ma.us/

All six schools in this exemplary district reflect a commitment to educating for social responsibility as an integral part of rigorous academic learning. Character education, social skills, ethical development, community service learning, inquiry-based learning, and a democratized learning environment all serve to support Hudson's core values of empathy, ethics, and service.

Mast Landing School—Soule Program
116 Bow Street, Freeport, Maine 04032
Phone: (207) 865-4561, ext. 4
Teaching Principal: Mr. Gene Berg

http://www.freeportpublicschools.org/mls/mlshome.html

The Soule Program (grades 3–5) is one of three programs of choice in this elementary school. Its philosophy emphasizes the importance of student, as well as teacher, choice. Soule is distinguished by an emphasis on decision making and responsibility, multigraded classrooms, and teachers as specialists in a particular subject area, with children seeing two main teachers each day.

Jefferson County Open School
7655 West 10th Avenue
Lakewood, Colo. 80215
Phone: (303) 982-7045
Principal: Bonnie Walters
http://jeffcoweb.jeffco.k12.co.us/high/jcos/

This is an alternative, public program consisting of a preschool, early learning center, intermediate area, middle and high school. Its educational philosophy is student-centered, emphasizing the whole person, learning by doing, a community service and social justice orientation, and the full development of each student's personal potential.

The Metropolitan Regional Career and Technical Center (The Met)
The Big Picture Company
275 Westminster Street
Suite 500, Providence, R.I. 02903
Phone: (401) 456-0600
Fax: (401) 456-0606
Co-directors: Dennis Littky and Elliot Washor
http://www.metcenter.org/

The Met is a small public high school open to all students in Rhode Island. The school educates one student at a time, so each student's curriculum is determined by his or her unique interests, background, and learning styles. All students work on projects in real-world settings related to their interests and develop strong relationships with teachers and project mentors.

The New School at SouthShore
8825 Rainier Avenue South
Seattle, Wash. 98118
Phone: (206) 252-6560
Principal: Gary Tubbs
http://www.seattleschools.org/schools/southshore/

This new K–8 public school's vision is to create a loving community of purposeful learning that focuses on the whole child: mind, body, and spirit. The school's mission is to view each child as a bright spirit on a magnificent journey in the quest to contribute powerfully to the healing of humanity and Mother Earth.

RESOURCE ORGANIZATIONS

Following is a list of organizations that help in shaping a progressive, holistic democratic vision for education and that are consistent with the values represented in this volume. Many of these organizations will provide technical assistance or training to schools and educators, as well as offering publications, research and conferences, and workshops.

Ecology, Environment, and Sustainability

Antioch New England Institute
40 Avon Street
Keene, N.H. 03431-3516
Phone: (603) 357-3122, ext. 344
Fax: (603) 357-0718
E-mail: ANEI@antiochne.edu
http://www.anei.org/

A nonprofit environmental and educational consulting organization of Antioch New England Graduate School, the Institute provides training and resources to communities and organizations in the following areas: environmental education, leadership training, environmental policy development, nonprofit management and governance, exhibit planning and design, public administration, facilitation, and democracy building.

Center for Ecoliteracy
2528 San Pablo Avenue
Berkeley, Calif. 94702
Fax: (510) 845-1439
E-mail: *info@ecoliteracy.org*
http://www.ecoliteracy.org/index.html

The Center for Ecoliteracy is dedicated to fostering a profound understanding of the natural world, grounded in direct experience, that leads to sustainable patterns of living. In providing support to educators, the Center for Ecoliteracy empowers them to help children learn the values and gain the knowledge and skills that are crucial to building and nurturing ecologically sustainable communities. They provide project support, grants, and publishing in service of their mission.

The Center for a Sustainable Future
Educating for a Sustainable Future
A Division of the Concord Consortium
1611 Harbor Road
Shelburne Farms
Shelburne, Vt. 05482
Phone: (802) 985-0789
E-mail: *keith@concord.org* (Keith Wheeler)
http://csf.concord.org/esf/

This project has experience-based research, curriculum, and training for schools on how to educate for a sustainable future.

Earth and Peace Education Associates
97-37 63rd Rd. 15e
Rego Park, N.Y. 11374
Phone: (718) 275-3932
E-mail: info@globalepe.org
http://globalepe.org/

This association consists of a global network of educators who aim to promote the recognition of the reciprocal relationship between ecological degradation and the violation of human rights on a local, national, and global level. Contextual sustainability, the organizing principle underlying the EPE's approach, defines this relationship. It assumes that the earth is the primary context and essential foundation of all social activity and that ecological sustainability is key to achieving a culture of peace.

Facing the Future: People and Our Planet
811 First Ave., Suite 454
Seattle, Wash. 98104
Phone: (206) 264-1503
Fax: (206) 264-1506
E-mail: admin@facingthefuture.org
www.facingthefuture.org

Facing the Future is a nonprofit organization providing teachers, students, and the public with dynamic and successful global issues education and action opportunities to shape our future. Its programs address the interconnected issues of population, poverty, consumption, peace and conflict, and the environment. It researches and writes curriculum materials that meet educational standards, encouraging and supporting the participation of students and the public in action and service learning projects, and delivering educational resources through local, national, and international educator conferences, school district in-services, university preservices, award winning websites, and strategic partnerships.

Portland International Initiative for Leadership in Ecology, Culture and Learning
Portland State University–Graduate School of Education
P.O. Box 751-ED
Portland, Ore. 97207-0751
Phone: (503) 725-4684
Fax: (503) 725-3200
E-mail: *pramodp@pdx.edu* (Pramod Parajuli)
www.piiecl.pdx.edu

The overall goal of the Portland International Initiative for Leadership in Ecology, Culture, and Learning (PIIECL) is to offer a world-class, cutting-edge program for higher education students and members in the community who are dedicated to making this world livable, sustainable, bio-culturally diverse, and socially just. PIIECL believes that through education, research, and curriculum development not only is such a world desirable, it is also achievable.

Holistic, Progressive, Democratic Education, Spirituality in Education

The Center for Teacher Formation
PMB 375, 321 High School Rd. NE
Bainbridge Island, Wash. 98110
Phone: (206) 855-9140
Fax: (206) 855-9143
E-mail: info@teacherformation.org
http://www.teacherformation.org/

Based on the work of Parker Palmer and *The Courage to Teach* book, the center oversees Courage to Teach programs across the United States that take groups of twenty-five teachers over an eight-weekend, two-year program of personal reflection, community building, and transformation.

Foundation for Educational Renewal
Great Ideas in Education
Box 328, Brandon, Vt. 05733-0328
Phone: 1 (800) 639-4122
E-mail: info@great-ideas.org
http://www.great-ideas.org

Great Ideas in Education is the joint website of Holistic Education Press, Psychology Press, and the publishing division of the Foundation for Educational Renewal. It features an excellent selection of books on holistic, progressive, and democratic education.

The Institute for Democracy in Education (IDE)
Department of Education
McCracken Hall, Ohio University
Athens, Ohio 45701
Phone: (740) 593-4531
E-mail: democracy@ohiou.edu
http://www.ohiou.edu/ide/

IDE is a partnership of all participants in the educational process—teachers, administrators, parents and students—who believe that restructuring for democratic education must come from those at the heart of education. IDE works to provide teachers committed to democratic education with a forum for sharing ideas, with a support network of people holding similar values, and with opportunities for professional development.

The Heritage Institute (THI)
Box 860, Clinton, Wash. 98236
Phone: (360) 341-3020
Fax: (360) 341-3070
E-mail: *mike@hol.edu* (Mike Seymour)
www.hol.edu

The Heritage Institute has been a leader in progressive continuing education programs for K–12 educators offering workshops, field studies, global travel studies, and distance education to educators in the Northwest, around the United States, and the world. Its philosophy of educating for humanity provides the framework and inspiration for our leading-edge perspective on teaching and learning and for our vision of schools as enriching and productive learning environments for all children. Its goal is to renew teachers with learning experiences that empower them to inspire children to become whole, compassionate and wise contributing citizens to a world that works for all.

Ontario Institute for Studies in Education (OISE)
University of Toronto
Department of CTL
252 Bloor Street West
Toronto, Ontario
M5S 1V6
Phone: (416) 923-6641, ext. 2633
Fax: (416) 926-4744
E-mail: jmiller@oise.utoronto.ca (Jack Miller)
http://www.oise.utoronto.ca/~skarsten/holistic/HAE.html

A graduate program in holistic and aesthetic education that recognizes the interconnectedness of body, mind, emotions, and spirit. Learning is viewed as an experiential, organic process; making connections is seen as central to curriculum processes. An aesthetic perspective and the process of building knowledge through inquiry are seen as integral to all forms of education and life itself. Creative tools and webs of communication are explored within this context. Courses in this program focus on arts education, creativity, contemplation, imagery, literature, mathematics and technology, and experience-based approaches to language.

PassageWays Institute Inc.
P.O. Box 19468
Boulder, Colo. 80308
Phone: (303) 247-0156
E-mail: info@passageways.org
http://www.passageways.org/

Founded by Rachael Kessler, author of *The Soul of Education,* PassageWays Institute provides materials, consultation and training in the "Passages" approach to social and emotional learning—a model that integrates heart, spirit, and community into curriculum, staff, and organizational development. It has also served as a catalyst and advocate for bringing the spiritual dimension into the educational mainstream.

Systemwide School Improvement

Coalition of Essential Schools
CES National
1814 Franklin St., Suite 700
Oakland, Calif. 94612
Phone: (510) 433-1451
Fax: (510) 433-1455
E-mail: *ksimon@essentialschools.org* (Kathy Simon, Co-director)
http://www.essentialschools.org/

A highly successful, reform initiative based on the work of Ted Sizer and basic coalition principles. Thousands of secondary and elementary schools worldwide have adopted CES principles, and over six hundred are formal affiliates. The CES mission is to create and sustain equitable, intellectually vibrant, personalized schools and to make such schools the norm of American public education.

Expeditionary Learning
Outward Bound USA
100 Mystery Point Road
Garrison, N.Y. 10524
Phone: (845) 424-4000
Fax: (845) 424-4280
E-mail: linda_collins@elob.org
http://www.elob.org/

Expeditionary Learning, Outward Bound is a proven model for comprehensive school reform for elementary, middle, and high schools. It emphasizes learning by doing, with a particular focus on character growth, teamwork, reflection, and literacy. Teachers connect high-quality academic learning to adventure, service, and character development through a variety of student experiences including interdisciplinary, project-based learning expeditions.

The George Lucas Educational Foundation
P.O. Box 3494
San Rafael, Calif. 94912
Phone: (415) 507-0399
Fax: (415) 507-0499
E-mail: edutopia@glef.org
http://www.glef.org/

This progressive foundation focuses on research, publishing in the areas of alternative and authentic assessment, project-based learning, school-to-career experience and technology integration, and other areas it feels contributes to powerful schools.

The Small Schools Project
900 East Greenlake Drive N., Suite 212
Seattle, Wash. 98103
Phone: (206) 616-0303
Fax: (206) 543-8250
http://www.smallschoolsproject.org/

The Small Schools Project, housed at the University of Washington College of Education, provides support to the many new small schools being established in Washington State and throughout the United States. The project, supported by a gift from the Bill and Melinda Gates Foundation, provides a range of services to new and emerging small schools that have an organizational structure and philosophical commitment compatible with the attributes of high-achieving schools.

Social and Emotional Learning, Ethics, Character Education, and Service Learning

The Collaborative for Academic, Social and Emotional Learning (CASEL)
Department of Psychology (M/C 285)
The University of Illinois at Chicago
1007 W. Harrison Street, Chicago, Ill. 60607-7137
Phone: (312) 413-1008

CASEL enhances children's success in school and life by promoting coordinated, evidence-based social, emotional, and academic learning as an essential part of education from pre-school though high school. CASEL publishes and maintains listservs and events for educators and parents in support of their mission.

Character Education Partnership
1025 Connecticut Ave., NW
Suite 1011, Washington, D.C. 20036
Phone: (800) 988-8081
E-mail: geninfo@character.org
www.character.org

The Character Education Partnership (CEP) is a nonpartisan coalition of organizations and individuals dedicated to developing moral character and civic virtue in our nation's youth as one means of creating a more compassionate and responsible society.

Committee for Children
2203 Airport Way South, Suite 5000
Seattle, Wash. 98134
Phone: (800) 634-4449
E-mail: info@cfchildren.org
www.cfchildren.org

Committee for Children, a nonprofit organization, is a leader in social and emotional learning and violence prevention. Its award-winning programs and prevention curricula focus on the topics of youth violence, bullying, child abuse, and personal safety. Each year its programs reach millions of children and educators throughout the world.

Communities in Schools (CIS)
http://www.cisnet.org/

CIS is the nation's leading community-based organization helping kids succeed in school and prepare for life. CIS provides schools with technical support. It champions the connection of needed community resources with schools to help young people successfully learn and stay in school.

Developmental Studies Center (DSC)
2000 Embarcadero, Suite 305

Oakland, Calif. 94606
Phone: (800) 666-7270
E-mail: info@devstu.org
www.devstu.org

For twenty-three years, DSC has worked with elementary schools to help its students become skilled, motivated readers and caring, principled people. Recognizing that children's academic, ethical, social, and emotional development are interrelated and interdependent, it has designed in-school and after-school programs that address those dimensions of children's learning in seamlessly coordinated, systemic ways.

Educators for Social Responsibility
23 Garden Street
Cambridge, Mass. 02138
Phone: (800) 370-2515
E-mail: educators@esrnational.org
www.esrnational.org

Educators for Social Responsibility (ESR) helps educators create safe, caring, respectful, and productive learning environments. ESR also helps educators work with young people to develop the social skills, emotional competencies, and qualities of character they need to succeed in school and become contributing members of their communities.

Facing History and Ourselves: Examining History and Human Behavior
16 Hurd Road
Brookline, Mass. 02146
Phone: (617) 232-6919
www.facinghistory.org

Facing History and Ourselves is based on the belief that education in a democracy must be what Alexis de Tocqueville called "an apprenticeship in liberty." Facing History helps students find meaning in the past and recognize the need for participation and responsible decision making. They do this through a professional development program that helps teachers master important pedagogy skills to immerse students in reflective, critical learning through reading, writing, speaking, and listening.

National Service-Learning Partnership (NSLP)
100 Fifth Ave.
New York, N.Y. 10011
Phone: (202) 367-4570
E-mail: nslp@aed.org
www.learningindeed.org/leadership/nslpnewaddr.html

NSLP is the only national membership organization bringing together practitioners, administrators, policymakers, researchers, community leaders, parents, and young people to support K–12 service learning. The Partnership serves as a national leadership hub for more than 2,000 individuals and organizations committed to raising the visibility and enhancing the quality of service learning in schools and communities across the country.

Northeast Foundation for Children
39 Montague City Road
Greenfield, Mass. 01301
Phone: (800) 360-6332
Phone: (413) 772-2066
Fax: (413) 772-2097
E mail: info@responsiveclassroom.org
www.responsiveclassroom.org

The Responsive Classroom, from the Northeast Foundation for Children, is an approach to teaching and learning that fosters safe, challenging, and joyful classrooms and schools, kindergarten through eighth grade. Developed by classroom teachers, it consists of practical strategies for bringing together social and academic learning throughout the school day.

The Stone Center, Wellesley College
Open Circle Program
106 Central Street
Wellesley, Mass. 02181-8268
Phone: (781) 283-2847
www.wellesley.edu/OpenCircle

Open Circle works with school communities to help children become ethical people, contributing citizens, and successful learners. By helping schools implement the unique open circle curriculum, it fosters the development of relationships that support safe, caring, and respectful learning communities of children and adults.

Social Justice and Multicultural Education

Center for Multicultural Education
110 Miller Hall, Box 353600
University of Washington
Seattle, Wash. 98195-3600
Phone: (206) 543-3386
Fax: (206) 543-8439
E-mail: centerme@u.washington.edu
http://depts.washington.edu/centerme/home.htm

The Center for Multicultural Education at the University of Washington focuses on research projects and activities designed to improve practice related to equity issues, intergroup relations, and the achievement of students of color. The center also engages in services and teaching related to its research mission

Justice Matters Institute—Educational Justice Program
1375 Sutter Street, Suite 110
San Francisco, Calif. 94109
Phone: (415) 353-5735
Fax: (415) 353-5733
E-mail: contact@edjustice.org
http://www.edjustice.org/

Its mission is to promote quality education for students of all races and cultures. To achieve this, the institute tackle issues of educational equity, culture, and institutional racism in education, providing research and events (in the Bay area) to support educators and schools.

ReThinking Schools
1001 E. Keefe Avenue
Milwaukee, Wis. 53212
Phone: (414) 964-9646 or (800) 669-4192
Fax: (414) 964-7220
E-mail: *rsleon@execpc.com* (Leon Lynn)

ReThinking Schools' newsletter, teaching resources, and website are committed to equity and to the vision that public education is central to the creation of a humane, caring, multiracial democracy. While writing for a broad audience, ReThinking Schools emphasizes problems facing urban schools, particularly issues of race.
http://www.rethinkingschools.org/

SUGGESTED READING

Cultural Analysis and the Human Future

Becker, Ernest. 1973. *The Denial of Death*. New York: Free Press Paperbacks.
Bellah, Robert et al. 1996. *Habits of the Heart: Individualism and Commitment in American Life*. Berkeley: University of California Press.
Capra, Fritjof. 1988. *The Turning Point: Science, Society and the Rising Culture*. New York: Bantam Books.
Capra, Fritjof. 1997. *The Web of Life: A New Scientific Understanding of Living Systems*. New York: Anchor Books.
Chomsky, Noam. 1994. *Manufacturing Consent: A Primer in Intellectual Self-Defense*. Cheektowga, N.Y.: Black Rose Books.
Eisler, Riane. *The Chalice and the Blade: Our History, Our Future*. San Francisco: Harper.
Elgin, Duane. 1993. *Awakening Earth: Exploring the Evolution of Human Culture and Consciousness*. New York: William Morrow & Co.
————. 2000. *Promise Ahead: A Vision of Hope and Action for Humanity's Future*. New York: HarperCollins.
Havel, Vaclav. 1987. *Living in Truth*. London: Faber & Faber.
Houston, Jean. 2000. *Jump Time: Shaping Your Future in a World of Radical Change*. New York: Jeremy P. Tarcher/Putnam.
Korten, David. C. 1995. *When Corporations Ruled the World*. San Francisco: Berrett-Koehler Publishers with Kumarian Press.
————. 1999. *The Post-Corporate World: Life after Capitalism*. San Francisco: Berrett-Koehler Publishers with Kumarian Press.
Kozol, Jonathan. 1995. *Amazing Grace: The Lives of Children and the Conscience of a Nation*. New York: Perennial.
Lappé, Frances Moore, and Paul Du Bois. 1994. *The Quickening of America: Rebuilding our Nation, Remaking Our Lives*. San Francisco: Jossey-Bass.

Prigogine, Ilya, and Isabelle Stengers. 1984. *Order Out of Chaos: Man's New Dialogue with Nature.* Boulder: New Science Library.

Putnam, Robert. 2000. *Bowling Alone: The Collapse and Revival of American Community.* New York: Simon & Schuster.

Ray, Paul, and Sherry Ruth Anderson. 2000. *The Cultural Creatives: How 50 Million People Are Changing the World.* New York: Harmony Books.

Rifkin, Jeremy. 1991. *Biosphere Politics: A New Consciousness for a New Century.* New York: Crown Publishers.

Schweitzer, Albert. 1987. *Philosophy of Civilization: Part I: The Decay and Restoration of Civilization.* New York: Promethean Books.

Swimme, Brian, and Thomas Berry (Contributor). 1994. *The Universe Story.* New York: HarperCollins.

Theobold, Robert. 1997. *Reworking Success: New Communities at the Millenium.* Gabriola Island, B.C.: New Society Press.

Williamson, Marianne. 1997. *The Healing of America.* New York: Simon & Schuster.

————, ed. 2000. *Imagine What America Could Be in the 21ˢᵗ Century: Visions of a Better Future from Leading American Thinkers.* New York: Rodale Books.

Ecology, Ecopsychology, Sustainability, and Simplicity

Abram, David. 1997. *The Spell of the Sensuous: Perception and Language in a More-Than-Human World.* New York: Vintage Books.

Berry, Thomas. 1990. *The Dream of Earth.* San Francisco: Sierra Club.

————. 1999. *The Great Work: Our Way into the Future.* New York: Crown Publishing.

Brown, Lester. 2001. *Eco-Economy: Building an Economy for Earth.* New York: W. W. Norton and Co.

Carson, Rachel. 1962. *Silent Spring.* New York: Houghton Mifflin Co.

Cavanagh, John, and Jerry Mander. *Alternative to Economic Globalization: A Better World Is Possible.* A report of the International Forum on Globalization. San Francisco: Berrett-Koehler Publishers.

Durning, Alan T. 1996. *This Place on Earth: Home and the Practice of Permanence.* Seattle, Wash.: Sasquatch Books.

Elgin, Duane. 1991. *Voluntary Simplicity: Toward a Way of Life That Is Outwardly Simple, Inwardly Rich.* New York: William Morrow.

Glendenning, Chellis. 1994. *My Name Is Chellis and I'm in Recovery from Western Civilization.* Boston: Shambala Publications.

Harrison, Roger Pogue. 1992. *Forests: The Shadow of Civilization.* Chicago: University of Chicago Press.

Hawken, Paul, Amory Lovins, and L. Hunter Lovins. 1999. *Natural Capitalism: Creating the Next Industrial Revolution.* Boston: Little, Brown & Co.

Jardine, David. 2000. *"Under the Tough Old Stars": Ecopedagogical Essays.* Brandon, Vt.: The Foundation for Educational Renewal.

Kaza, Stephanie, and Kenneth Kraft. 2000. *Dharma Rain: Sources of Buddhist Environmentalism.* Boston: Shambala.

Macy, Joanna. 1991. *World as Lover, World as Self.* Berkeley: Parallax Press.

————. 2000. *Widening Circles.* Gabriola Island, B.C.: New Society Publishers.

Metzner, Ralph. 1999. *Green Psychology: Transforming Our Relationship to the Earth.* Rochester, Vt.: Park Street Press.

Orr, David W. 1992. *Ecological Literacy: Education and the Transition to a Postmodern World.* Albany: State University of New York Press.

———. 1994. *Earth in Mind: On Education, Environment, and the Human Prospect.* Washington, D.C.: Island Press.

Roszak, Theodore, Mary E. Gomes, and Allen D. Kanner, eds. 1995. *Ecopsychology: Restoring the Earth, Healing the Mind.* San Francisco: Sierra Club Books.

Schlosser, Eric. 2001. *Fast Food Nation: The Dark Side of the All-American Meal.* New York: Perrenial.

Schumacher, E.F. 1989. *Small Is Beautiful: Economics as if People Mattered.* Vancouver: Hartley and Marks.

Seed, John, Joanna Macy, Pat Fleming, and Arne Naess. 1988. *Thinking Like a Mountain: Towards a Council of All Beings.* Gabriola Island, B.C.: New Society Publishers.

Thoreau, Henry D. 1971[1854]. *Walden. The Writings of Henry D. Thoreau.* Princeton: Princeton University Press.

Williams, Dilafruz, and Greg Smith, eds. 1999. *Ecological Education in Action: On Weaving Education, Culture and the Environment.* Albany: State University of New York Press.

Wilson, E. O. 1998. *Consilience: The Unity of Knowledge.* New York: Vintage Books.

Critical Pedagogy, Social Justice, Multicultural Education

Allen, JoBeth. 1999. *Class Actions: Teaching for Social Justice in Elementary and Middle School.* New York: Teachers College Press.

Ayers, William, Jean Ann Hunt, and Therese Quinn, eds. 1998. *Teaching for Social Justice.* New York: The New Press.

Delpit, Lisa. 1995. *Other People's Children: Cultural Conflict in the Classroom.* New York: The New Press.

Freire, Paulo. 2000. *Pedagogy of the Oppressed.* New York: Continuum.

Gatto, John T. 1992. *Dumbing Us Down: The Hidden Curriculum of Compulsory Schooling.* Gabriola, B.C.: New Society Press.

———. 2001. *The Underground History of American Education: An Intimate Investigation into the Problem of Modern Schooling.* New York: The Oxford Village Press.

Giroux, Henry A. 1997. *Pedagogy and the Politics of Hope: Theory, Culture, and Schooling.* Boulder, Colo: Westview Press.

hooks, bell. 1994. *Teaching to Transgress: Education as the Practice of Freedom.* New York: Routledge.

Howard, Gary. 1999. *We Can't Teach What We Don't Know: White Teachers, Multiracial Schools.* New York: Teachers College Press.

Kohl, Herbert. 1994. *"I Won't Learn from You": And Other Thoughts on Creative Maladjustment.* New York: The New Press.

Levine, David, Robert Lowe, Bob Peterson, and Rita Tenorio. 1995. *Rethinking Schools: An Agenda for Change.* New York: The New Press.

Lewis, Barbara. 1998. *The Kid's Guide to Social Action.* Minneapolis, Minn.: Free Spirit Publishing.

Loewen, James W. 1995. *Lies My Teacher Told Me: Everything Your American History Book Got Wrong.* New York: Touchstone.

———. 1999. *Lies across America: What Our Historic Sites Get Wrong.* New York: Touchstone.

McLaren, Peter. 1997. *Revolutionary Multiculturalism: Pedagogies of Dissent for the New Millennium.* Los Angeles: UCLA Press.

Nieto, Sonia. 1999. *The Light in Their Eyes: Creating Multicultural Learning Communities.* New York: Teachers College Press.

Noddings, Nel. 2002. *Educating Moral People: A Caring Alternative to Character Education.* New York: Teachers College Press.

Purpel, David E. 1989. *The Moral and Spiritual Crisis in Education: A Curriculum for Justice and Compassion in Education.* New York: Bergin & Garvey.

Simon, Katherine G. 2001. *Moral Questions in the Classroom: How to Get Kids to Think Deeply about Real Life and Their Schoolwork.* New Haven: Yale University Press.

Zinn, Howard. 1999. *People's History of the United States: 1492–Present.* New York: Perennial.

Holistic Education, Transformative Education, Spirituality in Education

Armstrong, Thomas. 1988. *The Radiant Child.* Wheaton, Ill: The Theosophical Publishing House.

———. 1991. *Awakening Your Child's Natural Genius: Enhancing Curiosity, Creativity, and Learning Ability.* New York: Jeremy P. Tarcher/Putnam.

Eisler, Riane. 2000. *Tomorrow's Children: A Blueprint for Partnership Education in the 21ˢᵗ Century.* Boulder, Colo.: Westview.

Kessler, Rachael. 2000. *The Soul of Education: Helping Students Find Connection, Compassion, and Character at School.* Alexandria, Va.: Association for Supervision and Curriculum Development.

Intrator, Sam. Ed. 2002. *Stories of the Courage to Teach: Honoring the Teacher's Heart.* San Francisco: Jossey-Bass.

Lantieri, Linda. 2001. *Schools with Spirit: Nurturing the Inner Lives of Children and Teachers.* Boston: Beacon Press.

Marshak, David.1997. *The Common Vision: Parenting and Educating for Wholeness.* New York: Peter Lang.

Mezirow, Jack et al. 2000. *Learning as Transformation: Critical Perspectives on a Theory in Progress.* San Francisco: Jossey-Bass.

Miller, John P. 1996. *The Holistic Curriculum.* Toronto: OISE Press.

Miller, John P., and Yoshiharu Nakagawa. 2002. *Nurturing Our Wholeness: Perspectives on Spirituality in Education.* Brandon, Vt.: Foundation for Educational Renewal.

Miller, Ron. 2000. *Caring for New Life: Essays on Holistic Education.* Brandon, Vt.: Foundation for Educational Renewal.

O'Reilley, Mary Rose. 1998. *Radical Presence: Teaching as Contemplative Practice.* Portsmouth, N.H.: Boynton/Cook Publishers.

O'Sullivan, Edmund. 2001. *Transformative Learning: Educational Vision for the 21ˢᵗ Century.* Toronto: University of Toronto Press.

Palmer, Parker. 1993. *To Know as We Are Known: Education as a Spiritual Journey.* San Francisco: Harper.

———. 1998. *The Courage to Teach: Exploring the Inner Landscape of a Teacher's Life.* San Francisco: Jossey-Bass.

———. 2000. *Let Your Life Speak: Listening for the Voice of Vocation.* San Francisco: Jossey-Bass.

Pearce, Joseph Chilton. 1992. *Magical Child.* New York: A Plume Book.

Wood, Chip. 1999. *Time to Teach, Time to Learn: Changing the Pace of School.* Greenfield, Mass.: Northeast Foundation for Children.

Zimmerman, Jack, and Virginia Coyle. 1996. *The Way of Council.* Las Vegas, Nev.: Bramble Books.

Zohar, Danah, and Dr. Ian Marshall. 2000. *Spiritual Intelligence: The Ultimate Intelligence.* New York: Bloomsbury.

Progressive Education: General

Bensman, David. 2000. *Central Park East and Its Graduates: "Learning by Heart."* New York: Teachers College Press.

Berman, Sheldon. 1997. *Children's Social Consciousness and the Development of Social Responsibility.* Albany: State University of New York Press.

Darling-Hammond, Linda. 1997. *The Right to Learn: A Blueprint for Creating Schools That Work.* San Francisco: Jossey-Bass.

Dewey, John. 1944. *Democracy and Education: An Introduction to the Philosophy of Education.* New York: The Free Press.

Gardner, Howard. 1999. *Intelligence Reframed: Multiple Intelligences for the 21st Century.* New York: Basic Books.

Gibboney, Richard A. 1994. *The Stone Trumpet: A Story of Practical School Reform 1960–1990.* Albany: State University of New York Press.

Goodlad, John I. 1984. *A Place Called School: Prospects for the Future.* New York: McGraw-Hill.

————. 1994. *What Schools Are For.* Bloomington, Ind.: Phi Delta Kappa Educational Foundation.

Hickman, Larry A., and Thomas M. Alexander, eds. *The Essential Dewey: Volume 2, Ethics, Logic, Psychology.* Bloomington, Ind.: Indiana University Press.

Kohl, Herbert. 1998. *The Discipline of Hope: Learning from a Lifetime of Teaching.* New York: The New Press.

Kohn, Alfie. 1998. *What to Look for in a Classroom: and other Essays.* San Francisco: Jossey-Bass.

————. 1999. *The Schools Our Children Deserve: Moving Beyond Traditional Classrooms and "Tougher Standards."* Boston: Houghton-Mifflin Co.

Levine, Eliot. 2002. *One Kid at a Time: Big Lessons from a Small School.* New York: Teachers College Press.

Meier, Deborah. 1995. *The Power of Their Ideas: Lessons for America from a Small School in Harlem.* Boston: Beacon Press.

Noddings, Nel. 1992. *The Challenge to Care in Schools: An Alternative Approach to Education.* New York: Teachers College Press.

Sergiovanni, Thomas J. 1994. *Building Community in Schools.* San Francisco: Jossey-Bass.

Sizer, Theodore R. 1992. *Horace's School: Redesigning the American High School.* Boston: Houghton-Mifflin.

Sizer, Theodore R., and Nancy Faust Sizer. 1999. *The Students Are Watching: Schools and the Moral Contract.* Boston: Beacon Press.

Tyack, David, and Larry Cuban. 1995. *Tinkering Toward Utopia: A Century of Public School Reform.* Cambridge, Mass.: Harvard University Press.

Wood, George H. 1993. *Schools That Work: America's Most Innovative Public Education Programs.* New York: A Plume Book.

Index

About the Editor

Mike Seymour is director of The Heritage Institute (THI), a progressive program of continuing education for K–12 teachers, in the Northwest, offering place-based earth and social history programs. The leading-edge educational curriculum includes field studies, workshops, distance courses, and foreign-travel programs that reach educators in the Northwest, around the United States, and the world. The mission of THI is to "Educate for Humanity"—it is a commitment to promote a vision of education that furthers a world that works for all. Previously, Mike was a family therapist treating children, couples, and individuals, as well as an organizational consultant to schools and small businesses.